CLASSICAL MUSIC

Classical Music

Contemporary Perspectives and Challenges

Edited by Michael Beckerman and Paul Boghossian

https://www.openbookpublishers.com

© 2021 Michael Beckerman and Paul Boghossian. Copyright of individual chapters is maintained by the chapters' authors.

This work is licensed under a Creative Commons Attribution-NonCommercial-NoDerivs license (CC BY-NC-ND 4.0). This license allows you to share, copy, distribute, and transmit the work providing you do not modify the work, you do not use the work for commercial purposes, you attribute the work to the authors, and you provide a link to the license. Attribution should not in any way suggest that the authors endorse you or your use of the work and should include the following information:

Michael Beckerman and Paul Boghossian (eds), *Classical Music: Contemporary Perspectives and Challenges*. Cambridge, UK: Open Book Publishers, 2021, https://doi.org/10.11647/OBP.0242

Copyright and permissions for the reuse of many of the images included in this publication differ from the above. This information is provided separately in the List of Illustrations.

In order to access detailed and updated information on the license, please visit, https://doi.org/10.11647/OBP.0242#copyright

Further details about CC BY-NC-ND licenses are available at https://creativecommons.org/licenses/by-nc-nd/4.0/

All external links were active at the time of publication unless otherwise stated and have been archived via the Internet Archive Wayback Machine at https://archive.org/web

Updated digital material and resources associated with this volume are available at https://doi.org/10.11647/OBP.0242#resources

Every effort has been made to identify and contact copyright holders and any omission or error will be corrected if notification is made to the publisher.

ISBN Paperback: 9781800641136
ISBN Hardback: 9781800641143
ISBN Digital (PDF): 9781800641150
ISBN Digital ebook (epub): 9781800641167
ISBN Digital ebook (mobi): 9781800641174
ISBN XML: 9781800641181
DOI: 10.11647/OBP.0242

Cover image: Photo by JRvV on Unsplash, https://unsplash.com/photos/NpBmCA065ZI
Cover design by Jacob More.

Table of Contents

List of Illustrations		vii
Author Biographies		xi
Preface *Paul Boghossian*		xxv
Introduction *Michael Beckerman*		xxxiii

PART I

1.	The Enduring Value of Classical Music in the Western Tradition *Ellen T. Harris and Michael Beckerman*	1
2.	The Live Concert Experience: Its Nature and Value *Christopher Peacocke and Kit Fine*	7
3.	Education and Classical Music *Michael Beckerman, Ara Guzelimian, Ellen T. Harris, and Jenny Judge*	15
4.	Music Education and Child Development *Assal Habibi, Hanna Damasio, and Antonio Damasio*	29
5.	A Report on New Music *Alex Ross*	39
6.	The Evolving Role of Music Journalism *Zachary Woolfe and Alex Ross*	47
7.	The Serious Business of the Arts: Good Governance in Twenty-First-Century America *Deborah Borda*	55
8.	Audience Building and Financial Health in the Nonprofit Performing Arts: Current Literature and Unanswered Questions (Executive Summary) *Francie Ostrower and Thad Calabrese*	63

9. Are Labor and Management (Finally) Working Together to Save the Day? The COVID-19 Crisis in Orchestras 75
Matthew VanBesien

10. Diversity, Equity, Inclusion, and Racial Injustice in the Classical Music Professions: A Call to Action 87
Susan Feder and Anthony McGill

11. The Interface between Classical Music and Technology 103
Laurent Bayle and Catherine Provenzano

PART II

12. Expanding Audiences in Miami: The New World Symphony's New Audiences Initiative 121
Howard Herring and Craig Hall

13. Attracting New Audiences at the BBC 143
Tom Service

14. Contemporary Classical Music: A Komodo Dragon? New Opportunities Exemplified by a Concert Series in South Korea 157
Unsuk Chin and Maris Gothoni

15. The Philharmonie de Paris, the *Démos* Project, and New Directions in Classical Music 177
Laurent Bayle

16. What Classical Music Can Learn from the Plastic Arts 183
Olivier Berggruen

Index 191

List of Illustrations

Chapter 4

Fig. 1   Aerial view of the brain from the top depicting white matter pathways connecting the left and the right hemisphere. Image from data collected as part of ongoing study at the Brain and Creativity Institute (2012–2020); post-processed by Dr. Hanna Damasio (2020), CC-BY-NC-ND.   34

Chapter 10

Fig. 1   African American and Latinx representation in higher education music programs. Data drawn from National Association of Schools of Music (NASM) 2015-16 Heads Report. © NYU Global Institute for Advanced Study. CC-BY-NC-ND.   95

Fig. 2   BIPOC musicians in community music schools. Data drawn from US Census Bureau, 2011 American Community Survey; National Guild for Community Arts Education Racial/Ethnic Percentages of Students Within Membership Organizations. © NYU Global Institute for Advanced Study. CC-BY-NC-ND.   95

Chapter 12

Fig. 1   New World Symphony's performance and research cycle for audience acquisition and engagement. Graphic by Howard Herring and Craig Hall (2012), © 2012, New World Symphony, Inc. All rights reserved.   125

Fig. 2	Jamie Bernstein narrates during an *Encounters* concert performed by the New World Symphony orchestra at the New World Center. This video as well as the graphics and animations featured as performance elements within the video were created in the Knight New Media Center at the New World Center campus in Miami Beach, FL. Knight Foundation and New World Symphony: Reimagining classical music in the digital age. © 2020, New World Symphony, Inc. All rights reserved. Duration: 1:35.	127
Fig. 3	NWS Fellow, Grace An, gives an introduction during a *Mini-Concert* (2012). New World Center, Miami Beach, FL. Photo courtesy of New World Symphony. © 2012, New World Symphony, Inc. All rights reserved.	128
Fig. 4	NWS Conducting Fellow, Joshua Gersen, leads *Pulse—Late Night at the New World Symphony*. Photo by Rui Dias-Aidos (2013), New World Center, Miami Beach, FL. © 2013, New World Symphony, Inc. All rights reserved.	129
Fig. 5	The chart indicates the variety of activities in which audiences engage throughout *Pulse—Late Night at the New World Symphony*. Research and results compiled by WolfBrown in partnership with New World Symphony. © WolfBrown dashboard, www.intrinsicimpact.org. All rights reserved.	130
Fig. 6	Luke Kritzeck, Director of Lighting at NWS, describes the technical production and audience experience of *Pulse—Late Night at the New World Symphony*. The video, as well as the video projections and lighting treatments featured within this video, were created in the Knight New Media Center. Knight Foundation and New World Symphony: Reimagining classical music in the digital age. © 2020, New World Symphony, Inc. All rights reserved. Duration: 1:49.	131
Fig. 7	WALLCAST® concert outside the New World Center. WALLCAST® concerts are produced in the Knight New Media Center at the New World Center campus. Photo by Rui Dias-Aidos (2013), New World Center and SoundScape Park, Miami Beach, FL. © 2013, New World Symphony, Inc. All rights reserved.	131

List of Figures ix

Fig. 8 Clyde Scott, Director of Video Production at NWS, gives an overview of aspects of a *WALLCAST*® concert. This video as well as the *WALLCAST*® production featured in this video were produced in the Knight New Media Center. Knight Foundation and New World Symphony: Reimagining classical music in the digital age. © 2020, New World Symphony, Inc. All rights reserved. Duration: 2:49. 133

Fig. 9 Percent of first-time attendees by concert format at New World Symphony. Graphic by Craig Hall (2015). © 2015, New World Symphony, Inc. All rights reserved. 133

Fig. 10 First-time attendees to alternate performance formats at NWS return at a higher rate than first-time attendees to traditional concerts at NWS. Graphic by Craig Hall (2018). © 2018, New World Symphony, Inc. All rights reserved. 134

Fig. 11 Blake-Anthony Johnson, NWS Cello Fellow, introduces the symphony's performance of Debussy's *Prelude to the Afternoon of a Faun* drawing on his personal experience with the music to contextualize the piece for the audience. Video created in the Knight New Media Center. Knight Foundation and New World Symphony: Reimagining classical music in the digital age. © 2020, New World Symphony, Inc. All rights reserved. Duration: 15:15. 136

Fig. 12 Project artists, contributors, and NWS staff members describe Project 305 and the culmination of the project in Ted Hearne and Jon David Kane's symphonic documentary, *Miami in Movements*. Project 305 was supported by the Knight Foundation. Video created in the Knight New Media Center. Knight Foundation and New World Symphony: Reimagining classical music in the digital age. © 2017, Ted Hearne and Jon David Kane, *Miami in Movements*. © 2020, New World Symphony, Inc. All rights reserved. Duration: 7:23. 137

Fig. 13 Explore NWS's 2018 Community Concerts conceived and created by NWS musicians in an interactive video highlighting four projects. Video produced in the Knight New Media Center. Knight Foundation and New World Symphony: Reimagining classical music in the digital age. Video features 'Suite Antique' by John Rutter © Oxford University Press 1981. Licensed by Oxford University Press. All rights reserved. © 2020, New World Symphony, Inc. All rights reserved. 138

Chapter 14

Fig. 1	ARS NOVA, Dress rehearsal for the Korean premiere of Pierre Boulez' Notations pour orchestra. © 2008, Seoul Philharmonic Orchestra. CC-BY-NC-ND.	166
Fig. 2	ARS NOVA, Korean premiere of John Cage's Credo in the US. © 2008, Seoul Philharmonic Orchestra. CC-BY-NC-ND.	169
Fig. 3	ARS NOVA, video installation of Hugo Verlinde. © Seoul Philharmonic Orchestra. CC-BY-NC-ND.	171
Fig. 4	ARS NOVA, preparations for the Korean premiere of György Ligeti's 'Poéme symphonique pour 100 metronomes". © 2007, Seoul Philharmonic Orchestra. CC-BY-NC-ND.	172
Fig. 5	ARS NOVA, audiovisual installation inspired by Mauricio Kagel's movie 'Ludwig van'. © 2006, Seoul Philharmonic Orchestra. CC-BY-NC-ND.	173

Author Biographies

Laurent Bayle is the General Manager of "Cité de la musique — Philharmonie de Paris," a public institution inaugurated in January 2015 and co-funded by the French State and the city of Paris. He started his career as Associate Director of the Théâtre de l'Est lyonnais, and was then appointed General Administrator of the Atelier Lyrique du Rhin, an institution which fosters the creation of contemporary lyric opera. In 1982, he created and became the General Director of the Festival Musica in Strasbourg, an event dedicated to contemporary music and still successful today. In 1987, he was appointed Artistic Director of Ircam (the Institute for Music/Acoustic Research and Coordination), then directed by Pierre Boulez, whom he would succeed in 1992. In 2001, he became General Manager of the Cité de la musique in Paris. In 2006, the Minister of Culture entrusted him with the implementation of the reopening of the Salle Pleyel and with the Mayor of Paris announced a project to create a large symphony hall in Paris. It marked the birth of a new public institution, "Cité de la musique — Philharmonie de Paris," a large facility including three concert halls, the Musée de la musique, an educational center focused on collective practice, and numerous digital music resources. In 2010, Laurent Bayle implemented a children's orchestra project baptized Démos, a social and orchestral structure for music education in disadvantaged neighborhoods, a project developed throughout the national territory with the aim of reaching sixty orchestras by 2020. In April 2018, Laurent Bayle was entrusted with the successful mission of integrating the Orchestre de Paris into the Cité de la musique — Philharmonie de Paris.

Paul Boghossian is Julius Silver Professor and Chair of Philosophy at New York University. He is also the Founding Director of its Global Institute for Advanced Study. He was previously Chair of Philosophy from 1994–2004, during which period the department was transformed from an MA-only program to being the top-rated PhD department in the country. He earned a PhD in Philosophy from Princeton University and a B.Sc. in Physics from Trent University. Elected to the American Academy of Arts and Sciences in 2012, his research interests are primarily in epistemology, the philosophy of mind, and the philosophy of language. He is the author of *Fear of Knowledge: Against Relativism and Constructivism* (Oxford University Press, 2006), which has been translated into thirteen languages; *Content and Justification* (Oxford University Press, 2008); and the recently published *Debating the A Priori* (with Timothy Williamson, Oxford University Press, 2020). In addition, he has published on a wide range of other topics, including aesthetics and the philosophy of music. At NYU since 1991, he has also taught at the University of Michigan at Ann Arbor, Princeton University, the École Normale Supérieure in Paris and has served as Distinguished Research Professor at the University of Birmingham in the UK.

Michael Beckerman is Carroll and Milton Petrie Professor and Collegiate Professor of Music at New York University where he is Chair of the Department of Music. His diverse areas of research include Czech and Eastern European music; musical form and meaning; film music; music of the Roma; music and war; music in the concentration camps; Jewish music, and music and disability. He is author of *New Worlds of Dvořák* (W. W. Norton & Co., 2003), *Janáček as Theorist* (Pendragon Press, 1994), and has edited books on those composers and Bohuslav Martinů. He is the recipient of numerous honors, from the Janáček Medal of the Czech Ministry of Culture in 1988 to an Honorary Doctorate from Palacký University (Czech Republic) in 2014, and most recently the Harrison Medal from the Irish Musicological Society. For many years he wrote for *The New York Times* and was a regular guest on *Live From Lincoln Center*. From 2016-18 he was the Leonard Bernstein Scholar-in-Residence at the New York Philharmonic Orchestra.

Born in Switzerland, **Olivier Berggruen** grew up in Paris before studying art history at Brown University and the Courtauld Institute of Art. As Associate Curator at the Schirn Kunsthalle Frankfurt, he organized major retrospectives of Henri Matisse, Yves Klein, and Pablo Picasso, and he has lectured at institutions including the Frick

Collection, Sciences Po, and the National Gallery in London. In addition to editing several monographs, he is the author of *The Writing of Art* (Pushkin Press: 2011), and his essays have appeared in *The Brooklyn Rail*, *Artforum*, and *Print Quarterly*. He is an adviser to the Gstaad Menuhin Festival in Switzerland and is a member of the board of Carnegie Hall.

Deborah Borda has redefined what an orchestra can be in the twenty-first century through her creative leadership, commitment to innovation, and progressive vision. She became President and CEO of the New York Philharmonic in September 2017, returning to the Orchestra's leadership after serving in that role in the 1990s. Upon her return, she and Music Director Jaap van Zweden established a new vision for the Orchestra that included the introduction of two contemporary music series and *Project 19*, the largest-ever women composers' commissioning initiative to celebrate the centennial of American women's suffrage. Ms. Borda has held top posts at the Los Angeles Philharmonic, The Saint Paul Chamber Orchestra, and the Detroit Symphony Orchestra. She currently also serves as Chair of the Avery Fisher Artist Program.

The first arts executive to join Harvard Kennedy School's Center for Public Leadership as a Hauser Leader-in-Residence, her numerous honors include a Lifetime Achievement Award at the Dallas Symphony Orchestra's Women in Classical Music Symposium (2020), invitation to join Oxford University's Humanities Cultural Programme Advisory Council (2020), being named a Woman of Influence by the *New York Business Journal* (2019), and election to the American Academy of Arts & Sciences (2018).

Thad Calabrese is an Associate Professor of Public and Nonprofit Financial Management at the Robert F. Wagner Graduate School of Public Service at New York University where he currently serves as the head of the finance specialization. Thad has published over thirty peer-reviewed articles and eight books on financial management, liability management, contracting, forecasting, and other various aspects of financial management in the public and nonprofit sectors. He currently serves on three editorial boards for academic journals. Prior to academia, he worked at the New York City Office of Management and Budget and as a financial consultant with healthcare organizations in New York City.

Thad currently serves as the Treasurer for the Association for Research on Nonprofits and Voluntary Action, and also the Chair-Elect of the Association for Budgeting and Financial Management, which he also represents on the Governmental Accounting Standards Advisory Council.

Unsuk Chin is a Berlin-based composer. She is Director of the Los Angeles Philharmonic's Seoul Festival in 2021, Artistic Director Designate of the Tongyeong International Music Festival in South Korea as well as Artistic Director Designate of the Weiwuying International Music Festival in Kaohsiung, Taiwan.

Antonio Damasio is Dornsife Professor of Neuroscience, Psychology and Philosophy, and Director of the Brain and Creativity Institute at the University of Southern California in Los Angeles.

Damasio was trained as both neurologist and neuroscientist. His work on the role of affect in decision-making and consciousness has made a major impact in neuroscience, psychology, and philosophy. He is the author of several hundred scientific articles and is one of the most cited scientists of the modern era.

Damasio's recent work addresses the evolutionary development of mind and the role of life regulation in the generation of cultures (see *The Strange Order of Things: Life, Feeling, and the Making of Cultures* (Random House, 2018-2019)). His new book *Feeling and Knowing* will appear in 2021. Damasio is also the author of *Descartes' Error* (Avon Books, 1994), *The Feeling of What Happens* (Vintage, 2000), *Looking for Spinoza* (Mariner Books, 2003) and *Self Comes to Mind* (Vintage, 2012), which are translated and taught in universities worldwide.

Damasio is a member of the National Academy of Medicine and a Fellow of the American Academy of Arts and Sciences. He has received numerous prizes, among them the International Freud Medal (2017), the Grawemeyer Award (2014), the Honda Prize (2010), and the Asturias Prize in Science and Technology (2005); he holds Honorary Doctorates from several leading universities, some shared with his wife Hanna, e.g. the École Polytechnique Fédérale de Lausanne (EPFL), 2011 and the Sorbonne (Université Paris Descartes), 2015.

For more information go to the Brain and Creativity Institute website at https://dornsife.usc.edu/bci/ and to https://www.antoniodamasio.com/.

Hanna Damasio M.D. is University Professor, Dana Dornsife Professor of Neuroscience and Director of the Dana and David Dornsife Cognitive Neuroscience Imaging Center at the University of Southern California. Using computerized tomography and magnetic resonance scanning, she has developed methods of investigating human brain structure and studied functions such as language, memory and emotion, using both the lesion method and functional neuroimaging. Besides numerous scientific articles (Web of Knowledge H Index is 85; over 40,620 citations), she is the author of the award-winning *Lesion Analysis in Neuropsychology* (Oxford University Press, 1990), and of *Human Brain Anatomy in Computerized Images* (Oxford University Press, 1995), the first brain atlas based on computerized imaging data.

Hanna is a Fellow of the American Academy of Arts and Sciences and of the American Neurological Association and she holds honorary doctorates from the École Polytechnique Fédérale de Lausanne, the Universities of Aachen and Lisbon, and the Open University of Catalonia. In January 2011, she was named USC University Professor.

Kit Fine is a University Professor and a Julius Silver Professor of Philosophy and Mathematics at New York University, specializing in Metaphysics, Logic, and Philosophy of Language. He is a fellow of the American Academy of Arts and Sciences, and a corresponding fellow of the British Academy. He has received awards from the Guggenheim Foundation, the American Council of Learned Societies and the Humboldt Foundation and is a former editor of the *Journal of Symbolic Logic*. In addition to his primary areas of research, he has written papers in the history of philosophy, linguistics, computer science, and economic theory and has always had a strong and active interest in music composition and performance.

Susan Feder is a Program Officer in the Arts and Culture program at The Andrew W. Mellon Foundation, where since 2007 she has overseen grantmaking in the performing arts. Among the initiatives she has launched are the Foundation's Comprehensive Organizational

Health Initiative, National Playwright Residency Program, National Theater Project, and Pathways for Musicians from Underrepresented Communities. Earlier in her career, as Vice President of the music publishing firm G. Schirmer, Inc., she developed the careers of many leading composers in the United States, Europe, and the former Soviet Union. She has also served as editorial coordinator of *The New Grove Dictionary of American Music* (Oxford University Press, 1878-present) and program editor at the San Francisco Symphony. Currently, Feder sits on the boards of Grantmakers in the Arts, Amphion Foundation, Kurt Weill Foundation, and Charles Ives Society, and is a member of the Music Department Advisory Council at Princeton University. She is the dedicatee of John Corigliano's Pulitzer-Prize winning Symphony No. 2, Augusta Read Thomas's *Helios Choros*, and Joan Tower's *Dumbarton Quintet*.

Maris Gothoni is currently Head of Artistic Planning of the Stavanger Symphony Orchestra in Norway. He is also Artistic Advisor Designate of the Tongyeong International Music Festival in South Korea, as well as Artistic Advisor Designate of the Weiwuying International Music Festival in Kaohsiung, Taiwan.

Ara Guzelimian is Artistic and Executive Director of the Ojai Festival in California, having most recently served as Provost and Dean of the Juilliard School in New York City from 2007 to 2020. He continues at Juilliard in the role of Special Advisor, Office of the President. Prior to the Juilliard appointment, he was Senior Director and Artistic Advisor of Carnegie Hall from 1998 to 2006. He was also host and producer of the acclaimed "Making Music" composer series at Carnegie Hall from 1999 to 2008. Mr. Guzelimian currently serves as Artistic Consultant for the Marlboro Music Festival and School in Vermont. He is a member of the Steering Committee of the Aga Khan Music Awards, the Artistic Committee of the Borletti-Buitoni Trust in London, and a board member of the Amphion and Pacific Harmony Foundations. He is also a member of the Music Visiting Committee of the Morgan Library and Museum in New York City.

Ara is editor of *Parallels and Paradoxes: Explorations in Music and Society* (Pantheon Books, 2002), a collection of dialogues between Daniel Barenboim and Edward Said. In September 2003, Mr. Guzelimian was awarded the title of Chevalier des Arts et des Lettres by the French government for his contributions to French music and culture.

Assal Habibi is an Assistant Research Professor of Psychology at the Brain and Creativity Institute at University of Southern California. Her research takes a broad perspective on understanding music's influence on health and development, focusing on how biological dispositions and music learning experiences shape the brain and development of cognitive, emotional and social abilities across the lifespan. She is an expert on the use of electrophysiologic and neuroimaging methods to investigate human brain function and has used longitudinal and cross-sectional designs to investigate how music training impacts the development of children from under-resourced communities, and how music generally is processed by the body and the brain. Her research program has been supported by federal agencies and private foundations including the *NIH, NEA* and the *GRoW @ Annenberg Foundation*, and her findings have been published in peer-reviewed journals including *Cerebral Cortex, Music Perception, Neuroimage,* and *PLoS ONE*. Currently, she is the lead investigator of a multi-year longitudinal study, in collaboration with the Los Angeles Philharmonic and their Youth Orchestra program (YOLA), investigating the effects of early childhood music training on the development of brain function and structure as well as cognitive, emotional, and social abilities. Dr. Habibi is a classically trained pianist and has many years of musical teaching experience with children, a longstanding personal passion.

Craig Hall worked at the New World Symphony (NWS) from 2007–2020, serving as Vice President for Communications and Vice President of Audience Engagement, Research and Design. During this time, NWS significantly developed its media and research programs, in addition to its audience, creative services and ticketing capacities. Throughout his career, Mr. Hall has sought to attract new audiences and increase engagement while developing an understanding and greater appreciation for classical music through a combination of program development, branding, creative and empathetic messaging, and patron services. Mr. Hall has also launched and developed extensive research programs to track NWS's new audience initiatives, the results of which have been shared in reports, publications and at conferences internationally.

Craig has been a featured presenter at conferences including the League of American Orchestras, Orchestras Canada and the Asociación Española de Orquestas Sinfónicas, and a guest lecturer for classes at Indiana University's School of Public and Environmental Affairs. In his own community, he has served as guest speaker at the Miami Press Club, grant panelist for Miami-Dade County and the City of Miami Beach, and as a Task Force Member of Miami-Dade County's Miami Emerging Arts Leaders program.

Ellen T. Harris, (eharris@mit.edu) B.A. '67 Brown University; M.A. '70, Ph.D. '76 University of Chicago, is Class of 1949 Professor Emeritus at MIT and recurrent Visiting Professor at The Juilliard School (2016, 2019, 2020). Her book, *George Frideric Handel: A Life with Friends* (Norton, 2014) received the Nicolas Slonimsky Award for Outstanding Musical Biography (an ASCAP/Deems Taylor Award). *Handel as Orpheus: Voice and Desire in the Chamber Cantatas* (Harvard, 2001) received the 2002 Otto Kinkeldey Award from the American Musicological Society and the 2002-03 Louis Gottschalk Prize from the Society for Eighteenth-Century Studies. December 2017 saw the release of the thirtieth-anniversary revised edition of her book *Henry Purcell: Dido and Aeneas*. Articles and reviews by Professor Harris concerning Baroque opera and vocal performance practice have appeared in numerous publications including *Journal of the American Musicological Society*, *Händel Jahrbuch*, *Notes*, and *The New York Times*. Her article "Handel the Investor" (*Music & Letters*, 2004) won the 2004 Westrup Prize. Articles on censorship in the arts and arts education have appeared in *The Chronicle of Higher Education* and *The Aspen Institute Quarterly*.

Howard Herring joined the New World Symphony (NWS) as President and Chief Executive Officer in 2001. His first charge was to guide the process of imagining and articulating a program for the long-term future of the institution. That program formed the basis for NWS's new home, the New World Center (NWC). Designed by Frank Gehry, the NWC opened to national and international acclaim in 2011 and is a twenty-first-century laboratory for generating new ideas about the way music is taught, presented and experienced. A specific initiative of interest is

WALLCAST® concerts – capture and delivery of orchestral concerts on the primary façade of the NWC offered at the highest levels of sight and sound and for free. Now with over 1,150 alumni, NWS continues to expand its relevance in South Florida and beyond, winning new audiences and enhancing music education.

Mr. Herring is a native of Oklahoma. A pianist by training, he holds a bachelor of music degree from Southern Methodist University and a master's degree and honorary doctorate from Manhattan School of Music. He was the pianist of the Claremont Trio, a winner of the Artists International Competition, and an active musician and teacher in New York City. In 1986 he became Executive Director of the Caramoor Music Festival. During his fifteen-year tenure, he guided the creation of the Rising Stars Program for young instrumentalists and Bel Canto at Caramoor for young singers. During that period, Caramoor also celebrated its fiftieth Anniversary and established an endowment.

Jenny Judge is a philosopher and musician whose work explores the resonances between music and the philosophy of mind. She holds a PhD in musicology from the University of Cambridge and is currently completing a second doctoral dissertation in philosophy at NYU. An active musician and songwriter, Judge performs and records with jazz guitarist Ted Morcaldi as part of the analogue electronic / folk duo, "Pet Beast". Judge also writes philosophical essays for a general audience, exploring topics at the intersection of art, ethics and technology. Her work has appeared in *The Guardian*, *Aeon*, *Medium*'s subscription site *OneZero*, and the *Philosopher's Magazine*. Selections can be found at www.jennyjudge.net.

Judge also works as a music writer. She regularly collaborates with flutist Claire Chase, most recently authoring an essay for the liner notes of Chase's 2020 album 'Density 2036: part v'.

Hailed for his "trademark brilliance, penetrating sound and rich character" (*The New York Times*), clarinetist **Anthony McGill** enjoys a dynamic international solo and chamber music career and is Principal Clarinet of the New York Philharmonic—the first African-American principal player in the organization's history. In 2020, he was awarded the Avery Fisher Prize, one of classical music's most significant awards given in recognition of soloists who represent the highest level of musical excellence.

McGill appears regularly as a soloist with top orchestras including the New York Philharmonic, Metropolitan Opera, Baltimore Symphony Orchestra, San Diego Symphony, and Kansas City Symphony. He was honored to perform at the inauguration of President Barack Obama, premiering a piece by John Williams and performing alongside Itzhak Perlman, Yo-Yo Ma, and Gabriela Montero. In demand as a teacher, he serves on the faculty of The Juilliard School, Curtis Institute of Music, and Bard College Conservatory of Music. He is Artistic Director for the Music Advancement Program at The Juilliard School. In May 2020, McGill launched #TakeTwoKnees, a musical protest video campaign against the death of George Floyd and historic racial injustice which went viral. Further information may be found at anthonymcgill.com.

Francie Ostrower is Professor at The University of Texas at Austin in the LBJ School of Public Affairs and College of Fine Arts, Director of the Portfolio Program in Arts and Cultural Management and Entrepreneurship, and a Senior Fellow in the RGK Center for Philanthropy and Community Service. She is Principal Investigator of Building Audiences for Sustainability: Research and Evaluation, a six-year study of audience-building activities by performing arts organizations commissioned and funded by The Wallace Foundation. Professor Ostrower has been a visiting professor at IAE de Paris/Sorbonne graduate Business School and is an Urban Institute-affiliated scholar. She has authored numerous publications on philanthropy, nonprofit governance, and arts participation that have received awards from the Association for Research on Nonprofit and Voluntary Action (ARNOVA) and Independent Sector. Her many past and current professional activities include serving as a board member and president of ARNOVA, and an editorial board member of the Nonprofit and Voluntary Sector Quarterly.

Christopher Peacocke is Johnsonian Professor of Philosophy at Columbia University in the City of New York, and Honorary Fellow of the Institute of Philosophy in the School of Advanced Study in the University of London. He is a Fellow of the British Academy and of the American Academy of Arts and Sciences. He writes on the philosophy of mind, metaphysics, and epistemology. He has been concerned in the past decade to apply the apparatus of contemporary philosophy of mind to explain phenomena in the perception of music. His articles on this topic are in the *British Journal of Aesthetics* and in the *Oxford Handbook of Western Music and Philosophy*, ed. by J. Levinson, T. McAuley, N. Nielsen, and A. Phillips-Hutton (Oxford University Press, 2020).

Catherine Provenzano is an Assistant Professor of Musicology and Music Industry at the UCLA Herb Alpert School of Music. Her scholarship focuses on voice, technology, mediation and labor in contexts of popular music production, with a regional specialty in North America. Catherine has conducted ethnographic research with software developers, audio engineers, music producers and artists in Los Angeles, Nashville, Silicon Valley and Germany. In addition to an article in the *Journal of Popular Music Studies*, Catherine has presented research at meetings of the Society for Ethnomusicology, EMP PopCon, Indexical, The New School, Berklee College of Music and McGill University.

In 2019, Catherine earned her Ph.D. in Ethnomusicology from New York University. At NYU and The New School, Catherine has taught courses in popular music, critical listening, analysis of recorded sound and music and media. Her dissertation, "Emotional Signals: Digital Tuning Software and the Meanings of Pop Music Voices," is a critical ethnographic account of digital pitch correction softwares (Auto-Tune and Melodyne), and their development and use in US Top 40 and hip-hop. She is also a singer, songwriter and performer under the name Kenniston, and collaborates with other musical groups.

Alex Ross has been the music critic of *The New Yorker* since 1996. His first book, *The Rest Is Noise: Listening to the Twentieth Century* (Harper, 2009), a cultural history of music since 1900, won a National Book Critics Circle award and the Guardian First Book Award, and was a finalist for the Pulitzer Prize. His second book, the essay collection *Listen to This* (Fourth Estate, 2010), won an ASCAP Deems Taylor Award. In 2020 he published *Wagnerism: Art and Politics in the Shadow of Music* (Farrar, Straus and Giroux, 2020), an account of the composer's vast cultural impact. He has received a MacArthur Fellowship, a Guggenheim Fellowship, and an Arts and Letters Award from the American Academy of Arts and Letters.

Tom Service broadcasts for BBC Radio 3 and BBC Television: programmes include *The Listening Service* and *Music Matters* on Radio 3, the BBC Proms and documentaries on television. His books about music are published by Faber, he wrote about music for *The Scotsman* and *The Guardian* for two decades, and he is a columnist for *The BBC Music Magazine*. He was the Gresham College Professor of Music in 2018-19, with his series, "A History of Listening". His Ph.D, at the University of Southampton, was on the music of John Zorn.

Matthew VanBesien has served as the President of the University Musical Society (UMS) at the University of Michigan since 2017, becoming only the seventh president in UMS's 142-year history. A 2014 recipient of the National Medal of Arts, UMS is a nonprofit organization affiliated with U-M, presenting over 80 music, theater, and dance performances, and over 300 free educational activities, each season.

Before his role in Michigan, he served as Executive Director and then President of the New York Philharmonic. Previously, Mr. VanBesien served as managing director of the Melbourne Symphony Orchestra, following positions at the Houston Symphony as Executive Director, Chief Executive Officer, and General Manager.

During his tenure at the New York Philharmonic, Matthew developed and executed highly innovative programs along with Music Director Alan Gilbert, such as the NY PHIL BIENNIAL in 2014 and 2016, the Art of the Score film and music series, and exciting productions such as *Jeanne d'Arc au bûcher* with Marion Cotillard, and *Sweeney Todd* with Emma Thompson. He led the creation of the New York Philharmonic's Global Academy initiative, which offered educational partnerships with cultural institutions in Shanghai, Santa Barbara, Houston, and Interlochen to train talented pre-professional musicians, often alongside performance residencies. He led a successful music director search, with Jaap van Zweden appointed to the role beginning in 2018, the formation of the Philharmonic's International Advisory Board and President's Council, and the unique and successful multi-year residency and educational partnership in Shanghai, China.

A native of St. Louis, Missouri, Matthew earned a Bachelor of Music degree in French horn performance from Indiana University, and holds an Honorary Doctorate of Musical Arts from Manhattan School of Music.

He serves as the Secretary and Treasurer of the International Society for the Performing Arts, and is a board member of Ann Arbor SPARK.

Zachary Woolfe has been the classical music editor at *The New York Times* since 2015. Prior to joining *The Times*, he was the opera critic of the *New York Observer*. He studied at Princeton University.

Preface[1]

Paul Boghossian

In the 1973 movie, *Serpico*, there is a scene in which the eponymous hero, an undercover detective, is in his back garden in the West Village drinking some coffee and playing at high volume on his record player the great tenor aria from Act 3 of *Tosca*, "E lucevan le Stelle." His neighbor, an appealing woman whom he doesn't know and who, it is later revealed, works as a nurse at a local hospital, comes out to her adjoining garden and the following dialogue ensues over the low wall separating them:

> Woman: "Is that Björling?"
> Serpico: "No, it's di Stefano."
> Woman: "I was sure it was Björling."

They continue chatting for a while, after which she goes off to work. This is virtually the only scene in the film at which opera comes up and there is no stage-setting for it: the filmmakers were able simply to assume that enough moviegoers would know without explanation who Björling and di Stefano were.

If one were looking for a poignant encapsulation of how opera's place in popular culture has shifted from the early 1970s to the 2020s, this would serve as well as any. Such a snippet of dialogue in a contemporary wide-release Hollywood movie would be unthinkable: with the exception of a few opera fanatics, no one would have any idea

---

[1] I am very grateful to Mike Beckerman for his prodigious efforts in helping run this project and edit the present volume. Many thanks, too, to Anupum Mehrotra, who provided administrative support, especially in the early stages. A very special debt of gratitude to Leigh Bond, the Program Administrator of the GIAS, without whose extraordinary judgment, organization, and firm but gentle coaxing, this volume would probably never have seen the light of day.

who these gentlemen were, or what it was that they were supposedly singing.

In the decades leading up to the 1970s, many opera stars, including di Stefano and Björling, appeared on popular TV programs sponsored by such corporate titans as General Motors and General Electric. Their romantic entanglements were breathlessly covered by the tabloid press. The National Broadcasting Corporation (NBC) had its own orchestra, one of the very finest in the world, put together at great expense specifically for the legendary conductor Arturo Toscanini, who had to be wooed out of retirement to take its helm. For the first radio broadcast of a live concert conducted by Toscanini, in December of 1937, the programs were printed on silk to prevent the rustling of paper programs from detracting from the experience.

Not long after *Serpico* was released, opera—and classical music more generally—started its precipitous decline into the state in which we find it today: as an art form that is of cultural relevance to an increasingly small, increasingly aging, mostly white audience. The members of this audience mostly want to hear pieces that are between two hundred and fifty and one hundred years old, over and over again. The occasional new composition is performed, to be sure, but always by placing even heavier stress on ticket sales. (Research shows that ticket sales for any given concert are inversely proportional to the quantity of contemporary music that is programmed.) The youth show up in greater numbers for new compositions, but not their parents or grandparents, who make up the bulk of the paying public.

Classical music's dire state of affairs is reflected in poor ticket sales at the major classical music institutions—for example, at the Metropolitan Opera and the NY Philharmonic, both of which have run deficits for many of their recent performing seasons. The contrast with its heyday in the 1960s could not be greater. The Met recently discovered in its archives a note from Sir Rudolf Bing, then the General Manager, which said, roughly: "The season has not yet started, and we have already sold out every seat to every performance to our subscribers. Could you please call some of them up and see if we can free up some single tickets to sell to the general public?" What a difference from the situation today, when the house is often barely half full. The sorry plight of classical music is also reflected in the large and increasing number of orchestra bankruptcies or lockouts. For many of these wonderful institutions, with their large fixed costs and declining revenues, already hugely financially fragile, the cancellation of months, and possibly years, of concerts induced by the current pandemic might well be the final blow.

It's true, of course, that even prior to the current public health crisis, the "Netflixization" of entertainment had already had a major impact on the performing arts. So much content is available to be streamed into a person's living room at the click of a button that the incentive to seek diversion outside the house has been greatly diminished in general. This has affected not only attendance at concerts, but also golf club memberships, applications for fishing licenses, and so on. However, classical music stands out for the extent to which it has lost the attention of the general public and so cannot be said to be merely part of a general decline in people seeking entertainment outside the home.

If further proof of this were wanted, one would only need to note the stark contrast between classical music and the current state of the visual arts. Problems caused by the current pandemic aside, museums nowadays are mostly flourishing, setting new attendance records on a frequent basis, and presenting blockbuster shows for which tickets are often hard to get. Most strikingly, the museums that are doing best are those that specialize in modern and contemporary art, rather than those which mostly showcase pre-twentieth-century art—in New York these days, the Museum of Modern Art outshines the Metropolitan Museum. So, whatever is going on in classical music, it's not merely part of a general decline of interest in the fine arts.

All of this formed the backdrop against which I decided that it might be a good idea to convene a think tank, under the auspices of NYU's Global Institute for Advanced Study, to study the phenomenon of classical music's decline and to investigate ideas as to how its fortunes might be revived. I had early conversations with Kirill Gerstein, Jeremy Geffen, Toby Spence and Matthew VanBesien, all of whom were enthusiastic about the idea, and all of whom made useful suggestions about who else it would be good to invite and what issues we might cover. At NYU, I had the good fortune to be able to convince Michael Beckerman and Kit Fine to join as co-conveners of the think tank. Together we assembled a truly illustrious group of musicologists, musicians, music managers, music journalists and, of course, musically inclined philosophers. (A full list of the members of the think tank can be found at the end of this preface.)

Over the course of three years, we looked at a number of questions:

1. What would be lost if we could no longer enjoy live concert experiences, at the very high level at which they are currently available, and had to listen to music mostly on playback devices?
2. Does the live concert experience, whose basic features date from the nineteenth century, need a major makeover? If so, what form should that makeover take?
3. Orchestras, as well as their audiences, are mostly white and affluent; how could this be changed so that classical music could come to better reflect the society which it serves?
4. To what extent is classical music's mausoleum-like character, mostly programming eighteenth- and nineteenth-century pieces over and over again, responsible for alienating new audiences; and what might be done about it?
5. To what extent are the business model, and governance and labor structures, of big classical music organizations, responsible for their current problems, and what might be done about them?
6. How has the decline in music education, both in schools and in private, impacted people's interest in classical music?
7. How might developments in technology help address some of the issues identified?
8. What is the role of classical music critics, especially as many newspapers face extinction and others drastically reduce their coverage of the arts?
9. What might music institutions learn from the relative success enjoyed by the institutions that serve the visual arts?

The presentations on these topics were given not only by members of the think tank but also by the occasional invited guest, such as Professor Robert Flanagan, a labor economist at Stanford University, whose book *The Perilous Life of Symphony Orchestras* gives a rigorous analysis of the challenges faced by these institutions. We were also fortunate in being able to include in our volume some specially commissioned pieces from experts who did not participate in the think tank (Chapters 4, 8, 12). Although our focus was primarily on the United States, we were able to make useful comparisons with other countries through the presentations of Laurent Bayle (France), Unsuk Chin (South Korea) and Huda Alkhamis-Kanoo (Middle East).

Initially, some of us harbored the hope that this group would issue a joint report, proposing solutions that might attract widespread attention and perhaps acceptance. This hope evaporated in the face of a lack of consensus amongst the members of the think tank, both as to what the central issues were, and on the various proposed remedies. Of course, if these problems had been easy, they would have been solved some time ago. In the end, we agreed to have individual members (or appropriate teams of them) write essays on topics on which they were particularly expert. In addition, we commissioned a few pieces on especially relevant topics, or case studies, by folks who had not participated in the meetings of the think tank. The resulting collection is by no means a poor second best to what we had originally envisioned. It offers a great deal of insight into an art form that is beloved by many and will, hopefully, contribute to the thinking of those who are charged with maintaining that art form for the generations to come.

***

Members of the NYU GIAS Classical Music Think Tank:[2]

- H.E. Huda Alkhamis-Kanoo (Founder, Abu Dhabi Music & Arts Foundation; Founder and Artistic Director, Abu Dhabi Festival)
- Laurent Bayle (Chief Executive Director, Cité de la Musique —Philharmonie de Paris)
- Michael Beckerman (Carroll and Milton Petrie Professor of Music and Chair; Collegiate Professor, New York University)

---

2   The opinions expressed in this publication are those of the authors. They do not purport to reflect the opinions or views of the NYU GIAS Think Tank members.

- Paul Boghossian (Julius Silver Professor of Philosophy and Chair; Director, Global Institute for Advanced Study, New York University)
- Deborah Borda (President and Chief Executive Officer, New York Philharmonic; former President and Chief Executive Officer, Los Angeles Philharmonic)
- Ian Bostridge (Tenor)
- Claire Chase (Flautist and Founder, International Contemporary Ensemble)
- Unsuk Chin (Composer; Director, Seoul Festival with the LA Philharmonic; Artistic Director Designate, Tongyeong International Music Festival, South Korea; Artistic Director Designate, Weiwuying International Music Festival, Kaohsiung, Taiwan)
- Andreas Ditter (Stalnaker Postdoctoral Associate, Department of Linguistics and Philosophy, Massachusetts Institute of Technology; PhD graduate, Department of Philosophy, New York University)
- Kit Fine (Julius Silver Professor of Philosophy and Mathematics; University Professor, New York University)
- Kirill Gerstein (Pianist)
- Jeremy N. Geffen (Executive and Artistic Director, Cal Performances; former Senior Director and Artistic Adviser, Carnegie Hall)
- Ara Guzelimian (Artistic and Executive Director, Ojai Festival; Special Advisor, Office of the President and former Provost and Dean, The Juilliard School)
- Ellen T. Harris (Class of 1949 Professor Emeritus of Music, MIT; former President, American Musicological Society)
- Jenny Judge (PhD candidate, Department of Philosophy, New York University)
- Anthony McGill (Principal Clarinet, New York Philharmonic; Artistic Director for the Music Advancement Program at The Juilliard School)

- Alexander Neef (General Director, Opéra national de Paris, former General Director, Canadian Opera Company)
- Alex Ross (Music Critic, *The New Yorker*)
- Esa-Pekka Salonen (Composer and Conductor; Principal Conductor and Artistic Advisor, Philharmonia Orchestra, London; Music Director, San Francisco Symphony; Conductor Laureate, Los Angeles Philharmonic)
- Christopher Peacocke (Johnsonian Professor of Philosophy, Columbia University; Honorary Fellow, Institute of Philosophy, University of London)
- Catherine Provenzano (Assistant Professor of Musicology and Music Industry, UCLA Herb Alpert School of Music; PhD graduate, Department of Music, New York University)
- Peter Sellars (Theater, Opera, Film, and Festival Director; Distinguished Professor, UCLA Department of World Arts and Cultures/Dance)
- Richard Sennett OBE FBA (Honorary Professor, The Bartlett School, University College London; Member, Council on Urban Initiatives, United Nations Habitat; Chair, Theatrum Mundi, Registered Charity 1174149 in England & Wales)
- Tom Service (Writer and Broadcaster, BBC)
- Toby Spence (Tenor)
- Matthew VanBesien (President of the University Musical Society, University of Michigan, Ann Arbor; former President and CEO of major orchestras including the New York Philharmonic, Melbourne Symphony Orchestra, and Houston Symphony)
- Julia Wolfe (Composer; Professor of Music Composition and Artistic Director of Music Composition at New York University Steinhardt, and co-founder of Bang on a Can)
- Zachary Woolfe (Classical Music Editor, *The New York Times*)

Introduction[1]

Michael Beckerman

This is the third, or possibly the fourth, time I have sat down to write an introduction to our volume about classical music. It was mostly complete by the beginning of 2020 when Covid-19 hit. As my co-editor Paul Boghossian makes clear in his Preface, our "think tank" approach to the subject had emerged from a strong sense that classical music, however it is defined, is both something of great value, and in various ways also in crisis. The early effects of the pandemic sharpened both of these perspectives. The almost three million views of the Rotterdam Symphony performing a distanced version of the Beethoven Ninth, or viral footage of Italians singing opera from their balconies, were a testament to the surprising power of the tradition, while its vulnerability quickly became apparent as live presentations vanished and virtually all institutions faced unprecedented and devastating challenges, both artistic and economic.[2]

---

1   I would like to thank the following people for their help in this project. Prof. Catherine Provenzano, who served as an assistant to the endeavor in several of its stages; Brian Fairley and Samuel Chan, who offered essential and critically important advice throughout; Prof. Lorraine Byrne Bodley of Maynooth University in Ireland, who offered encouragement and valuable ideas; and to Dr. Karen Beckerman, who has been supportive throughout even though she has been hearing about this for far too long. Of course, great thanks are due to all those who participated in the project, and particularly those who offered written contributions. As Paul Boghossian notes in the *Preface*, we genuinely could not have finished this project without the hard-nosed work, wisdom and thoughtful contributions of Leigh Bond, to whom we are extremely grateful. And of course at the end, I owe a great debt to Paul Boghossian for involving me in this project. It has been a great ride, and now it is an honor and a privilege to see it through to the end together.
2   See Rotterdam Philharmonic Orchestra (2020).

Yet no sooner had this reality been outlined in a fresh introduction, than we experienced the awful events of the late spring, with the murder of George Floyd and others, forcing a national reckoning about race which has had clear ramifications for the future of the country as a whole, and for our subject. So another rewrite—of both the introduction and parts of several chapters—was necessary to grapple with the legacy of classical music in the United States and its own very real history in relation to race and segregation.³

At this time, issues surrounding classical music seem almost quaint compared to the much more potent questions about the future direction of the United States. With ever-sharpening binaries it is difficult, if not impossible, to imagine what kind of impact all of the events of this roiled year 2020 will have on the future of classical music... and everything else. In New York City, the Metropolitan Opera House, the New York Philharmonic Orchestra and Carnegie Hall have cancelled their 2020-21 seasons, and all major houses in the country remain shuttered for anything resembling normal musical life. While many arts organizations have been enterprising in their use of online content, both live-streamed and recorded, considering the many hours people are already online (resulting in "Zoom fatigue" and other syndromes), it is not clear that this virtual world can ever take the place of live performances. At this particular moment there is a massive resurgence of the coronavirus with higher caseloads than ever, and while several vaccines have appeared, it is in no way clear when any kind of normal life—still less normal musical life—can begin again.

As we move forward to some new reality, discussions about systemic inequities have not only cast light on the history of classical music—and, to be fair, the entire music industry—but have raised questions about the extent to which the classical music world in particular is still very much a bastion of white privilege, and even further, the ways in which the musical substance itself may be tainted by some rotten core of racism, sexism and colonialism. These are not simple matters, and investigations of such things as the relationship between, say, racism, sexism, and musical content require enormous care and nuance to think through; shorthand slogans just will not do.

---

3   For other recent explorations of this topic, see Ross (2020); Tsioulcas (2020); Brodeur (2020); and Woolfe & Barone (2020).

Even though this volume is appearing in such a charged moment, it cannot and will not attempt to grapple fully with these issues, especially since much of it was written before the events of the late winter and early spring of 2020 shook the foundations of our world. But these issues of value, accountability, and context will not go away, and as several of our contributors write, finding solutions to them will be critical to the future of the enterprise.

In short then, questions along the lines of "what shall we do about 'the arts'?" that might have been raised in February 2020 have been ratcheted up to an entirely new level in almost every way.

The Experience of Classical Music

Yet even as we consider these thorny issues, for many of those who are reading this volume, as listeners, composers, performers, and presenters, the experience of encountering something they would call "classical music" has been, and is still one of the most valuable things in their lives. Remarkable in their power and immediacy are such things as sonic beauty and structural coherence; physical (in the case of opera), intellectual, and spiritual drama; the powerful connections between sound and philosophy; the sheer sweep of certain compositions; and breathtaking virtuosic skill. That these aspects of classical music, however, are not the focus of this volume, should not be taken as a sign that the writers here assembled lack strong and meaningful experiences with it, or are somehow ashamed of it, but rather that there are other things afoot at this particular moment.

It follows, then, that this collection of essays is not meant as a simple celebration of classical music—still less of only its elite composers, performers, and practitioners—but resulted at least as much from our sense of a community in crisis as it did from our sense of its value. As you will read in several chapters (and probably already know), audiences are aging and it is not clear that they are being replaced by younger members; the number of positions in arts journalism and serious criticism has dwindled dramatically; cycles of financial boom and bust have put large arts organizations, whose costs go up every year, in a precarious position, dependent on donors who may or may not be able to come up with the funds—and this was even before the pandemic. If this were not enough, the staggering and increasing amount of online content has kept viewers at their smartphones and laptops and away from concert halls more than ever. For some, these problems have been created by the classical music world itself: there is a view that it is outdated and out of touch, at best a kind of museum. It has therefore been our task to contemplate and test some of these ideas by putting together a group representing arts and academic administrators, performers, educators, critics, and composers to give their perspectives on these matters.

Some Non-Definitions

In *Henry V* Shakespeare famously has a character ask: "What ish my nation?" And we have struggled with the question, "What ish our subject?" Of course, narrow attempts to circumscribe precisely what we mean can be pointless. And yet if one is writing about classical music, one had better explain what is being spoken about. Despite our best efforts, as you will see in several chapters, we were not always able to agree exactly on just what "classical music" meant; whether in using that expression we were speaking, essentially, about the highly skilled professional caste of musicians in Europe, North America, and Asia performing the music (largely) of the Western canon, or really, the whole gamut of activities, institutions and individuals associated with it, involving a broad repertoire all over the world. Even after the conclusion of our discussions, it is not clear whether we would all agree that things like Yo-Yo Ma's "Songs of Comfort and Hope," an eight-year-old practicing Bach Inventions in Dubai, and a beginner string trio in Kinshasa are involved in the same classical music "enterprise," any more than it can be easily determined whether a performance of *Tosca* at the Metropolitan Opera in New York, an amateur staging of *Brundibár* in Thailand, a version of Monteverdi's *Orfeo* at the Boston Early Music Festival and Tyshawn Sorey's *Perle Noire* are part of the same operatic world. Could classical music then be merely anything one might find in the classical section of a miraculously surviving record store, or simply the music that appears under "classical" on your iTunes or Spotify app?

If there were contrasting views on these matters among our group, it was even more difficult when it came to weighing the material on the chronological endpoints of the "classical" spectrum. Several of us wondered how to characterize Early Music, whether as "classical music" or another, more self-contained subset. And if trying to decide whether such things as Gregorian chant and Renaissance motets were part of any putative "classical music world," things were even trickier when we considered what constitutes "New Music" or "Contemporary Music." The jury is out on the basis of extended discussions with composers, performers, and critics, some of whom are insistent that what they do is part of, and dependent on, the ongoing tradition of Western classical music, while others are equally adamant about distancing themselves (some vehemently so) from that tradition.

It would be easy to get out of all this by making the platitudinous claim that "classical music" is but a mirror in which everyone sees themselves as they want to be, either in harmony with or opposed to, or to say that classical music is simply the sum total of everything people think it is. Part of the quandary, as my philosopher colleagues know, is the problem of making sets. One thinks one knows what belongs in the set called "classical music,"—say, Bach's *Goldberg Variations*—and what does not—Freddy and the Dreamers' recording of "I'm Telling You Now." But what about all those things that might or might not belong: light classics, film music, Duke Ellington's *Black, Brown and Beige*, the Three Tenors, nineteenth-century parlor songs, Croatian folksong arrangements? When confronted by a set with fuzzy edges one can either say that such a thing poses no problem at all, or argue more dangerously that the fuzzy edges are ultimately destabilizing and, like the voracious Pac-Man, always eat their way to the center of the set, destroying it. In this case the resulting conclusion would be that there is simply no such thing as classical music. At that point, someone is always bound to step in and say, "look, we all know what we're talking about, so let's stop the nonsense!" Yet after all this time, and considerable effort on the part of our group, we cannot and do not speak with a single voice about such things. This is not something negative, for it is our view that the tension, the problem of what comprises classical music and how we should regard it, refuses to disappear. Far from being a drawback, we believe that this dissent has contributed to the vitality of this cohesive yet diverse collection of essays.

Classical Music and the Academy

Since this report comes out of a project sponsored by a university, it is worth noting that attitudes towards classical music have changed dramatically in the academy in the last decades. As observed several times in this volume, under the influence of such things as feminist and queer theory, cultural studies, critical theory and critical race theory, the notion of a traditional canon has been relentlessly problematized, and dismissed outright by many as a massive impediment, or even fraud, both inaccurate and reactionary. It is argued in many quarters that the virtual monopoly classical music has had on curricula at many universities needs to be drastically dismantled, and many music departments have made fundamental changes to address this. At their most polemical, such approaches attack the classical tradition for everything from its white supremacy to misogyny, and consider it something like a sonic advertisement for imperialism, sexism, and colonialism. While more than half of our contributors come from outside the academic world, and while one should not necessarily overrate the influence of such ideas about classical music, they cannot be ignored, nor completely defended. It is, however, worth noting that many criticisms of classical music are written in a kind of opaque idiolect which makes a Beethoven quartet seem like Doo-wop by comparison. This is not incidental: to the extent that much academic writing fails to acknowledge the complicity between itself and the very things it sets itself against, it does not always need be taken as seriously as it would like to be. Yet other aspects of these arguments about the implications of classical music are thoughtfully couched and raise compelling questions that cannot be sidestepped; we have addressed them here when appropriate.

The Volume, Part 1

In **Chapter 1**, Ellen T. Harris and I have tried to tackle a central question about the "enduring value" of classical music. This is a thorny problem for many reasons. Even if we could "define" classical music, which presents challenges for the reasons suggested above, discussions of *value* inevitably trigger subjectivist and relativist impulses. Thus arguing for the value of classical music, even if carefully done, often comes close to proclaiming its superiority over other kinds of music—clearly an argument that is neither sensible, sustainable or correct.

In **Chapter 2** a pair of noted philosophers, Kit Fine and Chris Peacocke, take on another question which has become of considerable moment since the onset of the Covid-19 pandemic: wherein lies the power of live music? This is always a vexed question, especially since we clearly are capable of deriving enormous pleasure from recorded works. When we look at a "Rembrandt painting" in a book, we absolutely know it is a reproduction, but I am not sure we have that sense when listening to a recording of a Bartók string quartet. In fact, recorded music usually feels like the real thing rather than a copy of it. This has, of course, become even more confused over the last months, where we find ourselves making distinctions between live-in-person, recorded video, recorded audio, and live-streamed presentations. Yet the authors of this chapter make a powerful argument that "There is literally a world of difference between experiencing an event for real and experiencing a copy or simulacrum of the event; and this difference is of great value to us."

Preliminary data from a serious study of the effects of music education on everything from socialization to brain development and "connectivity" strongly suggests a correlation between music lessons and a host of positive attributes. While no evidence attaches this specifically to classical music, what obviously matters most is that some form of serious and even rigorous music education contributes to the process of becoming a mature individual. Both **Chapter 3** and **Chapter 4** address this issue of education in different ways. The former gives an overview of the way education plays out in various groups and categories, resisting the temptation to make global claims about what a music education should look like, especially in a period of major change. Yet the four authors of this chapter agree without hesitation that change must come. Chapter 4 is both a highly detailed scientific study of music training from the Brain and Creativity Institute at the University of Southern California, and an advocacy document for music education more broadly. It argues persuasively that access to quality music education "[s]hould not have to be on the grounds of research proven benefits…" but, rather, that "music and other arts are essential components of childhood development that will promote skill learning and will give children access to creative imagination in a fundamentally enjoyable and interactive context."

Few writers have had greater opportunity to track developments in new music than Alex Ross, who has chronicled them in *The New Yorker* and elsewhere for the last twenty-five years. In **Chapter 5**, writing about the field at large, he states simply that "the sheer quantity of music being produced from year to year defeats any attempt to encompass it." Nonetheless he describes a "thriving culture" that is "distinct from mainstream classical music" and he makes the further suggestion that finding some kind of rapprochement between this classical mainstream and the "kaleidoscopic" world of New Music is key to the future health and survival of this tradition.

It is not clear that either Alex Ross or Zachary Woolfe are able to sustain an equally optimistic tone about the world of musical journalism. They note, at the beginning of **Chapter 6**, that "since the advent of the digital age, journalism has encountered crises that have severely affected the financial stability of the business," with the decline of readership and advertising. That same technology, measured in clicks, reveals just how small the audience for, say, music criticism actually is, further resulting in the loss of positions and prestige. Zachary Woolfe suggests, in relation to *The New York Times*, that today's more national (and international) audience is less interested in local New York events than they once were, while Alex Ross muses that "journalism as we have long known it is in terminal decline." While he self-deprecatingly describes himself in jest as "a member of a dying profession covering a dying art," he also asserts that important voices will continue to appear and have their say.

While it is not clear that the survival of classical music as a sounding thing is identical to the survival of music journalism, the question of the health of large arts organizations is a different matter. These institutions—opera companies, symphony societies, presentation venues, and music festivals—are something like the major leagues in the sport of classical music, or perhaps more accurately, the aircraft carriers of the arts. While often criticized for the way they reinforce conservative tastes in programming, they also set a standard for skill, excellence, style and quality that plays a powerful role in everything from pedagogy to criticism. And it was the strong sense of our group that these organizations face unique dangers. For this reason, several essays in our collection focus on the importance of boards, audiences, management, and unions in creating the optimal conditions for the survival of these organizations. In **Chapter 7** Deborah Borda writes with great clarity about the significance and responsibility of governance for the financial health of large arts organizations, although many of her ideas might well be absorbed by anyone in a position of leadership, even the odd department chair. In fact, her ideas are so vitalizing that one can come to two different conclusions: the first, that organizations can indeed thrive and survive if they have highly skilled, honest, and visionary managers; the second, how difficult it is to find the kinds of leaders in any profession who can combine such things as intuition, faith, calculation, and charisma in order to move things in the right direction.

Chapter 8, by Ostrower and Calabrese, presents the results of a good deal of research based on two fundamental questions: what is the state of attendance at non-profit performing arts events, and how do we evaluate the financial health of the organizations which make those events possible? Through a careful review of the literature, the authors outline the ways in which various non-profit arts organizations are responding, and conclude that audience building "is not an isolated endeavor, but an undertaking that is related to other aspects of organization culture and operations." In **Chapter 9**, Matthew VanBesien draws on his experience in both labor and management to wrestle with questions concerning the relationship between orchestras and unions. In doing so he highlights several kinds of institutional response to the Covid-19 pandemic; some more inspiring than others. At the core of the issue lies a paradox which will continue to cause difficulties between unions and managers, that is, the irreconcilable tensions between the acknowledged need to pay players a fair wage and provide appropriate benefits, on the one hand, and, on the other, the unsustainable financial model of these large organizations, which lose more money each year and have to figure out where and how to pay for everything.[4]

Chapter 10 is concerned with one of the most pressing and difficult matters facing the world of classical music and the United States as a whole: diversity, equity and inclusion. Subtitled "A Call to Action," the chapter

---

4   For other recent exploration of this topic, see Jacobs (2020).

opens with a powerful autobiographical reflection by Anthony McGill, Principle Clarinetist of the New York Philharmonic, followed by Susan Feder's honest, painful and entirely accurate discussion of the history of racism in classical music and serious discussion of what needs to be done. While acknowledging that there has been change in such matters, Feder also raises issues with regard to mentoring, the lack of diversity on boards, whether the unions are prepared to make changes about such things as auditions and tenure in order to be fairer, and finally asks "[t]o what extent do the internal cultures of classical music organizations allow for mistreatment to be acknowledged and acted upon?"

In **Chapter 11** Laurent Bayle and Catherine Provenzano take on the broad question of the relationship between classical music and technology. While arguing that this particular moment of "estrangement" from concert life offers an opportunity to improve the quality of the online experience, there is a parallel longing "for something a livestreamed concert or a remote learning environment might never provide." Looking at everything from digital innovations to concert hall design, and from pedagogy to creativity, the authors offer a broad overview of the possibilities—and perils—of technology. The chapter concludes with Provenzano's peroration around Black Lives Matter, making it clear that "no digital tool is going to change the white-dominated and deeply classist lineage and current reality of the North American classical music world."

The Volume, Part 2

The second part of the volume offers five case studies related to specific venues, audiences and artforms. In the first of these, **Chapter 12**, Howard Herring and Craig Hall offer a view of the thorough, careful, and innovative approaches that can be used to attract and retain audiences. They focus on everything from venue type to programming, and also keep careful track of everything from age demographics to who returns and who does not. Taking advantage of everything from the weather in Miami to the presence of the charismatic Michael Tilson Thomas, the New World Symphony offers an example of a successful and thriving organization.

Tom Service begins **Chapter 13** wondering pessimistically whether anything called "classical" can attract the young audiences any medium needs to survive. Yet, in the end, he argues that there is much to be hopeful about. Noting the connection—pursued also today in the fields of musical scholarship—between music and gaming, he suggests that the sooner classical music loses its exclusive and elite status, the better. In his view, however, this push rarely emerges from the major classical music organizations but, in his words comes, "from the ground up," referring to contemporary composers, gamers, cinema audiences, and even to sampling by pop artists. Service goes on to trace the many different attempts of the BBC to connect with its audiences, whether through programs such as Slow Radio, the Ten Pieces Project or Red Brick Sessions, noting that there has never been a time where there has been both greater opportunity and more at stake.

Another important subject is what might broadly be called "classical music as world music." Our central focus on larger arts organizations in Europe and North America means that, with the exception of **Chapter 14**, which looks at contemporary music events in South Korea, we have not highlighted the considerable and profound impact of classical music in such places as China and Japan. Nor have we emphasised the emerging classical music cultures in the Middle East, Africa and India, or important practices throughout Latin America. How this plays out over the coming decades, with millions of music students in China alone, remains to be seen, but for this reason it is doubtful that the actual survival of classical music is in jeopardy.

In Chapter 14, Unsuk Chin and Maris Gothoni offer this trenchant observation: "In a way, the COVID-19 crisis could be likened to a macabre litmus test which mercilessly exposes the level of importance our societies attribute to non-functional and not immediately accessible art." After a rich meditation on the lot of the composer, from the historic past to the present day, the authors look at the enormously successful Ars Nova festival of the Seoul Philharmonic, which Unsuk Chin curated for more than a decade. Taking the challenge of difficult new music seriously, they make the simple but powerful point that "cutting-edge works had to be put into specific contexts in order to create a point of orientation for listeners and musicians alike."

In **Chapter 15** Laurent Bayle outlines new conceptions of programming, artistic space, and especially the question of placing performing arts organizations away from elite downtown districts. Documenting robust debates within France around the question of "classical music as an art of the past," the activities of the Philharmonie de Paris and the Démos project for children demonstrate the opposite: the vitality of the tradition when thoughtfully planned and presented. In particular, the creation of orchestras for children, combined with free training and musical instruments, along with the mixing of traditional repertoire with compositions reflecting different genres and a global reach, offers another model for revitalizing and sustaining the tradition.

Lest one think somehow that classical music is all about genius, we may mention that there is a great deal of it which is considered "mediocre" at best, by *aficionados* of that world. Ironically though, the very works whose greatness is most agreed upon are often derogated as "museum pieces," implying both a certain objectified immobility, and the lack of an organic connection to the rest of the world. So perhaps it is appropriate that our collection ends in museums and galleries, with a provocative meditation which contrasts the extraordinary popularity and success of the visual and plastic arts over the last several decades with the more problematic status of classical music. Noting that museums have been wonderfully adept at merging the traditional and the new, and alluding to the sexiness of the astonishing prices that have emerged for contemporary art, in **Chapter 16** Olivier Berggruen suggests several ways in which the classical music world might model that success. Of course, there is at least one nagging difference between a painting and a musical composition, and that is how much more time one usually invests in the latter. While one might easily move on in a matter of seconds from, say, a sculpture that does not resonate, sitting for the duration of a live new music performance can require a different level of patience.

***

We who love music, whether we call it classical, pop, hip hop, jazz, world music or anything else, like to believe that there are sounds for every occasion, and that no matter how dark or difficult the situation, music can in some way ease our burden or frame our experience. The last months—of Covid, of George Floyd, and the Capitol insurrection—remind us that there are some moments where no music of any kind seems appropriate. During such crises we may even yearn for a time when grappling with the challenges faced by classical music, and the other performing arts, seemed among the most urgent of matters. Let us hope those days will return in the not too distant future and that, when they do, this volume will make a modest contribution to helping us think of new ways of meeting those challenges.

Michael Beckerman
Berkeley, California
January, 2021

References

Brodeur, Michael Andor. 2020. "That Sound You're Hearing Is Classical Music's Long Overdue Reckoning with Racism", *The Washington Post*, 16 July, https://www.washingtonpost.com/lifestyle/style/that-sound-youre-hearing-is-classical-musics-long-overdue-reckoning-with-racism/2020/07/15/1b883e76-c49c-11ea-b037-f9711f89ee46_story.html

Jacobs, Julia. 2020. "Even When the Music Returns, Pandemic Pay Cuts Will Still Linger", *The New York Times*, 17 December, https://www.nytimes.com/2020/12/17/arts/music/performing-arts-unions-pandemic.html

Ross, Alex. 2020. "Black Scholars Confront White Supremacy in Classical Music", *The New Yorker*, 14 September, https://www.newyorker.com/magazine/2020/09/21/black-scholars-confront-white-supremacy-in-classical-music

Rotterdam Philharmonic Orchestra. 2020. "From Us, For You: Beethoven Symphony No. 9", 3:59, posted online by Rotterdam Philharmonic Orchestra, 20 March, *YouTube*, https://www.youtube.com/watch?v=3eXT60rbBVk

Tsioulcas, Anastasia. 2020. "Classical Music Tries to Reckon with Racism - on Social Media", *NPR*, 29 July, https://www.npr.org/2020/07/29/896200557/classical-music-tries-to-reckon-with-racism-on-social-media?t=1613753876393

Woolfe, Zachary, and Joshua Barone. 2020. "Musicians on How to Bring Racial Equity to Auditions", *The New York Times*, 10 September, https://www.nytimes.com/2020/09/10/arts/music/diversity-orchestra-auditions.html

PART I

1. The Enduring Value of Classical Music in the Western Tradition

Ellen T. Harris and Michael Beckerman

Any serious discussion of "the enduring value of classical music in the Western tradition" must jump a number of significant hurdles. We begin with definitions. What does "classical" mean? Even within the field of music the answer is confused. Sometimes it is used to denote a period of time (generally 1750 to 1800 or thereabouts). Charles Rosen in *The Classical Style* (1971/1998) defined it by composer: Haydn, Mozart, and Beethoven. Lawrence Kramer, in his book *Why Classical Music Still Matters* (2007), extends this definition to mean music "since the eighteenth century" (11), but his range doesn't reach much beyond 1900. More broadly, the word is used to encompass what for the lack of a better term can be called the European musical tradition stretching from the beginning of written music in the Middle Ages to the present, embracing music of vastly different styles, nationalities, and purposes.

The common method of defining Western classical music by antonym also never fully succeeds. The frequent contrast with "folk" music, for example, implies a sense of "folk" traditions as simple and the "classical" tradition as more complex. Although this has some merit (depending on how one defines "complexity"), it denigrates the intricacy of many folk traditions and overlooks the simplicity of much classical music. Defined as the opposite of "vernacular" music, classical music becomes akin to a "foreign" or, worse, "dead" language, an idea that may have more currency today than we would like to acknowledge. Richard Taruskin, in *The Oxford History of Western Music* (2005), suggests that classical music may have as its most distinguishing feature a largely written (literate) tradition, but oral and improvisatory practices coexist alongside notated scores (as Taruskin is quick to point out), and Western music is neither the only nor first tradition to have developed notation; further, the term "literate" for Western classical suggests that music in other traditions is "illiterate," which is not the case.

Even such seemingly specific words as "European" and "Western" need to be queried. Although these geographical markers may have had pertinence in earlier centuries in terms of music production—that is, where the music was written, who wrote it, and who performed it—the terms no longer carry any geographical significance given the creation and performance of so-called "Western" classical music around the globe. Joseph Auner, in *Music in the Twentieth and Twenty-First Centuries* (2013) for the series entitled "Western Music in Context," includes not only music influenced by music traditions from around the world, such as the gamelan-inspired music of Colin McPhee, Lou Harrison, and Evan Ziporyn, but also compositions from the global community of composers writing so-called Western classical music, including Toru Takemitsu and Chen Yi.

One of the more persistent definitions of classical music is that it is an elite tradition in opposition to popular music. Without doubt, this is also true in part. The Western classical tradition was principally created and preserved through the wealth of the Church and royal court, and to a large extent performed for the upper classes. However, there has always been exchange between court and street (e.g., with vocal music, later including opera, and dance music in particular), and composers from at least the fourteenth century engaged the vernacular traditions of their time (as in Dufay's masses, Haydn's symphonies, and Dvořák's dances). But that doesn't change the overall historical picture of how classical music was generally produced and heard.

If classical music remains elite today, it is because those concerned with its production and performance have enjoyed its historical prestige and fostered it in large and often forbidding institutions. And yet, we, the authors of this chapter, have seen the joy and serenity that live performance of classical music can bring to people from all walks of life—including children without any prior exposure to its sounds, the homeless,[1] and the frail and aged. In this book, Western classical music is examined in terms of the issues it is confronted with today: live performance in the face of sound recording and reproduction, failing music education, shaky financial stability, and audience expectations. It is examined in these terms because of our belief in the enduring value of this music for all.

But how can we ascribe "enduring value" to something so difficult to define? Classical music ranges from medieval chant and sacred works best heard in reverberant places of worship, to symphonies and operas performed in great purpose-built halls and opera houses, to the song heard in the privacy of a home, to marching bands in the streets, to contemporary compositions incorporating multiple compositional practices performed in untraditional venues. The musical traditions of North America have pushed the boundaries still further with such contributions as the Great American Songbook, Blues and Jazz, the Broadway musical, and the rise of film music. And the influence of global musical traditions has expanded the field of Western classical music still further. For those who decry the Western classical tradition as elite and hegemonic, the embrace of popular and global stylistic elements within the classical tradition becomes a form of neo-colonialism, appropriation, and commodification. For others, the openness to different ideas and styles is, and always has been, a strength of Western music. Although the geographical range of classical music was largely limited to Europe until the twentieth century, composers were always on the lookout for new stylistic ideas across borders (whether it was the Flemish eyeing the English in the fifteenth century; the English learning from the Italians in the early seventeenth century; or the Italians adopting French and German approaches in nineteenth-century opera).

When we assert the "enduring value" of "classical music in the Western tradition," we do not, therefore, privilege any single element of this music, nor claim the superiority of classical music over other musical traditions at least as old and complex (although we are aware of those attitudes existing within the field). Rather, we argue that a great deal of music produced within the broadly construed Western tradition has intrinsic worth, giving it value that does not necessitate invidious

---

1   Shelter Music Boston is one such example. Its website lists many others with the same values.

comparisons. Nor does "enduring" for us indicate the immortalization of a core repertoire. The irony is that with few exceptions (Gregorian chant being one), and until the nineteenth century, the goal and history of Western classical music lay in contemporary performance rather than a tradition preserved in performance through time (in the way that some traditional folk musics—the Japanese shamisen tradition, and Senegalese sabar music, for example—have been passed on through generations of performers). That is, the predominant feature of classical music until the nineteenth century, with its development of large-scale performance venues, "Complete Works" editions, and the growth of technology, was a desire to constantly supersede itself. Around 1476, Johannes Tinctoris applauded "musica nova" and rejected any music written before 1430; Claudio Monteverdi defended the apparent stylistic solecisms in his music by calling them the "seconda prattica" as opposed to the older, more rigid practice; and in the eighteenth century the Academy of Ancient Music described "ancient music" as that which was at least thirty years old. The inherent strength of the Western musical tradition is not that it is "better" than other musical traditions, but rather its freedom of construction over centuries that has permitted a wide range of intellectual rigor, emotional depth, light-hearted frivolity, and spiritual intensity whose potency and communicative power is not restricted to the period of its composition, however much it may reflect it. Western classical music cannot, therefore, be thought of as stable or as a single type of music; the music of Palestrina, Bach, Stravinsky, and Glass co-exist within a musical framework of continual and contemporary rejuvenation.

As classical music is largely a literate tradition, the preservation of musical scores from centuries past allows for the continuing performance of music today apart from its original temporal and social context. This survival, akin to an architectural heritage, surely comprises one of the world's great artistic legacies, but the *intrinsic value* of classical music lies rather in its continual reimagining. Previously considered a "universal language," this older repertoire is now more properly recognized as a particular outgrowth of Western culture that has not always translated easily to other cultures, even though many cultures have embraced it. Its circumscribed geographical origin makes it no less valuable; indeed, the continuing use of the word "Western" in our nomenclature for this music is obsolete. Classical music of today is no longer limited by geography, nationality, or race, but global in its freedom and inclusion of difference (think, say, of Scott Joplin, Osvaldo Golijov, Tan Dun, Wynton Marsalis, or Thomas Adès). Classical music (based on a European tradition of explicit notation enabling replication) continues to thrive best—in both composition and performance—on exploration and innovation; it grows ever more meaningful through repeated, close listening and, like all types of music, endures through live performance and technology well beyond the context of its creation.

References

Auner, Joseph. 2013. *Music in the Twentieth and Twenty-First Centuries: Western Music in Context* (New York: W. W. Norton).

Kramer, Lawrence. 2007. *Why Classical Music Still Matters* (Berkeley: University of California Press), https://doi.org/10.1525/california/9780520250826.001.0001

Rosen, Charles. 1970/1988. *The Classical Style: Haydn, Mozart, Beethoven* (New York: W. W. Norton).

Shelter Music Boston, https://www.sheltermusicboston.org/

Taruskin, Richard. 2005. *The Oxford History of Western Music*, 6 vols (New York: W. W. Norton).

2. The Live Concert Experience: Its Nature and Value[1]

Christopher Peacocke and Kit Fine

After the introduction of social distancing in response to the COVID-19 pandemic, there was, for several months, no live performance in Europe and the United States. This essay aims to analyze the nature of what it was that we were missing so much in those months. When the BBC resumed the broadcast of live performance on 1 June 2020 from the Wigmore Hall in London, the pianist on that occasion, Stephen Hough, said in an interview with Jon Snow, "The audience is not just a passive thing when you're going to a concert, it's a very active involvement in the music. I think that a performer senses this [...] you feel an electricity there you cannot replicate".

Virgil Thomson, the composer and music critic, wrote that we never enjoy a recorded performance in the same way as we enjoy a live performance (2014: 251). The same applies to live performance in the theatre and to attendance at a sports event, as opposed to seeing a performance or game on DVD or a TV recording. This difference is of great value to us. But why?

One point of difference lies in the lower level of quality of the reproduction. Much recorded music is heard through headphones from mp3 files. But this cannot be a full explanation of the difference. Listening even to lossless files through speakers connected to the most sensitive equipment remains a significantly different experience from that of hearing the same music live in a concert hall. So we should not succumb to the temptation to think that the only significant difference between

---

1   We thank Paul Boghossian for advice, both expository and substantive.

live and recorded music lies in the quality of the auditory signal. Even when this difference is completely eradicated, there remains a special value in listening to a live performance. We suggest that this is so for several reasons.

When we sit in the concert hall or sports arena, we know from the very circumstances of our situation that we are experiencing the events for real. This is a crucial element of our experience. There is literally a world of difference between experiencing an event for real and experiencing a copy or simulacrum of the event; and this difference is of great value to us. We suggest that the difference is rooted in our deep need for authenticity and a relation to the very event or object produced by the performer or artist. Consider a similar case of viewing the real *Mona Lisa* versus a clever forgery. The one experience is far more valuable than the other. We might be willing to travel many miles to go to the Louvre for the one experience but unwilling to get out of our armchair for the other.

Another important aspect of live performance concerns joint awareness. In live performance, the performers and the audience are present to one another, and not merely in the sense of occupying the same place. Each is aware of and responsive to the other. The performer intends the audience to hear the music in a certain way; the audience is aware of and responsive to this intention; and the performer, in his or her turn, is aware of—and, in many cases, responsive to—the audience's response; and so on. There is in this way an ongoing and symbiotic link between the two, of which both sides are at some level aware. One might say that the listener is not a mere participant. Rather, both musician and listener contribute in their own way to the musical performance.

Joint awareness and activity of this sort pervades many aspects of our life. It is present from the moments we share with family or friends to our participation in the culture or society at large. This sharing—the act of our doing these things together—is a large part of what gives these activities meaning and makes them so enjoyable to us. Indeed, as noted by such neuroscientists as Mona Chanda and Daniel Levitin (2013), they are correlated with raised levels of the hormone, oxytocin.

This joint awareness is also something from which the audience and the performers, separately, can benefit. Consider an audience in a cinema watching a "Live in HD" broadcast from an opera house. The audience in this case will not be involved in joint activity and awareness with the performers. But they will be involved in a joint activity with one another. This is a shared experience of some value, one from which they can learn. Seeing how the rest of the audience reacts to the various elements of the opera, they can begin to appreciate how they themselves might react.

Many performers (though not all) also value and benefit from the presence of an audience. Alfred Brendel described the experience of playing in the recording studio as performing "as in a tomb" (1990: 202). Wilhelm Furtwängler is reported to have been reluctant to record Beethoven's 9th Symphony under studio conditions (Cook, 1995). Recording experts such as Michael Haas speak of "'the great arc' that mysteriously disappears in takes, sapping all force from once-animated performances" (2009: 61).

Herbert von Karajan (Thielemann, 2015), Daniel Barenboim (2002), and Christian Thielemann (2015) have all spoken of the importance of spontaneity in live performance. Spontaneity has several dimensions, but one aspect of it is the feeling that "This is it!"—that what is done cannot be undone or redone. That feeling could, of course, be present in the recording studio in which there is a requirement to record in a single take. But live performance seems to bring out other, perhaps even more important, aspects of spontaneity.

For any performance may be adjusted in the light of the context in which it takes place. Even the background awareness that an audience is perceiving the performance in real time can enhance the performer's awareness of the possibilities for adjusting the current performance. This adds to the level of excitement and engagement when even the smallest adjustment in timing, volume, or phrasing can produce utterly different results. Barenboim writes, "No performance should be allowed to pass without the performer having gained some degree of further understanding" (2002: 218). That may be a little strong. But any performance, be it musical, theatrical, sporting, or even academic, that is done before an audience will involve an element of felt uncertainty and the possibility of a new or renewed understanding of what is being performed. Indeed, the ability to produce a spontaneous performance is a kind of socially embedded skill, whose exercise is best produced only in the presence of an audience.

By listening with others, we become better listeners and by performing with, and to, others we become better performers. It is hard to see how a musical performer could flourish if he or she never played before a live audience. It is also hard to believe that a musical listener could flourish without ever having attended a live performance. The very vitality of our musical traditions rests upon the continued role of live performance.

We have so far emphasized the auditory qualities of music. However, an important part of our enjoyment of a musical performance is visual. When a pianist makes a leap in the left hand in the opening notes of Beethoven's Hammerklavier Sonata, we literally see his or her virtuosity, something that could not be appreciated from the sounds themselves. But the visual aspects of performance may be far more pervasive than we ever expected. Experiments by Chia-Jung Tsay (2013) show that even expert musicians were much better at judging which contestants were winners of music competitions when given video of the performance in addition to sound. The visual aspects were adding, in a significant way, to their whole musical experience.

The total visual context can also matter. The experience of hearing a Josquin motet is enhanced by hearing it in a cathedral rather than a concert hall, even if the concert hall is adjusted to reproduce the acoustic effects of the cathedral. Of course, a recording may also provide video as well as audio information. The subjects in Tsay's experiments were provided with video. But it is unlikely that we will ever successfully reproduce the fully rounded experience which combines elements of both; and even though virtual reality may make our total experience more realistic, it can never make it real.

Another important part of our enjoyment of a musical performance is its social or cultural role. The music we listen to belongs to a long and distinguished tradition. In attending live performances that offer new works or provide new insights into existing works, we experience and contribute to the renewal and extension of our cultural heritage. Attendance is, in this way, an affirmation of our common culture. This is something that could hardly be done from our own home or the confines of a listening booth.

Another important part of music's social role is its role as a unifier. By bringing people together musically in a public context we bring them together in other ways as well. Under apartheid in South Africa, young blacks said that, for them, the songs of struggle of the period "broke the sense of non-belonging" (Mohare, 2017). It was presumably for this reason that the songs were banned from broadcasts by the nationalist South African government in the time of apartheid. The freedom anthems of the civil rights movement in the United States had the same powerful effect. A live performer expressing the emotions involved in these anthems engages the empathy of the audience all the more directly. Martin Luther King was well aware of the power in public performance of Nina Simone singing "I wish I know how it would feel to be free". Another well-known example is provided by the performance of Shostakovich's 7th Symphony during the siege of Leningrad. In all of these cases, it is the public and political aspects of the performance that are paramount. But even when politics are not in question, shared musical experience can still play an important role in shaping our shared values and interests.

None of these points is meant to denigrate or to detract from the value of recorded music. There are respects in which recorded music has its own advantage. Sometimes a recording can bring out features that it would be hard or impossible to bring out under conditions of live performance. In multiple takes, one can achieve a level of perfection that would be generally impossible in a live performance; and, of course, a recording is, by its very nature, reproducible at very little cost. Recordings can provide a practically indispensable stepping stone to the appreciation of live performance.

Nonetheless, recorded music can never be a substitute for the real thing. Not only is live performance of great value as a musical experience in itself, it is also of great benefit to musicians and listeners alike; and not only does it play an important musical role, it also plays a broader cultural and social role. Without it, we and the society to which we belong would be much poorer.

References

Barenboim, Daniel. 2002. *A Life in Music*, ed. by M. Lewin, revised by P. Huscher (London: Weidenfeld and Nicolson).

Brendel, Alfred. 1990. "A Case for Live Recordings", in *Music Sounded Out: Essays, Lectures, Interviews, Afterthoughts* (London: Robson), pp. 200–207.

Chanda, Mona, and Daniel Levitin. 2013. "The Neurochemistry of Music", *Trends in Cognitive Sciences*, 17(4): 179–193, https://doi.org/10.1016/j.tics.2013.02.007

Cook, Nicholas. 1995. "The Conductor and the Theorist: Furtwangler, Schenker and the First Movement of Beethoven's Ninth Symphony", in *The Practice of Performance: Studies in Musical Interpretation*, ed. by J. Rink (Cambridge: Cambridge University Press), pp. 105–125.

Haas, M. 2009. "Broadening Horizons: 'Performance' in the Studio", in *The Cambridge Companion to Recorded Music*, ed. by Nicholas Cook et al. (Cambridge: Cambridge University Press), pp. 59–62, https://doi.org/10.1017/ccol9780521865821.010

Mohare, Thabiso. 2017. "The Sound of Soweto: Part Two", BBC World Service, 25 May, https://www.bbc.co.uk/programmes/p0534ps9

Snow, Jon. 2020. "Classical Music Concerts without Audiences Streamed Live", *Channel 4 News*, 1 June, https://channel4.com/news/classical-music-concerts-without-audiences-streamed-live

Thielemann, Christian, with Christine Lemke-Matwey. 2015. *My Life with Wagner*, transl. by A. Bell (London: Weidenfeld and Nicolson).

Thomson, Virgil. 2014. "Processed Music", in *Music Chronicles 1940-1954*, ed. by T. Page (New York: Library of America, Penguin Random House), pp. 249–252.

Tsay, Chia-Jung. 2013. "Sight over Sound in the Judgment of Music Performance", *Proceedings of the National Academy of Sciences*, 110(36): 14580–14585, https://doi.org/10.1073/pnas.1221454110

Additional Reading

The importance of experiencing the relation to the performer in live music is brought out vividly by those suffering from what is usually called "depersonalization syndrome". These subjects accurately perceive the world around them, but say that it does not seem real to them. The sense of reality that is, by contrast, present in healthy subjects is a necessary condition for appreciating the relations enjoyed in live performance. Any account that omits this is missing a crucial component of the phenomenology of live music. For discussion of the philosophical interest of depersonalization syndrome, see:

Dokic, Jérôme, and Jean-Rémy Martin. 2017. "Felt Reality and the Opacity of Perception", *Topoi*, 36: 299–309, https://doi.org/10.1007/s11245-015-9327-2

On the significance of live performance in the theatre, see:

Fischer-Lichte, Erika. 2008. *The Transformative Power of Performance: A New Aesthetics*, trans. by S. Jain (Abingdon: Routledge), https://doi.org/10.4324/9780203894989

3. Education and Classical Music

*Michael Beckerman, Ara Guzelimian,
Ellen T. Harris, and Jenny Judge*

The question of classical music education is broad and multifaceted; this chapter covers four significant areas, each of which plays a part in the creation of a "classical music culture," and each of which may be instrumental in the evolution of this culture in the future. The first section, "Musical Education and Childhood Development," examines the current state of research concerning the effects of musical education on everything from the brain to social systems; the second section, "Music Education in the United States," provides an overview of the recent history of K-12 arts education (that is, education from kindergarten to 12th grade); the third part, "Educating Professional Musicians," discusses traditions of conservatory training in the United States and North America; and the concluding topic, "Musicology in the Twenty-First Century" looks at developments in the way music is presented and taught at university level.

1. Musical Education and Childhood Development

It is easy to forget that there was a time when the only way to hear music was to be present while somebody played or sang. In much of Europe and North America, the parish church was the only readily accessible public music venue for many: for reasons spanning the geographical and the socioeconomic, regular attendance at public performances was not an option for most. It was thus natural for the music-lover of modest means to learn to play and sing, and to ensure that the children of the household were given the opportunity to do likewise.

But the advent of recording technology changed all that. The affordability of playback devices, and, in particular, the preponderance of high-quality recordings available for free (or close to it) on the Internet, threatens domestic music-making with extinction. Why bother stumbling amateurishly through a Mozart sonata, a jazz standard from the Real Book or some Beatles arrangements for Easy Piano when one could at any moment hear the real thing, in glorious high fidelity, for free? And more to the point: why pay for expensive music lessons so that one's children can do likewise?

It is clear that music lessons are no longer the obvious way to ensure the presence of music in the home. But does this mean that there's no point in a musical education any more? A growing body of evidence from developmental psychology suggests that this is far from being the case.

Musical training brings with it a range of perceptual and motor advantages, first of all (for a parallel view of this issue see Chapter 4). Adults that have had musical training are more sensitive to pitch (Tervaniemi et al., 2005; Micheyl et al., 2006) and duration of sounds (Musacchia et al., 2007), as well as more accurate at synchronising their movements to a beat than adults that have not had such training (Drake, Penel, & Bigand, 2000). These sensorimotor benefits are reflected in striking anatomical differences: the brain of a musician tends to have more gray matter in the auditory cortex (Schlaug, Jäncke, Huang, & Steinmetz, 1995), and also in regions involved in integrating multisensory information (Bangert et al., 2006). Musical training also seems to be correlated with enlarging of the corpus callossum (Schlaug, Jäncke, Huang, Staiger, & Steinmetz, 1995), which facilitates communication across brain hemispheres, and the arcuate fasciculus, a region that mediates between sound perception and vocal control. Evidence suggests that these advantages have already begun to manifest in the brains of six-year-olds (Hyde et al., 2009).

While the widespread intuition that musical training can improve mathematical competence is probably baseless, there is growing evidence that music lessons can help linguistic and verbal skills. Those with musical training tend to be more sensitive to sequential and syntactic structure in spoken language (François & Schon, 2011), and remarkably, children that have taken music lessons for eighteen months tend to outperform their non-musician peers on vocabulary tests (Forgeard et al., 2008). Musical training is also correlated with enhanced verbal memory (Kilgour, Jakobson, & Cuddy, 2000), and associations between musical training and reading skills have been documented, even when the musical training involved does not involve learning to read musical notation (Moreno et al., 2011). In general, musical training is thought to lead to enhanced executive functioning—a set of processes involved in goal-directed planning, problem-solving, inhibitory control, working memory, and attention—though the precise nature of the interaction is still somewhat unclear.

It is unlikely that musical training makes you "smarter" in the sense of IQ scores, despite the ballyhoo surrounding the initial reporting of the roundly-debunked "Mozart effect". And many of the developmental benefits cited above are unlikely to be unique to musical education, still less a Western "classical" one. That being said, learning to play an instrument, or to sing, does afford distinctive advantages, and the quantifiable developmental advantages listed above may turn out to be the least compelling ones. Scholars have proposed that music-making evolved as a powerful tool for social cohesion. As our pre-Spotify forebears knew very well, playing and singing together, even in an amateurish way, is one of the most fulfilling and sometimes even profound experiences anyone can have.

A "classical" education in singing or performance is, of course, very far from being the only option on the table in this respect. In turn, it is undeniable that information technology, even as it undermines the case for learning an instrument as a way of ensuring the presence of music in the home, at the same time places a host of valuable resources at the disposal of the would-be domestic performer: YouTube tutorials, crowd-sourced guitar tabs, not to mention high-powered recording software for home studios. That being said, the emphasis on discipline and technical facility that the traditional pedagogical systems embody places one in a good position not just to play some of the greatest pieces of music written within the "classical" genres, but also to try one's hand at jazz, folk and much more besides.

The conception of music as something to be passively consumed is a very recent one. For most of our history, music has been something we do: a profoundly social activity that binds communities together. A classical music education is by no means the only way to learn to play music with others, but it's a good place to begin.

2. K-12 Music Education in the United States

A general consensus exists among educators, parents, and students in the United States that "many schools today are falling far short of providing students with a full experience of the arts" (PCAH, 2011: 3), but meaningful and detailed statistics are difficult to find. The US Department of Education reports that the percentage of public elementary schools offering instruction in music remained the same in 2009–2010 as in 1999–2000 at 94% (Parsad & Spiegelman, 2012: 5), but this was based on self-reporting from the schools, "most" of which provided this instruction "at least once a week" (Ibid.: 6). Questions about the adequacy of instruction, preparation of the teachers, and student outcomes were left unaddressed. Further, as reported by the President's Committee on the Arts and Humanities, "Recent results from a survey in Washington State show that 33% of elementary students receive less than one hour a week on the average of arts instructions, and almost 10% offer no formal arts instruction at all" (PCAH, 2011: 31). One is left to wonder how many of such schools are included in the stated 94% of elementary schools reporting music instruction in the Department of Education report.

The No Child Left Behind Act, passed in 2001 and signed into law in 2002, mandated the teaching of arts as a core education subject (Ibid.: 48, n. 31) but only required standards-based testing in grades 3–8 for English, mathematics, science, history, and geography. Because the results of this testing continue to determine future funding for the school or district, school curricula have increasingly focused on these tests to the detriment of other required core subjects (and, as some have argued, to the instruction in the subjects being tested). As a consequence of the "subsequent economic pressures on the finances of many school districts, music and arts education programs have been subject to significant budget cuts and de-emphases" (NAMM Foundation and Grunwald Associates LLC, 2015: 4).

Substantive programs in the arts in K-12 education offer the possibility of a lifetime of inspirational listening and performing experiences. In addition, there are "substantial studies indicating strong correlations between arts education and academic achievement, especially for the country's growing number of at-risk children" (Ibid.: 4). Unfortunately, the primary goal of No Child Left Behind to make American students first in the world in science and mathematics was not achieved, so that the subsequent national education plan focused K-12 education even more narrowly on STEM subjects (science, technology, engineering, mathematics) without asking whether the lack of a strong arts component in No Child Left Behind may have played a role in its failure. Instead, taking no notice and making no mention of the arts or the humanities, the plan of the National Science and Technology Council seeks to "prepare 100,000 excellent new K-12 STEM teachers by 2020," "support a 50 percent increase in the number of US youth who have an authentic STEM experience each year," and "graduate one million additional students [from college] with degrees in STEM fields over the next 10 years" (2013: viii).

It might be useful in closing, therefore, to consider the role of arts education at Massachusetts Institute of Technology (MIT), a premier American institution with a focus on STEM subjects. Not only do successful high school applicants to MIT present a very strong arts background (suggesting an important synergy of the arts and STEM subjects in K-12 education), but also the arts are viewed as a strong curricular partner at the Institute in innovation and creativity. L. Rafael Reif, President of MIT, could not have expressed these values more clearly (2013): "Today, unprecedented numbers of incoming students—80 percent—arrive at MIT with deep experience in the arts, *especially in music* [italics added]. In that context, the arts have never been more integral to the life of MIT nor more deserving of our focus and attention. We believe that our students and faculty in the performing arts deserve their own 'laboratory', an inspiring space for experimentation, collaboration, apprenticeship, and performance."

3. Educating Professional Musicians

The modern history of advanced degree-granting education for musicians in the United States dates to the mid-nineteenth century, with the founding of the Peabody Institute in 1857, the Conservatory at

Oberlin College in 1865, and the New England Conservatory in 1866. The most ambitious effort centered on the National Conservatory of Music of America, founded in 1885 by Mrs. Jeannette Thurber, a crusading philanthropist with the mission of establishing a federally funded national conservatory (chartered by Congress in 1891) dedicated to creating "a national musical spirit".

Like most American institutes of musical education, the newly formed National Conservatory modeled itself on a European standard (in this case, the Paris Conservatory) and Mrs. Thurber scored a major coup by enticing one of the most prominent European composers of the era, Antonín Dvořák, to serve as its director. The National Conservatory was most unusual in its time for its progressive admissions policies welcoming women and African-American students.

Despite this attempt to create a uniquely American institution, much of the history of American musical education relies on the presence of great European teachers and musicians well into the twentieth century. To take but one example, the violinist Franz Kneisel (1865–1926) is emblematic of so much in the transference of European tradition to American music life. After his formative education in Europe, he was appointed concertmaster of the Boston Symphony in 1885, formed the Kneisel Quartet (which gave the premiere of Dvořák's "American" Quartet in 1894), founded Kneisel Hall in 1902, an immersive summer school focused on chamber music which continues to this day, and, in 1905, became the first head of the violin department at the newly founded Institute of Musical Art in New York City, which later evolved into the Juilliard School.

Great European musicians like Kneisel occupied key leadership positions in most of the major American orchestras, became highly influential teachers, helped define the leading conservatories by validating their stature, and created summer programs and festivals which are central to American musical life. A subsequent infusion of musicians fleeing war and persecution in Europe in the 1930s further solidified this European core of American musical education and concert life. Again, one need only look at even the smallest sampling of influential teachers and performers from this era—Rudolf Serkin, Ivan Galamian, Artur Schnabel, Gregor Piatigorsky—to measure the centrality of these artists to American musical life.

Inevitably, a major focus of American musical education well into the twentieth century was the preservation and continuation of this great tradition, a direction which has created an inherently conservative or, more accurately, conservationist approach. Much of the teaching relied heavily on the relationship between teacher and student, master and apprentice. The relatively small number of major conservatories and university-based performance programs combined with the striking growth of American orchestras, opera companies, and teaching positions provided a relatively stable pipeline to employment opportunities.

But there also existed a narrow, rather monastic approach to the schooling of musicians in many places. It was assumed that by locking a young musician away for hours in a hermetically sealed practice room or studio, enough devotion and hard work would eventually lead students to success in a world ready to receive them. The iconic triumph of Van Cliburn at the 1958 Tchaikovsky Competition greatly heightened this sensibility. Music theory and musicianship skills were taught only as needed to enhance performance. A major divide existed between the superb musical scholarship found in the academic programs of major universities and the successful practitioners of the art itself in conservatories and university performance programs.

In the past forty years, there has been significant progress in the best practices of the most forward-looking institutions, moving towards a broader, more comprehensive approach to educating a "complete musician". There is a greater presence and integration of significant music history and liberal arts curricula. A focus on arts advocacy, social engagement and the role of citizen-artist continues to grow. The core repertoire, once focused tightly on Bach to the mid-twentieth century at best, has expanded to include early music and period instrument programs on one end of the historic spectrum to thriving new music ensembles at the other. There is far more meaningful interaction between scholarship and practice.

We are witnessing an expansion of important programs for the education of musicians, with major new schools (i.e. the Colburn School), much expanded and invigorated programs at existing schools (i.e. the Shepherd School of Music at Rice University) and substantially improved scholarship or tuition-free programs at long-established schools (i.e. the Yale School of Music). Paradoxically, there has been a contraction in the traditional career outlets, with orchestras and opera companies facing serious financial challenges, some reducing their scale of operation and even shutting down outright.

The growth of a more entrepreneurial model for present-day musicians has been a necessary response. The most progressive schools now teach, encourage and, in some cases, even fund student-created musical initiatives. These newly created collective ensembles are often nimbler and more wide-ranging in their programming, more imaginative in their choice of venues (witness the emergence of alternative and often intimate concert spaces in several major cities), and less bound by burdensome fixed costs. It's no surprise that enterprising ensembles such as The Knights (Juilliard), ICE, and Eighth Blackbird (Oberlin) all began as once-student initiatives at their respective schools.

It remains to be seen if the field of advanced education for musicians can respond to the many challenges of a changing environment. Applications and admissions remain robust and even growing at many major schools. But the financial burdens, in particular the troubling growth of student debt, loom very large at a time when employment opportunities may be declining and are certainly less immediately remunerative in the case of entrepreneurial ventures. Although the best of the schools have endorsed the important value of social engagement, diversity and inclusion remain unrealized hopes at best. It is essential that America's great schools of music constantly question and reimagine how the education of a twenty-first-century musician must continue to evolve.

4. Musicology in the Twenty-First Century

Up until the 1960s, academic programs in musicology (the research-based study of music) reliably contained an in-depth sequence of classes on the Western tonal (major–minor) system, its modal predecessors, and written notational practices in parallel with a similar sequence focusing on the written musical record from medieval chant (or even the musical systems of classical Greece) to the present as understood through a sequence of great (mostly male) composers (Léonin to Boulez).

As with so much else, the 1960s ushered in a thorough examination and re-evaluation of this approach that continues to evolve and develop.

Poststructuralism (or deconstructionism) shifted the focus of study from "the music itself" to a broader contextual and societal approach, and Roland Barthes' "death of the author" meant that deciphering the "intent" of individual composers through detailed source studies of sketches and individual notes was increasingly supplanted by studies of societal meaning and audience response.

Much of this shift was inflected by the growth of ethnomusicology, the study of worldwide musical systems, many of which were older and more sophisticated than Western practice (such as those of India and China). Ethnographical and anthropological approaches were widely adopted, placing Western music in its global context. That is, Western music was seen less as a "universal language," than as an example of a universal desire for music as part of community structure and social fabric. To some degree, scholarly interest in world music had been previewed at the beginning of the twentieth century by the growth of global (and also folk) musical traditions as a significant force in Western composition, making an understanding of non-Western music necessary even in the study of Western composers: Debussy (pentatonic scale), Stravinsky (African rhythmic patterns), and Britten (Japanese Noh theater) are only three of the most obvious examples.

There can be no question about the worth and importance of this broader focus in music scholarship, except that some older and valuable forms of close reading have been largely given up or even discredited. One of the great ironies of this change worldwide is that while many music departments in North American institutions of higher learning are eliminating any requirement for the specific study of Western music (Harvard University is only the most recent school to adopt this approach), the history and practice of Western music is increasingly fundamental to the study of music-making in China, Japan, and parts of Africa to the same extent that the global study of music is necessary for an understanding of Western classical music from at least the beginning of the twentieth century.

The issue before us is not how to reinstate in North America the practice of music study from before 1960, which would be to adopt a blinkered approach that would make it difficult even to understand the rich diversity of contemporary classical music, but whether higher education can (or should) preserve a way to interrogate musical value and understanding within a global context.

Realities and Fictions

Our investigations in these matters are not helped by the reality that, as has been noted, "classical music" is essentially a fiction. Referring to it as a coherent body of material, is, in fact, a "classic" example of a set with fuzzy edges; it contains both miniatures and works of monster length, compositions intended for the most serious contemplation and light dance pieces; works created for amateurs and those intended for virtuosi—there is hardly a generalization about it that will hold.

Further, as we have noted, "education" in relation to classical music involves at least four strands: training for those intending to be professional musicians; serious musical study for those engaging with the subject as an important part of their education (everything from piano lessons to theory courses); music as part of a general college curriculum and more "incidental" uses of music in K-12 settings; and the kinds of music education involving arts organizations and institutions—program notes, pre-concert talks, etc. Each of these has played some part in the creation of what might broadly be described as a "classical music culture," and each of these may play a significant role in how this culture unfolds in the future.

On this matter we also raise the question of whether some current trends in higher education that associate classical music negatively with everything from elite high culture to structural racism and a shifting focus to other genres and international musical traditions will necessarily have a dampening effect on audiences, or whether something more dynamic and challenging might evolve that rather situates the Western classical tradition more broadly as part of world culture.

Concluding Remarks

The unrealized hopes of classical music education gained overwhelming urgency in the summer of 2020, as the deep underlying fissures of American society burst unstoppably with the brutal death of George Floyd, another moment in centuries of such horrifying incidents laying bare the disease of racism. At the time of this writing, classical music in America is facing a reckoning of its neglect of Black composers and performers, as well as a broader neglect of women composers and composers of diverse ethnicities and national origins beyond the European tradition.

In addition, the coronavirus pandemic has forced a painful pause in virtually all in-person musical performance, with musical education largely moving to an online format. It is a time that severely tests the capacity for innovation and flexibility in these institutions. And yet, there have been glimmers of successful adaptations to digital transmission that may offer different avenues forward to complement the return to live performance.

The urgency of the moment makes it essential that America's great schools of music question and reimagine how to educate an evolving twenty-first-century musician.

References

Bangert, Marc, Thomas Peschel, Gottfried Schlaug, Michael Rotte, Dieter Drescher, Hermann Hinrichs, Hans-Jochen Heinze, and Eckhart Altenmüller. 2006. "Shared Networks for Auditory and Motor Processing in Professional Pianists: Evidence from FMRI Conjunction", *Neuroimage*, 30: 917–926, https://doi.org/10.1016/j.neuroimage.2005.10.044

Drake, Carolyn, Amandine Penel, and Emmanuel Bigand. 2000. "Tapping in Time with Mechanically and Expressively Performed Music", *Music Perception*, 18: 1–23, https://doi.org/10.2307/40285899

Forgeard, Marie, Ellen Winner, Andrea Norton, and Gottfired Schlaug. 2008. "Practicing a Musical Instrument in Childhood Is Associated with Enhanced Verbal Ability and Nonverbal Reasoning", *PLoS ONE*, 3(10): 1–8, https://doi.org/10.1371/journal.pone.0003566

François, Clément, and Daniele Schon. 2011. "Musical Expertise Boosts Implicit Learning of both Musical and Linguistic Structures", *Cerebral Cortex*, 21(10): 2357–2365, https://doi.org/10.1093/cercor/bhr022

Hyde, Krista L., Jason Lerch, Andrea Norton, Marie Forgeard, Ellen Winner, Alan C. Evans, and Gottfried Schlaug. 2009. "Musical Training Shapes Structural Brain Development", *The Journal of Neuroscience*, 29: 3019–3025, https://doi.org/10.1523/jneurosci.5118-08.2009

Kilgour, Andrea R., Lorna S. Jakobson, and Lola L. Cuddy. 2000. "Music Training and Rate of Presentation as Mediators of Text and Song Recall", *Memory & Cognition*, 28(5): 700-710, https://doi.org/10.3758/bf03198404

Micheyl, Cristophe, Karine Delhommeau, Xavier Perrot, and Andrew J. Oxenham. 2006. "Influence of Musical and Psychoacoustical Training on Pitch Discrimination", *Hearing Research*, 219: 36–47, https://doi.org/10.1016/j.heares.2006.05.004

Moreno, Sylvain, Ellen Bialystok, Raluca Barac, E. Glenn Schellenberg, Nicholas J. Cepeda, and Tom Chau. 2011. "Short-Term Music Training Enhances Verbal Intelligence and Executive Function", *Psychological Science*, 22: 1425–1433, https://doi.org/10.1177/0956797611416999

Musacchia, Gabriella, Mikko Sams, Eriko Skoe, and Nina Kraus. 2007. "Musicians Have Enhanced Subcortical Auditory and Audiovisual Processing of Speech and Music", *Proceedings of the National Academy of Sciences*, 104: 15894–15898, https://doi.org/10.1073/pnas.0701498104

NAMM Foundation and Grunwald Associates LLC. 2015. *Striking a Chord: The Public's Hopes and Beliefs for K–12 Music Education in the United States*, https://www.nammfoundation.org/educator-resources/striking-chord-publics-hopes-and-beliefs-k-12-education-united-states-2015

National Science and Technology Council. 2013. *Federal Science, Technology, Engineering, and Mathematics (STEM) Education: 5-Year Strategic Plan* (Washington, DC: Office of the President, 2013), https://obamawhitehouse.archives.gov/sites/default/files/microsites/ostp/stem_stratplan_2013.pdf

Parsad, Basmat, and Maura Spiegelman. 2012. *Arts Education in Public Elementary and Secondary Schools: 1999-2000 and 2009-10* (Washington, DC: NCES, IES), https://nces.ed.gov/pubs2012/2012014rev.pdf

President's Committee on the Arts and the Humanities (PCAH). 2011. *Reinvesting in Arts Education: Winning America's Future through Creative Schools* (Washington, DC: PCAH), https://www.giarts.org/sites/default/files/Reinvesting-in-Arts-Education-Winning-Americas-Future-Through-Creative-Schools.pdf

Rife, L. Rafael. 2013. "The Arts at MIT", *Spectrum* (Spring), http://spectrum.mit.edu/wp-content/images/2013-spring/spectrum-2013-spring-web.pdf

Schlaug, Gottfried, Lutz Jäncke, Yanxiong Huang, and Helmuth Steinmetz. 1995. "In Vivo Evidence of Structural Brain Asymmetry in Musicians", *Science*, 267: 699–701, https://doi.org/10.1126/science.7839149

Schlaug, Gottfried, Lutz Jäncke, Yanxiong Huang, Jochen F. Staiger, and Helmuth Steinmetz. 1995. "Increased Corpus Callosum Size in Musicians", *Neuropsychologia*, 33: 1047–1055, https://doi.org/10.1016/0028-3932(95)00045-5

Tervaniemi, Mari, Viola Just, Stefan Koelsch, Andreas Widmann, and Erich Schroger. 2005. "Pitch Discrimination Accuracy in Musicians vs.

Nonmusicians: An Event-Related Potential and Behavioral Study", *Experimental Brain Research*, 161: 1–10, https://doi.org/10.1007/s00221-004-2044-5

4. Music Education and Child Development[1]

*Assal Habibi, Hanna Damasio,
and Antonio Damasio*

Over the past two decades there has been an increase of research on the role of music in child development (Herholz & Zatorre, 2012; Swaminathan & Schellenberg, 2016). There are reports suggesting that learning to play music may further strengthen the intellectual and social development of children. In spite of this, many students in the current USA educational system have limited access to theatre, dance, visual arts, or music classes, and students from ethnic and racial minorities and from low-income communities bear a disproportionate share of this decline in art education (National Endowment for the Arts, 2011). In California, for example, during a period when the total public-school student population increased by 5.8%, the percentage of all public-school students involved in music education courses declined by 50%—the largest decline in any academic subject area (Music for All Foundation, 2004). Several factors, including overemphasis on standardized testing in the areas of reading, math, and science and an ongoing crisis of diminishing budgets for public education, contribute to this decline in enrolment and access to music over the last two decades. To ensure that all children have access to a full and balanced education that includes

---

1 The Brain and Music Program at the Brain and Creativity Institute is supported by the GRoW at Annenberg Foundation, the Los Angeles Philharmonic Association, the Van Otterloo Family Foundation, the National Institute of Health and the National Endowment for the Art.
Correspondence concerning this article should be addressed to Assal Habibi, Brain and Creativity Institute, University of Southern California, 3620 A McClintock Avenue, Suite 262, Los Angeles, California, 90089-2921, USA. E-mail: ahabibi@usc.edu.

music, we believe that policymakers, legislators, educators, and parents need to hear directly from scientists about the new and truly significant findings concerning music education and child development so that they can make informed decisions about the place of music in the school curriculum.

The Brain and Creativity Institute at the University of Southern California (USC) has been involved in music, neuroscience, and education research for the past decade; in this chapter, we summarize some of the most important findings on music training and child development drawn from our work and from the work of other groups. Advocating for access to quality music education should not have to be on the grounds of research proven benefits, such as improved language skills cognitive abilities or brain health. The plain consequences of music experience on the enjoyment of life and on humans are justification enough. We firmly believe that music and other arts are essential components of childhood development that will promote skill learning and will give children access to creative imagination in a fundamentally enjoyable and interactive context.

The Measurable Benefits of a Music Education

Playing a musical instrument typically requires a child to learn to continuously switch between reading musical notes and translating them into meaningful sounds by monitoring and adjusting fine finger movements to an instrument. When playing in a group, children also have to learn to attend to new and competing streams of sound as produced by their own playing and by other performers. Playing a musical instrument, as is the case with the acquisition of other complex skills, requires focused attention, self-discipline and prioritizing practice over more instantly gratifying activities. It is likely that mastering such skills can benefit a variety of processes including executive functions, cognitive abilities and prosocial behaviors. Furthermore, playing music entails not only the recruitment of the auditory, somatosensory, and visual systems but also the interaction of these sensory systems with the motor, executive, and affective systems. The combination of such demands is likely to influence the differential development, maintenance, and function of certain brain structures and systems.

A Longitudinal Study of the Effects of Music Education on Child Development

In the hope of uncovering the effects of musical education on the developing brain, we undertook a longitudinal study of school children (2012–2020). We opted for a population from deprived socioeconomic backgrounds convinced that such backgrounds could eliminate cultural factors which might otherwise contaminate the data. Here, we review the impact of this classical music training program comparing the target group with control groups not involved in music training but with comparable socioeconomic and cultural background.

We recruited eighty-eight participants, with an average age of 6.8 years from community music and sports programs and from public elementary schools in the Greater Los Angeles area. The participants came from three groups: the first group constituted children who had enrolled and were about to begin participation in the Youth Orchestra of Los Angeles at the Heart of Los Angeles program, known as YOLA at HOLA. The Youth Orchestra of Los Angeles is a signature education program of the Los Angeles Philharmonic. It is inspired by the Venezuelan approach to music studies known as "El Sistema". It offers free group-based classical music instruction 4–5 days a week to children from underserved communities of Los Angeles. The program emphasizes systematic, high intensity group music training. It focuses on rhythm, melody, harmony, and ensemble practice with the goal of promoting social inclusion. The curriculum includes group string instrument practice, group singing, the Orff Approach, and musicianship (ear training and theory skills), totaling 6–7 hours of music instruction per week.

The second group of children had enrolled and were about to begin participation in community-based soccer or swimming programs. The soccer and swimming programs offered free or low-cost training in a community setting to all children whose parents choose to enroll. The sports training group was selected as a comparison group to control for aspects of musical training that would likely be shared by those in a regular, extra-curricular activity. These include social engagement, discipline, and sustained effort. Sports training was also chosen because of its attendant sensory motor learning, a component that is widely shared with music training. These aspects alone may have beneficial effects on development of both cognitive and social skills, and it was thus essential to include an active comparison group.

The third group of children was recruited from public elementary schools in the same Los Angeles areas. At the time of recruitment, the children in the third group were not engaged in any organized and systematic after-school programs (Habibi et al., 2014).

All participants came from equally underprivileged backgrounds. Their family incomes were predominately below the federal poverty guidelines. All resided in geographical regions of Los Angeles affected by well-known common problems: large urban areas, high levels of poverty, drug trafficking, and violence. Most child participants were of Latino background and were being raised in bilingual households. They attended English-speaking schools that did not offer comprehensive music or sports education programs.

The children visited our laboratories at USC's Brain and Creativity Institute once a year, for six cumulative years, and participated in series of psychological and behavioral probes assessing cognitive, social, and emotional development. Furthermore, they completed neuroimaging assessments including Magnetic Resonance Imaging (MRI) and electroencephalography (EEG) designed to assess maturation of brain structures and connectivity of brain structures (Habibi, Sarkissian, Gomez, & Ilari, 2015).

At the beginning of the study, when children did not yet have any music or sports training, we found that the children in the music training group were not different from the children in the other two groups. Specifically, there were no differences between groups in brain measures and in intellectual, motor, musical, and social measures.

Music Education and Children's Cognitive, Social, and Brain Development

The findings concerning the influence of music training on the children's development are first reported in terms of the impact of music training on musical and auditory skills followed by the impact on nonmusical skills, cognitive abilities, and socioemotional maturation.

We found that children who received music training perform better than children in both comparison groups on tasks measuring pitch and rhythm discrimination (Ilari et al., 2016). The children were also better at perceiving temporal regularity in musical rhythm—what is commonly known as beat perception—which is a fundamental skill for music perception and production. The children in the music group, but not the children in the two comparison groups, showed enhanced ability to detect changes in tonal environment and displayed an increased functional development of the auditory pathways as measured by cortical auditory evoked potentials to musical notes (Habibi et al., 2016). The development of these skills in childhood is critical for music training and also contributes significantly to the development of language and communication skills.

In relation to cognitive abilities, we found that children who received music training show improvements in executive function skills when compared to their peers who did not receive music education. Executive functions are top-down processes related to goal acquisition and decision making that primarily recruit the brain's prefrontal areas (Miller & Cohen, 2001). These skills have been shown to be predictive of academic success (Alloway et al., 2005), career success (Bailey, 2007), positive socioemotional wellbeing (Eisenberg et al., 2005), reduced substance abuse risk and incarceration (Moffitt et al., 2011), and physical health (Miller, Barnes, & Beaver, 2011).

We also observed that children who received music training are better at decision making and at controlling their impulses. For example, compared to their control counterparts, they are capable of rejecting a small reward in favor of larger and better rewards at a later time (Hennessy et al., 2019). They reach this level of maturity earlier than the children who did not receive music training. They also perform better in assessments requiring task switching skills and they display stronger engagement of the brain's prefrontal network while performing these tasks inside the MRI scanner at an earlier age (Sachs et al., 2017). These findings suggest that music training during childhood is associated with beneficial changes in the brain's cognitive control and decision-making networks.

In the context of this study, we also conducted annual interviews with the parents of the participating children. Our goal was to examine parental views on the potential effects of music education program on children's socio-emotional skills and personality. What we observed is that parents held the impression that children who participated in the music as well as in sports programs in their communities were less aggressive and hyperactive, and showed more emotional stability over time than children who did not attend such programs. This is noteworthy considering that there were no differences in such measures at the beginning of the study and prior to the children's entry into these programs (Ilari et al., 2019). These findings suggest that access and participation in community-based programs can affect children, families, and their communities in positive ways. In relation to other social skills, we also observed that children musicians who show higher synchronization with others in a joint-drumming task were more willing to share their resources (e.g., stickers, toys) with others, suggesting that formal music training not only enhances rhythm synchronization skills in children but also generates positive affect and pro-social behavior towards others (Ilari, Fesjian, & Habibi, 2018).

Finally, in relation to brain development and in line with reports from others, we observed that children who received music training show more robust connectivity (larger fractional anisotropy) in the white matter pathways connecting the left and the right hemisphere, via the corpus callosum (see Fig. 1) (Habibi et al., 2018). Given that playing a musical instrument requires processing of sound, coordination of both hands, and integration of actions of auditory and motor systems, it is possible that these demands lead to a higher interhemispheric interaction and communication, which, in turn, might promote an accelerated maturation of the connections that join them.

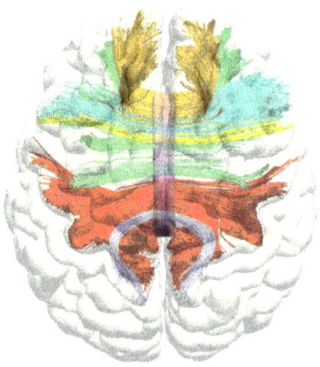

Fig. 1 Aerial view of the brain from the top depicting white matter pathways connecting the left and the right hemisphere. Children who received music training showed more robust connectivity in the frontal, sensory and motor segments of these interhemispheric connections. Image from data collected as part of ongoing study at the Brain and Creativity Institute (2012–2020); post-processed by Dr. Hanna Damasio (2020), CC-BY-NC-ND.

Concluding Remarks

The findings from this multi-method interdisciplinary research program indicate that music education induces a degree of brain and behavioral changes in developing children that cannot be attributable to pre-existing biological traits and developmental abilities. Considering these findings, the idea of reducing or removing music lessons from education curriculum is unjustifiable. However despite the unequivocal evidence indicating that participation in music education programs can positively benefit children, schools will continue to adopt a take-it-or-leave-it approach as long as legislators and policymakers view music participation as relatively inconsequential, and do not allocate the necessary budgets to support implementation and maintenance of music programs. Neuroscience and psychology research now show that music and arts in general can play an important role in developing the intellectual and emotional well-being of our children. We believe that it is the responsibility of every education policymaker to consider these findings seriously and to ensure that we keep in place the financial and educational structures that provide all students—irrespective of their socio-economic status, ethnic, or geographic background—access to a complete and balanced education with high standards for every subject including music and arts.

References

Alloway, Tracy Packiam, Susan Elizabeth Gathercole, Anne-Marie Adams, Catherine Willis, Rachel Eaglen, and Emily Lamont. 2005. "Working Memory and Phonological Awareness as Predictors of Progress towards Early Learning Goals at School Entry", *British Journal of Developmental Psychology*, 23(3): 417–426, https://doi.org/10.1348/026151005x26804

Bailey, Charles E. 2007. "Cognitive Accuracy and Intelligent Executive Function in the Brain and in Business", *Annals of the New York Academy of Sciences*, 1118(1): 122–141, https://doi.org/10.1196/annals.1412.011

Eisenberg, Nancy, Adrienne Sadovsky, Tracy L. Spinrad, Richard A. Fabes, Sandra H. Losoya, Carlos Valiente, Mark Reier, Amanda Cumberland, and Stephanie A. Shepherd. 2005. "The Relations of Problem Behavior Status to Children's Negative Emotionality, Effortful Control, and Impulsivity: Concurrent Relations and Prediction of Change", *Developmental Psychology*, 41(1): 193–211, https://doi.org/10.1037/0012-1649.41.1.193

Habibi, Assal, B. Rael Cahn, Antonio Damasio, and Hanna Damasio. 2016. "Neural Correlates of Accelerated Auditory Processing in Children Engaged in Music Training", *Developmental Cognitive Neuroscience*, 21: 1–14, https://doi.org/10.1016/j.dcn.2016.04.003

Habibi, Assal, Antonio Damasio, Beatriz Ilari, Ryan Veiga, Anand Joshi, Richard Leahy, Justin Haldar, Divya Varadarajan, Chitresh Bhushan, and Hanna Damasio. 2018. "Childhood Music Training Induces Change in Micro and Macroscopic Brain Structure; Results from a Longitudinal Study", *Cerebral Cortex*, 28(12): 4336–4347, https://doi.org/10.1093/cercor/bhx286

Habibi, Assal, Beatriz Ilari, Kevin Crimi, Michael Metke, Jonas T. Kaplan, Anand A. Joshi, Richard M. Leahy, David W. Shattuck, So Y. Choi, Justin P. Haldar, Bronte Ficek, Antonio Damasio, and Hanna Damasio. 2014. "An Equal Start: Absence of Group Differences in Cognitive, Social, and Neural Measures prior to Music or Sports Training in Children", *Frontiers in Human Neuroscience*, 8(SEP), https://doi.org/10.3389/fnhum.2014.00690

Habibi, Assal, Alissa Der Sarkissian, Martha Gomez, and Beatriz Ilari. 2015. "Underprivileged Communities: Strategies for Recruitment, Participation, and Retention", *Mind, Brain, and Education*, 9(3): 179–186, https://doi.org/10.1111/mbe.12087

Hennessy, Sarah L., Matthew E. Sachs, Beatriz Ilari, and Assal Habibi. 2019. "Effects of Music Training on Inhibitory Control and Associated Neural Networks in School-Aged Children?: A Longitudinal Study", *Frontiers in Neuroscience*, 13: 1–16, https://doi.org/10.3389/fnins.2019.01080

Herholz, Sibylle C., and Robert J. Zatorre. 2012. "Musical Training as a Framework for Brain Plasticity: Behavior, Function, and Structure", *Neuron*, 76(3): 486–502, https://doi.org/10.1016/j.neuron.2012.10.011

Ilari, Beatriz, Cara Fesjian, and Assal Habibi. 2018. "Entrainment, Theory of Mind, and Prosociality in Child Musicians", *Music & Science*, 1: 2059204317753153, https://doi.org/10.1177/2059204317753153

Ilari, Beatriz, Priscilla Perez, Alision Wood, and Assal Habibi. 2019. "The Role of Community-Based Music and Sports Programmes in Parental Views of Children's Social Skills and Personality", *International Journal of Community Music*, 12(1): 35–56, https://doi.org/10.1386/ijcm.12.1.35_1

Ilari, Beatiz S., Patrick Keller, Hanna Damasio, and Assal Habibi. 2016. "The Development of Musical Skills of Underprivileged Children Over the Course of 1 Year: A Study in the Context of an El Sistema-Inspired Program", *Frontiers in Psychology*, 7, https://doi.org/10.3389/fpsyg.2016.00062

Miller, Earl K., and Jonathan D. Cohen. 2001. "An Integrative Theory of Prefrontal Cortex Function", *Annual Review of Neuroscience*, 24(1): 167–202, https://doi.org/10.1146/annurev.neuro.24.1.167

Miller, Holly Ventura, J. C. Barnes, and Kevin M. Beaver. 2011. "Self-Control and Health Outcomes in a Nationally Representative Sample", *American Journal of Health Behavior*, 35(1): 15–27.

Moffitt, Terrie E., Louise Arseneault, Daniel Belsky, Nigel Dickson, Robert J. Hancox, HonaLee Harrington, Renate Houts, Richie Poulton, Brent W. Roberts, Stephen Ross, Malcolm M. Sears, W. Murray Thomson, and Avshalom Caspi. 2011. "A Gradient of Childhood Self-Control Predicts Health, Wealth, and Public Safety", *Proceedings of the National Academy of Sciences*, 108(7): 2693–2698, https://doi.org/10.1073/pnas.1010076108

Music for All Foundation. 2004. *The Sound of Silence: The Unprecedented Decline of Music Education in California Public Schools: A Statistical Review* (Warren, NJ: Music for All Foundation), https://www.americansforthearts.org/by-program/reports-and-data/legislation-policy/naappd/the-sound-of-silence-the-unprecedented-decline-of-music-education-in-california-public-schools-a

Rabkin, Nabkin, and E. C. Hedberg. 2011. *Arts Education in America: What the Declines Mean for Arts Participation. Based on the 2008 Survey of Public Participation in the Arts. Research Report 52* (Washington, DC: National Endowment for the Arts), https://www.arts.gov/sites/default/files/2008-SPPA-ArtsLearning.pdf

Sachs, Matthew, Jonas Kaplan, Alissa Der Sarkissian, and Assal Habibi. 2017. "Increased Engagement of the Cognitive Control Network Associated with Music Training in Children during an FMRI Stroop Task", *PLoS ONE*, 12(10): e0187254, https://doi.org/10.1371/journal.pone.0187254

Swaminathan, Swathi, and E. Glenn Schellenberg. 2016. "Music Training", in *Cognitive Training*, ed. by Tilo Strobach and Julia Karbach (Cham: Springer International Publishing), pp. 137–144, https://doi.org/10.1007/978-3-319-42662-4

5. A Report on New Music

Alex Ross

The state of new music in the classical-music sphere can only be described as lively. It is difficult to guess how many composers might be active around the world, but the number surely runs into the tens of thousands, if not hundreds of thousands. The sheer quantity of music being produced from year to year defeats any attempt to encompass it. For example, one can go to the website of the Australian Music Centre and see listings for some 700 "composers, sound artists and improviser performers". Although few of those untold thousands of composers make a living entirely from their music, the productivity is astounding, and encouraging, to behold. It is difficult to make generalizations about the stylistic profile of such a geographically and culturally diverse community of creators. In the twentieth century, clear divisions existed between composers of "progressive" reputation—modernist, avant-garde, experimental—and those who hewed to more traditional harmonic languages and forms. Such divisions still exist, but polemics are no longer so heated on either side. Furthermore, the definition of composition has steadily expanded to include improvisation, performance art, sound art, and myriad technologies (Rutherford-Johnson, 2017).

All this activity occurs in the face of a mainstream classical-music public that continues to resist new work, particularly work that fails to resemble music of the past. Our discussions of this hostility to contemporary music have made clear that it is a problem of long standing, reaching back to the nineteenth century. The scholar William Weber has established that the increasing veneration of Bach, Handel, Haydn, Mozart, and Beethoven in nineteenth-century concert culture began to crowd out the work of living composers. As early as 1861, organizers of a Paris series were observing that their subscribers "get upset when they see the name of a single contemporary composer on the programs" (Weber, 2008: 259). Concertgoers sometimes blame composers for the overrepresentation of the past on programs. It is often assumed that in the twentieth century composers alienated audiences to the point where they were driven back to the classics. But the research of Weber and others shows that new work had diminished in importance—and aroused suspicion in audiences—well before Arnold Schoenberg and allied thinkers adopted non-tonal languages. The intensity of this obsession of the past is an issue peculiar to classical music. In the visual-arts world, contemporary artists dominate the marketplace, and exhibitions of abstract painters continue to draw huge crowds.

The resistance to new music seems largely confined to the established institutions of symphony orchestras, opera houses, and long-standing chamber-music series. Elsewhere, we have seen the emergence of a thriving culture of new-music performance, one that is distinct from mainstream classical music. Forty or fifty years ago, the phenomenon of the new-music ensemble was relatively limited, and was often confined to university campuses. In the 1970s and 1980s, the emergence of dedicated new-music groups—such as the Kronos Quartet, Tashi, Bang on a Can, the Ensemble Intercontemporain, the London Sinfonietta, and such composer-led groups as the Fires of London, Steve Reich and Musicians, the Philip Glass Ensemble, and Meredith Monk's Vocal Ensemble—changed the landscape (Robin, 2018). In Europe, large-scale festivals of new music—such as the Donaueschingen Festival in Germany, Warsaw Autumn in Poland, and Big Ears in Knoxville, Tennessee—draw thousands of loyal listeners each year. The spectacle of new-music enthusiasts driving to Donaueschingen in campervans, or long lines of listeners waiting to hear, say, Anthony Braxton at Big Ears, is one that the wider community of classical music should take into account (Ross, 2012, 2016).

The role of composers in creating their own ensembles and concert series is especially significant. Given the paltry representation of new music at most larger institutions, composers realized that they would have to create their infrastructure for performance, and, to a great extent, their own audience. While both Reich and Monk have dabbled in orchestral writing, their main vehicle for realizing work has been their own ensembles. Begun largely out of necessity, this path has sustained careers across many decades. Alongside these self-sufficient composers, we have seen a huge growth in the number of musicians specializing in contemporary music. As opportunities in the classical world diminish, some young players see new music as a viable career path. Composers, performers, and institutions have together developed an audience that hardly resembles the traditional "classical music" audience, with its preponderance of older people. The new-music audience is much younger, and tends to come from a cohort of intellectually curious people who are receptive to current trends in various art forms.

At an NYU Global Institute for Advanced Study (GIAS) meeting in Florence, Claire Chase reported on the activities of the International Contemporary Ensemble (ICE), which she founded in 2001. Chase points out that many of the struggles reported in the orchestra and opera world—declining audiences, ageing audiences, poor representation of women and minorities—do not exist in her sphere. ICE has steadily expanded its performances to more than a hundred concerts a year. The audience is dominated by people under thirty-five (low ticket prices and free concerts have played a significant role). Of ninety-one world premières, thirty-five have been by women. The path is not an economically easy one: it took thirteen years before ICE's principals were able to make a living, and, even then, financial challenges remain. It will be crucial to cultivate models of patronage for new music. At the same meeting in Florence, Julia Wolfe, one of the founders of Bang on a Can, spoke about the importance of flexibility in the profile of a new-music group. Bang on a Can has found great success presenting concerts in non-traditional spaces—clubs, galleries, public areas—and, at the same, raised its profile by associating itself with Lincoln Center for the Performing Arts. She also highlighted the importance of forging links with other art forms, in which audiences are more responsive to the new. For fifteen years Bang on a Can has had a summer residence at Mass MoCA, the contemporary museum in western Massachusetts. Crucial to such efforts is the cultivation of an enduring space for new music within institutions. An audience comes to expect new work within a given space, rather than a fixed repertory.

As for the larger institutions, they have made some progress in bringing new music to reluctant audiences. One outstanding example is the Los Angeles Philharmonic, which has made an international calling card of its devotion to new and recent music. Esa-Pekka Salonen, during his tenure at the orchestra (1992 to 2009), demonstrated to a skeptical American-orchestra community that regular programming of modern music need not be a disadvantage at the box office; indeed, it assisted in the orchestra's rise to the international first rank. At another GIAS meeting, Salonen noted that he had the advantage of administrators—first Ernest Fleischmann, then Deborah Borda—who supported him, especially in the early years of his tenure, when he encountered skepticism from audiences and performers. Too often, poor box-office and audience complaints lead to the premature cancellation of such efforts. Another example is the Seoul Philharmonic's Ars Nova series, founded by Unsuk Chin a decade ago (see Chapter 14 in this volume). Addressing the fact that progressive twentieth-century music had been greatly neglected in Korean concert culture, she has programmed more than 170 Korean premieres, both of contemporary and "classic" modern work. In order to forge links between leading international figures and younger Korean composers, there are composition master classes twice a year, with selected composition students given the rare opportunity to have their rehearsed and read through by the Seoul Philharmonic under such guest conductors as Susanna Mälkki, François-Xavier Roth, and Stefan Asbury. The series has brought in a new and younger public and held the interest of more tradition-minded listeners. One other notable trend is that a number of high-profile instrumental soloists have seen new music as a way of furthering their careers. Yo-Yo Ma, Hilary Hahn, Johannes Moser, and Leila Josefowicz, among others, have broken the stereotype of the "new-music specialist" (i.e., one lacking in box-office appeal).

In stylistic terms, new music seems more diverse than it was several decades ago. As recently as the 1970s and 1980s, contemporary music was often seen as a closed, constricted world, defined by fierce polemics. In New York, for example, the compositional world was said to be split between the "uptown" school, which carried on the legacy of Schoenberg's twelve-tone method of composition, and the "downtown" school, which followed the avant-garde precepts of John Cage and his followers (Gann, 2006). In fact, these divisions were somewhat exaggerated: composers of many other persuasions were active throughout that period. All the same, one often encountered a clubbish dogmatism, and the discourse tended to be highly technical. Composers acquired the reputation of being disdainful of the ordinary listener. A series of developments at the end of the twentieth century shook up the existing order of new music and brought new perspectives to the fore. Until around 1950, composers were almost always of European or American origin. The ascendancy of composers from the Middle East, Asia, and Australia—the likes of Toru Takemitsu, Isang Yun, Yoji Yuasa, Franghiz Ali-Zadeh, Chou Wen-chung, and Liza Lim—permanently changed the complexion of so-called classical music. Furthermore, composition has ceased to be an almost exclusively all-male preserve, although one would not necessarily know this from some major orchestra seasons (several leading ensembles announced all-male seasons for 2018–2019 period). That said, there is still a great deal of work to be done in bringing more diversity to new-music programs, especially in terms of ethnic background. The extraordinary array of composer-musicians around the collective AACM, straddling African-American and European traditions, deserves more notice in the classical field. The work of the younger composer Tyshawn Sorey demonstrates the degree to which the jazz-classical divide is fictitious.

In American music, the signal event of the late twentieth century was the phenomenon of minimalism. Terry Riley, Steve Reich, and Philip Glass reasserted fundamental tonal harmonies and regular rhythmic patterns without displaying nostalgia for a bygone age. This was a fresh, modern tonality, often inflected by South Asian, African, and African-American. György Ligeti, in his late period, made his own rapprochement with tonality, employing a fragmented, kaleidoscopic version of the familiar harmonic language. In Europe, the Spectralist composers dealt with the question of tonality in a quite different way. They used advanced computer software to analyze the spectra of overtones that accompany any resonating tone, and then they extrapolated a new kind of music from the complex patterns that they found. Familiar intervals such as fifth and the major third can be heard alongside harmonies of much greater density, including microtones outside of the standard twelve-note chromatic scale. The modernist cult of complexity has, however, by no means abated. Many younger composers have avidly embraced the legacies of Stockhausen, Xenakis, Cage, or the great German avant-gardist Helmut Lachenmann. Yet these next-generation modernists seem less fixated on process, on the working out of an inflexible system. Instead, they are often drawn to a raw intensity of sound, and are not immune to influences from popular music—less in terms of melody or harmony than with regard to instrumental timbre. Thus, one finds electric guitars and a guttural vocal manner in the work of Olga Neuwirth, or a sound evocative of black-metal bands in the music of Raphaël Cendo. At another extreme, the Wandelweiser group of composers, who take inspiration from Cage, exudes a withdrawn, otherworldly quality, cultivating quiet, sparse sounds and meditative silences (Rutherford-Johnson, 2017).

The variegated world of new music can baffle first-time listeners. The challenge of coming years will be to make sense of the present-day explosion of compositional activity: there will be a need for curatorial voices guiding audiences through the field. Perhaps the most significant question is whether we can bring about a deeper integration between these distinct worlds of new music and mainstream classical music, so that traditional classical audiences open their ears to new work, and, likewise, so that new-music listeners can become part of the cohort supporting the older institutions. Our wider discussions of concert venues, formats, and protocols can readily be linked to the phenomenon of separate audiences for new and older music. The architecture of so many concert halls seems to militate against contemporary works, which feel out of place amid Gilded Age décor. Latter-day spaces like Disney Hall in Los Angeles, the Philharmonie de Paris (see Chapter 15 in this volume), and the Elbphilharmonie in Hamburg have proved more hospitable to contemporary voices. Marketing campaigns at mainstream institutions often fail to give attention to premières, and, indeed, often conceal their existence, for fear of alienating subscribers. New-music ensembles can seek out more opportunities to incorporate older works into their programs and collaborate with established institutions. Collaborations with museums have proved particularly fruitful for ICE and Bang on a Can.

In all, the historic split between old and new in the classical-music sphere seems one of the most important questions—possibly the most important question—confronting us as we move forward in the twenty-first century.

References

Australian Music Centre. "Represented Artists", https://www.australianmusiccentre.com.au/artists

Gann, Kyle. 2006. *Music Downtown: Writings from the Village Voice* (London: University of California Press).

Robin, William. 2018. "Balance Problems: Neoliberalism and New Music in the American University and Ensemble", *Journal of the American Musicological Society*, 71(3): 749–793, https://doi.org/10.1525/jams.2018.71.3.749

Ross, Alex. 2012. "Blunt Instruments", *The New Yorker*, 5 November, https://www.newyorker.com/magazine/2012/11/12/blunt-instruments

Ross, Alex. 2016. "Embrace Everything", *The New Yorker*, 25 April, https://www.newyorker.com/magazine/2016/04/25/the-big-ears-festival-embraces-all-music

Rutherford-Johnson, Tim. 2017. *Music After the Fall: Modern Composition and Culture Since 1989* (Oakland: University of California Press), https://doi.org/10.1525/california/9780520283145.001.0001

William Weber, William. 2008. *The Great Transformation of Musical Taste: Concert Programming from Haydn to Brahms* (New York: Cambridge University Press).

6. The Evolving Role of Music Journalism

Zachary Woolfe and Alex Ross

The field of classical-music criticism and journalism faces challenges that are quite distinct from the issues that surround classical music as a whole. Since the advent of the digital age, journalism has encountered crises that have severely affected the financial stability of the business: namely, a twin decline in both readership and advertising. The easy availability of vast quantities of information on the Internet has meant that many readers have fallen out of the habit of paying for news, and most publications have suffered as a result. Moreover, the ability to measure, by way of clicks, exactly how many readers are paying heed to a particular article has revealed that most cultural criticism has a seemingly quite limited audience. Thus, not only classical-music critics but also dance critics, book critics, pop-music critics, and even movie critics have been under pressure to demonstrate the value of their work. Many have not been able to convince editors of their usefulness, and have lost their jobs as a result.

In America, fewer than ten newspapers now have a full-time classical-music critic on staff: a couple of generations ago, the number was in the dozens (Ross, 2017a). In many cities, a general arts reporter is called upon to cover some combination of classical music, dance, theatre, and the art world. In the United Kingdom and Europe, most papers still carry classical reviews on a regular basis, but the space for these has been greatly reduced. Most general-interest magazines no longer employ a regular classical critic or regularly feature stories on classical music. Those who labor in this field have to confront the possibility that their line of work might vanish altogether.

Why the art of criticism has encountered such a severe drop-off in interest has sparked a great deal of anxious discussion, from which no clear consensus has emerged. It is possible that the audience for criticism was always limited, and click-counting has simply brought those limits to light. But the enormous influence wielded by—to make an eclectic list—George Bernard Shaw, Eduard Hanslick, Virgil Thomson, Edmund Wilson, Arlene Croce, Pauline Kael, Frank Rich, and Roger Ebert suggests that critics have long commanded a large audience and held considerable sway over cultural activity. Alternatively, it may be that digital culture has brought about a fundamental erosion in the authority of the critic. In an age where anyone can articulate critical judgments through social media, the need for expert judgment is perhaps diminished. Nonetheless, it is difficult to believe that as long as classical music continues to be composed and played there will not be a demand for informed discussion of it. The question is what form that discussion will take. Individual reports from two working critics follow.

The View from a Newspaper
Zachary Woolfe

As with large twenty-first-century classical-music institutions, the problem for large twenty-first-century newspapers is one of revenue. For decades, *The New York Times*, where I serve as classical-music editor and critic, was a print product that paid for its operations through a mixture of (mostly) advertising, (also) subscribership, and (a bit of) newsstand sales. The almost total shift in the consumption of journalism to digital formats—mostly, now, mobile phones—has shaken that model to its core. The trouble is not just on the revenue side. Creating *The New York Times* is now, and will remain for at least the next few years, a substantially more complex and expensive proposition than it once was, demanding resources for simultaneous digital and print products

This is the situation in which the *Times* and competitors like *The Washington Post* and *The Wall Street Journal* have found themselves. Each paper has its own strategy to try to survive and prosper. While pursuing other potential revenue streams, *The New York Times* has largely placed its bet on digital subscribership, hoping that the old reality—for argument's sake, say it was one million readers paying $100 a month—can be replaced by ten million readers paying $10 a month.

So, the charge that has been placed on everyone at *The New York Times*—not just classical music journalism, and not just culture journalism more broadly, but critics writing on sports, politics, science, business, everything—is that the key to the sustainability of the operation in the long term is a dramatic rise in digital subscribers. The print edition and print readers remain important to us, and we make plans—including a page in the Arts section every Saturday devoted to classical music—with them in mind. But our research shows that most print subscribers are in fact now reading *The New York Times* online, either wholly or in part. And print is not our future; we have to be creating an organization that is going to still be alive in fifty or one hundred years' time, and that is going to be one that exists ever more fully online.

There are many salient facts about the hypothetical digital subscriber. The person may be located in Los Angeles, and may be in Minnesota, and may be in Toronto, and might be in Vienna, and might be in Melbourne. They all access the same Facebook. They all access the same Twitter. We need to create journalism that people in Melbourne and Minneapolis and Buenos Aires would all be interested in reading frequently enough, and valuing enough, that they are motivated to subscribe to the service.

And while people in all of those places care about what's going on in New York, a center of many industries, and particularly culture, they do not—and I don't blame them—care about every single quartet performance in every single church on the Upper West Side, the "beat" that was once *The New York Times'* bread and butter, back when it was a fundamentally local paper, as opposed to a fundamentally global one. Those fifteen or twenty performance reviews per week, roughly four-hundred words apiece, often fluent and informative but by and large moderately—read: blandly—positive, simply get lost in a digital environment.

Writing now takes different paths through that digital ecosystem. Pieces are either promoted on *The New York Times* homepage or on the Arts or Music section fronts; there's Twitter, there's Facebook; there are various other social networks in which links are being shared; there's Google search. The emphasis is therefore on the ability to write and package pieces—in terms of the headline, the tweets, the photos that all support the text—so that *The New York Times* can promote them on its platforms and people will want to share them on those never-ending feeds. They exist through and on social networks.

The print newspaper is an amazing technology for many small aspects. It comes in one package, and there is so much serendipity involved in reading it: the layout creates little pockets of content that works especially well. Super-urgent and just-keeping-up things coexist, and are received in a single oomph, delivered to your doorstep. Whereas in an environment in which URL after URL of news story is flung out into the ether to rise and fall in readership individually, we see much more vividly which are the things that people are actually reading. Any kind of story requiring incremental coverage—a small business piece, a little report on a farm bill's journey through Congress—is generally trouble. Again, not only classical-music writers are having to change their methods of approach.

The New York Times does not expect classical coverage to get the same sheer readership numbers as stories on, say, Beyoncé or Trump, but we have demonstrated that even esoteric articles can have striking success in this digital environment. One of our recent popular successes was a 1000-word feature about a three-hour drone piano piece composed by Randy Gibson, consisting only of the note D (Walls, 2017). And reviews are still an integral—perhaps *the* integral—element of what we do. What is key is a sense of intention, of curation. No longer do we have the luxury of covering things out of habit or responsibility, merely because we've done so for years and years. If there is not a sense of urgency behind the journalism we're doing, we shouldn't be doing it.

What I have told *The New York Times*' critics—and myself, as one of them—is that we should be going to more and writing about less. Our writers might not be writing about everything they see, but they're taking it in, making decisions, synthesizing it. And if they see something and want to say something, it remains *The New York Times*' job to give them the platform to say it, whether it's an artist at the Met or at a tiny space in Brooklyn.

What this strategy requires is skilled, experienced critics, who are going to a broad range of performances. And it requires creativity and flexibility, not just in terms of content, as ever, but in form. Is the right way to cover a performance a preview? An interview after the fact? An interview before? A standard review? A brief description of a particularly memorable moment, packaged with other such "moments"? Inclusion in a later piece about a certain composer or playing style? Performances are not created equal, and we shouldn't treat them all the same way. All in all, the major struggle I now perceive as an editor planning *The New York Times*' classical coverage is the recruitment of capable writers, not the lack of opportunities for them once they've begun to contribute.

What keeps me up at night? I worry about missing superb rising artists. But our commitment to "seeing more and writing less" will allow us to be at many of those debut recitals, ready to write about performances and performances that excite us. Yes, those cursory mentions—"the poised young bassoonist" and the like—that often end up in the first sentences of artists' bios will be fewer and further between. But we will not be abnegating our responsibility to be looking for special young musicians; if anything, devoting ourselves to "curating" the classical scene has amplified our sense that one of our key responsibilities is to bring to our readers the talents that we think might define the future.

One way to do this is as follows: Anthony Tommasini, *The New York Times*' chief classical critic, recently attended a few debut recitals, and instead of taking the old approach (which would have resulted in a 300- or 350-word review of a concert), we decided it would be better to concentrate on a larger point that had struck Tony. He had noticed that more and more artists, especially the ones that he was admiring, had made New York debuts with quieter, more poetic repertoire rather than key-pumping bombast—the idea being that everyone can play everything now, so no one needs to prove their technical bona fides. So he reviewed the recital performances, but his piece had the feel of an essay. And the headline—"How Should a Musician make a Debut? Try Going Low-Key"—issued a broader invitation to the readership, making a more sweeping statement about the field and the way it's changed (Tommasini, 2017). The article became more than the sum of its parts.

Obviously, I worry about our responsibility to the music field. The sense I get from many conversations with artists, managers, impresarios, and presenters is that *The New York Times* coverage is meaningful less in terms of attracting audiences than in attracting (and keeping) donors. Particularly for smaller groups, the Internet has provided many ways to stimulate ticket-buying and keep a sizable amount of interested people aware of activities and events. But donors, by and large, are of the age and class for whom mention of an artist or company in *The New York Times* has been for decades a seal—even *the* seal—of approval. Some people still think that if it wasn't mentioned in *The New York Times*, it didn't happen. When the Cincinnati Symphony, say, comes to Carnegie Hall, it's the result of intensive fundraising work, and many givers expect a *The New York Times* review as part of the package.

I don't have an easy answer regarding how organizations should handle this period of transition as those expectations change, other than to clearly elucidate an artistic vision to donors and to have frank discussions about how the media environment has shifted.

The View from a Magazine
Alex Ross

Since 1996, I have been the music critic of *The New Yorker*. Before that, I served for four years as a freelance critic at *The New York Times*. It is difficult to generalize from my position: I am one of two classical critics still writing regularly for an American general-interest magazine. My colleague Justin Davidson, at *The New York Magazine*, is the other, and writes about classical music and architecture/urban design.

Many of the challenges that Zack describes above also apply to the magazine field. *The New Yorker* still has a strong subscriber base; indeed, it has more subscribers than ever before. These readers seem generally content with the format of the magazine as it has existed since the 1920s, although it has undergone many changes along the way. Thus, we feel less pressure to reinvent the magazine's identity. However, the magazine has experienced a fall-off in advertising, as has almost every other publication. The magazine's website, in particular, has become the focus for a wider range of offerings, which are designed to broaden the magazine's reach and attract more advertising.

I find myself in the lucky position of writing more or less the same kinds of reviews, at the same length and with the same frequency, as I did when I joined the magazine two decades ago. Each year I produce fourteen columns and three or four longer pieces, in the form of essays and profiles. I travel often and report periodically on American and international events. I also write twelve or so commentaries for the magazine's website. I have always felt that my role is not to respond overnight to musical events, in the style of a daily newspaper critic, but to step back and survey the entire field, intervening as a kind of color commentator. I attempt to assemble a portrait of the musical world piece by piece, in mosaic fashion. I alternate between major events at big institutions—the magazine wishes me to report regularly on the latest ups and downs of the Met and the New York Philharmonic—and the activities of smaller groups, unknown young composers, enterprising projects in unlikely locations. In June, 2017, I wrote about Renée Fleming and Alan Gilbert's farewell appearances at the Met and the Philharmonic (Ross, 2017b); in the same month, I went to Rangely, Colorado, to see a defunct water tank that has been converted into a hyper-resonant performance space (Ross, 2017c). That zig-zag motion between the famous and the obscure exemplifies my mission.

In other ways, my work has changed. In 2004, I started a blog, called The Rest Is Noise, named after a book that I was then in the process of writing. I initially saw this as an amusing sideline, but it turned into a fresh medium of critical expression, as I joined the wave of blogs that proliferated in the early aughts. Such activity has now subsided, as energy has shifted toward social media, but the rapidity and flexibility of communication on the Internet has changed the way I work. In particular, I have tried to take advantage of the technological ability to incorporate audio and video samples into online pieces. I've also profited from the international scope of conversations across blogs and, more recently, on Twitter. On social media, one finds considerable attention paid to questions of diversity and social justice in classical music. Those themes have assumed increasing prominence in my writing. Although the Internet can be an incomparable medium of distraction and stupefaction, it can also shove to the forefront issues that staider journalistic and institutional cultures have kept in the background.

What the future holds is impossible to know. At times I have the feeling that journalism as we have long known it is in terminal decline. I like to joke that I am a member of a dying profession covering a dying art. But the vigor of analysis and discussion among musicians like Jeremy Denk (Denk, 2013) and musicologists like Richard Taruskin (Taruksin, 2009), some of whom write for newspapers and magazines, suggests to me that critical voices will continue to emerge, whether or not full-time professional criticism survives. Institutions in every part of the music field should be asking: how can we maintain the public conversations that critics have long led? How can we train musicians and composers to speak and write effectively about their work? Music criticism has always been a limited affair: writing about music, talking about music, is far wider in scope, and more essential to musical life than many people realize. In the coming years, I hope to pass along whatever experience I have gained in the hope of keeping that conversation vital.

References

Denk, Jeremy. 2013. "Every Good Boy Does Fine", *The New Yorker*, 1 April, https://www.newyorker.com/magazine/2013/04/08/every-good-boy-does-fine

Ross, Alex. 2017a. "The Fate of the Critic in the Clickbait Age", *The New Yorker*, 13 March, https://www.newyorker.com/culture/cultural-comment/the-fate-of-the-critic-in-the-clickbait-age

Ross, Alex. 2017b. "Renée Fleming and Alan Gilbert Take their Bows", *The New Yorker*, 3 July, https://www.newyorker.com/?post_type=article&p=3718750

Ross, Alex. 2017c. "A Water Tank Turned Music Venue", *The New Yorker*, 17 July, https://www.newyorker.com/magazine/2017/07/24/a-water-tank-turned-music-venue

Taruskin, Richard. 2009. *The Danger of Music and Other Anti-Utopian Essays* (Berkeley: University of California Press).

Tommasini, Anthony. 2017. "How Should a Musician make a Debut? Try Going Low-Key", *The New York Times*, 10 February, https://www.nytimes.com/2017/02/10/arts/music/how-should-a-musician-make-a-debut-try-going-low-key.html

Walls, Seth Colter. 2017. "Listen to Three Hours of Music, from a Single Note", *The New York Times*, 16 June, https://www.nytimes.com/2017/06/16/arts/music/listen-to-three-hours-of-music-from-a-single-note.html

7. The Serious Business of the Arts:
Good Governance in Twenty-First-Century America

Deborah Borda[1]

Philanthropy has been part of the fabric of American society since the founding and settlement of its earliest colonies. Its roots were established when settlers had to rely on their communities to establish basic human services such as hospitals, schools, libraries, and, indeed, arts organizations. They gave, and they gave generously for the public good. This historical precedent still shapes American institutions in the twenty-first century.

The first professional music organization in the then-British colonies was the Handel and Haydn Society of Boston, founded in 1815 and supported by the merchant descendants of the pilgrims. Today, in the United States, orchestras and opera companies operate as nonprofit organizations granted tax-exempt status under section 501(c)(3) of the Internal Revenue Code. This exemption is awarded to arts organizations for their "educational value" and allows them to accept donations from individuals or institutions, which are in turn provided with a significant tax deduction. Nonprofit arts organizations in the US typically receive 4% or less of their annual budgets from governmental sources and raise more than half of their budgets via contributions, making this deduction a critical incentive and unique aspect of American fundraising.

---

[1] The views, thoughts, and opinions expressed in this chapter belong solely to the author, and not to the author's employer, organization, committee, or other group or individual.

While arts organizations employ professional staffs, maintaining tax-exempt status requires that they have a volunteer governing Board of Directors. The key responsibilities of the board include:

- approving organizational by-laws;
- determining mission and purpose;
- establishing goals and priorities for the chief executive and conducting an annual review;
- promoting fiscal responsibility, protecting assets, and evaluating an annual outside audit;
- overseeing the legal and ethical standing of the organization and its staff;
- and providing financial support or in-kind services in an amount set by the board. Serving on a volunteer board is a job you pay to do!

Nonprofit Literature: Governance Essentials

Countless books and articles have been written about good governance, and consulting on the subject is now an industry unto itself. By the early 1980s, the challenges of effective governance became a topic of greater focus as nonprofit institutions faced serious finance, labor, and audience development challenges. During this era, Kenneth Dayton, then-Chairman of the much-revered Dayton Hudson Corporation and volunteer chair of the Minnesota Orchestral Association, wrote *Governance Is Governance* (1987). In this prescient monograph, which maintains its pertinence still today, he clearly delineated the conviction that good board governance is *not* management.

Dayton laid out the primary responsibilities of the board as consistent oversight of an institution's mission and financial objectives, the ongoing evaluation of its CEO, and adherence to the basic practices of governance. These practices include maintaining active board committees, fostering an optimal relationship between the board and management, and implementing real rotation policies and regular evaluations to ensure that the board's composition remain healthy and diverse.

Today the "gold standard," which honors and builds off Dayton's work, is the impressive *Governance as Leadership: Reframing the Work of the Nonprofit Board* by Richard Chait, William Ryan, and Barbara Taylor (2005). Their work identified three modes of governance that any high-functioning board must work in: the fiduciary, strategic, and generative. They espouse the need for a new covenant between boards and executives that focuses volunteers on macro issues rather than micromanagement.

Governance Challenges: Examples and Queries

Tectonic shifts in society, particularly as they relate to the consumption and support of the arts, have made the role of boards ever more critical. Consider some recent examples in the music world where boards did not execute their responsibilities over a period of years because information was not sought, was not honestly presented, or was presented and then ignored. The demise of the once vibrant New York City Opera in 2013 is a prime example of a board's loss of focus on mission, planning, and financial accountability, resulting in a failure to protect the Opera's existing assets and the dissolution of the company. This sad drama was publicly played out over a period of almost a decade.

More recently, the seemingly successful Gotham Chamber Opera was suddenly dissolved when the board realized that the organization was literally out of money following the "discovery" of hundreds of thousands of dollars of unpaid bills. One might ask how a board with fiduciary responsibility could be so far out of the loop that such an occurrence was possible.

These trends are not reserved for opera companies alone. The board of a major American orchestra exercised a controversial form of responsibility when it declared bankruptcy and then withdrew from the musicians' pension plan for pennies on the dollar. The legal fees to process the bankruptcy were close to $10,000,000, and more than six years later, the orchestra's recovery plan is still not "recovered". What resulted were profound organizational challenges, including an ongoing disconnect from the region's philanthropic community.

These are dramatic examples, but on a smaller scale, such events have increased, and there is concern that they are harbingers of a diminished future for classical music. Critical questions must be asked.

What is a board responsible for when professional management is in place? How can it focus on the macro issues that will shape the future, and how will it evolve to meet the demands of today? What precisely are the challenges being faced by what are essentially nineteenth-century institutions, and how can they find a place of resilience in the twenty-first century? Clearly, boards, through their enlightened governance, have a prominent role to play in this journey. Taking these questions as a point of departure, the remainder of this chapter considers some of the basics of good governance today.

Guiding Good Governance: Transparency, Accountability, and Engagement

Arguably the two most crucial aspects to the operation of a functioning board are transparency and accountability. A board must ensure that management is providing an ongoing flow of accurate information in all financial matters, but also in strategic and long-term planning. They should review and approve reasonable, well-crafted plans and hold management—the CEO, in particular—and themselves accountable. There can be numerous barriers to this end, including poor information, unrealistic plans or projections, minimal communication, and faulty execution. Underlying each of these barriers is a lack of true engagement from the board to recognize and confront such issues.

It is serious work to serve on a board of directors. In addition to the accompanying legal, institutional, and ethical responsibilities, board members are typically expected to provide significant financial support. These requirements for participation, combined with the growing complexity of the challenges faced by nonprofit arts organizations today, can lead to a passionately dedicated, but small number of board members taking on too great a burden of responsibility. While it is generally true that a smaller group will have more time to invest, interest in the work, and the will to get things done, such "telescoping" can result in a larger segment of the board feeling uninformed and becoming disengaged. Over time, these members can begin to feel disaffected, powerless, and alienated from the organization itself. Critical decisions made by a few insiders that are not developed and syndicated with the full group create real problems.

Fostering Engagement: The Role of Leadership, Training, and Structure

Successful institutions have invariably invested time and capital on practicing responsible, transparent, and engaged governance. Board meetings are informative, participatory, and frequently augmented by an annual planning retreat. Engaged and educated board members can easily relay the institution's mission, key objectives, critical programs, current successes, and, just as importantly, its challenges. Even if smaller groups are more deeply involved (which is quite normal), there are systems and efforts in place to engage other board members. In an ideal world, this is the work of the board chair, but key leaders need recruitment and training.

The groundwork for engagement is laid early in the recruitment process and supported by essential board development and training practices. Among these practices are new member orientations, assigned mentors, letters of agreement detailing a board member's responsibilities, and active committees with job descriptions. Since American boards can sometimes have as many as sixty to seventy members, these smaller committees are key to fostering engagement. In general practice, committees include executive, finance, audit, nominating, marketing, education, development, compensation, investment, and community affairs. Committee reports to the full board should generally be presented by the committee's volunteer chair as opposed to the staff liaison. For example, an organization's annual audit report should be presented by the board chair of the audit committee and not the CFO. There are, of course, many other examples, but the important take-away is that these kinds of opportunities for participation and ownership are critical to cultivating a responsible and committed board.

Shifting Philanthropic Models: From "Art for Art's Sake" to Social Impact Investment

While older generations supported arts and culture, a major trend has emerged among donors—both the old guard and newly wealthy—towards supporting social service or related organizations that can offer a clear, evidence-based demonstration of their impact. As philanthropy is increasingly cast as an "investment" in social change, questions are being posed to orchestras and opera companies that were never imagined in the past. This can leave arts organizations vulnerable both in terms of attracting the support necessary to sustain their core artistic work and recruiting younger board members.

It takes a great deal of philanthropic muscle to support large arts institutions, and donors today routinely and rigorously question the worth of their investments. They are asking for what might be termed an institution's "value proposition": what is the social value of the artistic product, and what is the ultimate impact of a donor's giving on the community? This is especially true of younger philanthropists who are looking to make impactful social investments and demand quantifiable return on investment (ROI) for their contributions. Indeed, many major foundations have also moved away from support of the arts unless it is directly linked to community development. Operating support and core artistic funding is harder and harder to come by. Art for pure art's sake may be viewed by some as an outdated concept.

Board Leadership and Recruitment: Promoting Access and Inclusion

An emerging subtext is the discomforting perception that the boards of major arts institutions are largely comprised of older white men drawn from high-income brackets. This assertion is not without merit. According to the League of American Orchestras' *Racial/Ethnic and Gender Diversity in the Orchestra Field*, conducted by James Doeser (2016: 7), more than 90% of all orchestra boards are comprised of white men. As nonprofit arts institutions throughout the United States confront the need to diversify their volunteer leadership, they face another challenge indicative of our changing times: service on a symphony or opera board is not as prestigious or socially powerful as it once was. In the past, wealth and traditional connections were the primary requirements for board membership. How can this fact—that board members have been a critical source of core operational funding—be negotiated while addressing the call for access, inclusion, and equity?

Now, and even more so in the future, boards will be asked to consider the diversity of their composition and their programs. Doing so means that boards will have to engage in organized, honest, and sometimes uncomfortable discussions, resulting in strategies that will require broad buy-in and substantial energy to actualize. This is an essential first step and must be led from within the board. It cannot be imposed by staff if it is to succeed.

Once a path towards accessibility and inclusivity is genuinely endorsed and embarked upon, recruitment issues will still be encountered as individuals from traditionally underrepresented communities may not be eager to join what they may see as "imperial" institutions out of step with current social complexities. Ironically, current union hiring regulations in the United States make diversifying membership in major orchestras difficult. This has a very real impact on board recruitment. Having an orchestra onstage that barely reflects the community in which it resides can be a serious impediment to attracting new volunteer leaders. Addressing the diversity of board members, staff members, and musicians is critical future work but will require considerable effort and commitment.

Serving the Arts: The Importance of Passion

Having detailed the challenges of change, it is worth highlighting one final idealistic requirement for board service: a passion for and some knowledge of the art form. Although the other issues outlined here must be called out as we evolve orchestral institutions for the twenty-first century, in the end, there must also be true caring for the art form, and, as a result, the will to support and sustain it.

In closing, there are basic ground rules for good governance as boards chart a much-needed evolutionary course forward for orchestras and opera companies. Chief among these are transparency, accountability, and a willingness to recognize and change along with our bold new world. Technically, these rules can be expressed as fiduciary and strategic in nature, but the challenges contained within these terms are complex, varied, and far-reaching. What is undeniable is that the work of the board is a critical piston of the institutional engine. No matter how great the artistic achievements or how stellar the staff, board service and oversight is required for success, resilience, and longevity.

References

Chait, Richard, William Ryan, and Barbara Taylor. 2005. *Governance as Leadership: Reframing the Work of Nonprofit Boards* (Hoboken: John Wiley & Sons).

Dayton, Kenneth N. 1987. *Governance Is Governance* (Washington, DC: Independent Sector), https://independentsector.org/resource/governance-is-governance/

Doeser, James. 2016. *Racial/Ethnic and Gender Diversity in the Orchestra Field* (New York: League of American Orchestras), http://www.ppv.issuelab.org/resources/25840/25840.pdf

8. Audience Building and Financial Health in the Nonprofit Performing Arts:
Current Literature and Unanswered Questions (Executive Summary)[1]

Francie Ostrower and Thad Calabrese

Even before the COVID-19 pandemic shuttered performances, many nonprofit performing arts organizations faced challenges. This chapter examines literature relevant to challenges in two areas, audience building and financial health. The chapter is based on the executive summary from a full report by the same name. The interested reader will find more extensive references and examples of our points in that report. It is based on research commissioned and funded by The Wallace Foundation (The Building Audiences for Sustainability: Research and Evaluation study, of which the lead author is principal investigator).

National statistics show stagnant or declining attendance across many art forms associated with the nonprofit performing arts. Newspaper headlines report financial crises at established arts organizations. These

---

1   This chapter is based on research commissioned and funded by The Wallace Foundation. This chapter is an adapted version of the executive summary of a full report by the same name, available at https://www.wallacefoundation.org/knowledge-center/pages/audience-building-and-financial-health-nonprofit-performing-arts.aspx. A selection of citations from the literature review are included in this chapter. For all relevant references, please see the full report (Ostrower & Calabrese, 2019).

reflect the significant challenges nonprofit performing arts organizations face today when it comes to engaging audiences and achieving financial sustainability. Although there is a widespread acknowledgement that a problem exists, there is less consensus or confidence about how to address the problem. In this chapter, we review recent literature on audience building, financial health in the nonprofit performing arts, and the relationship between the two, to see what it tells us about the current state of attendance and finances, how organizations are responding, and which approaches have proven more or less successful.

The full report on which this summary chapter is based was the first in a series of publications being released as part of a study of the audience-building efforts of the twenty-five performing arts organizations in The Wallace Foundation's $52 million Building Audiences for Sustainability initiative.[2] The initiative awarded grants to the organizations to try to engage new audiences while retaining existing ones and to see whether these audience-building efforts contribute to organizations' financial health. The foundation then commissioned and funded The University of Texas at Austin to conduct an independent evaluation of these audience-building efforts. The lead author of this essay is the study's principal investigator.

This chapter summarizes our literature review and presents its major themes and arguments, identifies gaps in the literature, and suggests areas for future research to address unanswered questions. We provide references for the reader who wishes to pursue individual publications in greater depth. In the case of the audience-building literature, we found many relevant publications but not a cohesive line of inquiry whose studies reference and build upon one another. In the case of financial health, we found so little literature specifically on the performing arts that we considered other potentially relevant literature on nonprofit financial health more generally. With respect to the relationship between audience building and financial sustainability, we found virtually no literature.

Our purpose is not only to summarize the literature, but to assess what it has to say about a set of issues that we view as key to understanding

---

2   The second publication in the series is Ostrower, 2020.

audience building and financial health. We bring the following orienting questions to this review:

- *What is the definition and scope of "audience building" and "financial health" addressed in the literature?*
- *What does the literature say about the current state of attendance and financial health?*
- *What does the literature say about why nonprofit performing arts organizations are experiencing declines in audience? What does it say about why nonprofit performing arts organizations are experiencing financial problems?*
- *What does the literature say about how organizations are responding, and which approaches are more successful or less successful?*
- *What are the major gaps and unanswered questions?*

These questions structure the presentation of literature in this chapter and the full report, and help us to identify not only what the literature addresses, but what is missing. Since the audience-building and financial health literatures are distinct (with virtually no exploration of the relationship between the two), we present the reviews of each separately. The small amount of literature that addresses the relationship between audience building and financial health is included under the section on financial health. The major points from our reviews are summarized below.

Summary of Findings from the Review of Literature on Audience Building

While many relevant publications exist, there is not a cohesive line of inquiry about audience-building efforts among performing arts organizations whose authors cite one another and build on each other's work, or even necessarily address similar questions. By contrast, there is a more dedicated and distinct line of inquiry on individuals' engagement in the arts. Taking together the wide array of literature reviewed, the following major points and themes emerge:

- Attendance at multiple performing arts forms has declined or is stagnant. The National Endowment for the Arts' *Survey of Public Participation in the Arts* (2015a) indicates that fewer people are attending, and those that do attend are attending less often. Less is known about the reasons for these declines.

- Among the hypothesized drivers of the above declines are declines in school-based arts education (Brown & Novak-Leonard, 2011; Rabkin & Hedberg, 2011; Zakaras & Lowell, 2008), technological changes, generational shifts, an overemphasis on policies promoting supply rather than demand for the arts (Kushner & Cohen, 2016; Tepper, 2008; Zakaras & Lowell, 2008), and outmoded ways of operating on the part of arts organizations themselves (Borwick, 2012; Brown & Novak-Leonard, 2011; Conner, 2013; Nytch, 2013; Pulh, Marteaux, & Mencarelli, 2008; Reidy, 2014; Stallings & Mauldin, 2016). The literature offers suggestive links for some of these drivers, but raises doubts about others (e.g., on technological changes see National Endowment for the Arts, 2010 and Robinson, 2011 and on generational shifts see Stern, 2011).

- The literature proposes a wide array of audience-building techniques, but is inconclusive with respect to their results. One problem is that empirical support is often slim. To expand that empirical base, we need more studies that collect outcome data, follow audience-building efforts over time, and use larger samples to determine which audience-building approaches are more or less likely to achieve intended results under different circumstances and which are sustainable over the long term. We also need studies about the costs and benefits (both financial and mission-related) of implementing and sustaining different audience-building strategies.

- A widespread theme in the literature is that audiences do not attend solely, or even primarily, for the art presented, but for an *arts experience*, and that arts organizations are not currently responsive to this desire. Answers vary, however, as to what experiences audiences seek and how organizations could provide these. Strategies proposed include providing opportunities for more active audience engagement (Brown & Novak-Leonard, 2011; Conner, 2013; Glow, 2013; Pulh, Marteaux, & Mencarelli, 2008); performing in non-traditional venues (Walker & Sherwood, 2003; Reidy, 2014); creating a more welcoming, social, and/or informal environment (Brown & Ratzkin, 2013; Pulh, Marteaux, & Mencarelli, 2008; on socializing as a motivation see National Endowment for the Arts, 2015b; Ostrower, 2008); making increased use of technology and digital media (Bakhshi & Throsby, 2012; Preece, 2011; Turrini, Soscia, & Maulini, 2012; Walmsley, 2016); and better understanding audiences through market research (Grams, 2008; Harlow, 2014).

- The literature suggests that audience building is not an isolated endeavor, but an undertaking that is related to other aspects of organizational culture and operations. Efforts at audience building may place pressures on conducting business as usual and require shifts in culture and operations. Therefore, more research on the organizational conditions for successful audience-building activities is needed. The audience-building literature would therefore benefit from forging more bridges with the general literature on organizational learning and change.

- While some literature speaks about "audiences" in general, other literature observes that neither audiences nor the world of arts organizations are homogenous. This implies that different approaches may be better suited to engaging different audiences and serve different goals, and that organizations may need to make tradeoffs in their audience-building efforts depending on which goals they prioritize. For instance, McCarthy and Jinnett (2001) distinguish those already inclined to participate in the arts from those who are disinclined, and argue that different barriers need to be overcome to attract these two groups. One intriguing observation, made by Jennifer Wiggins (2004), is that audience-building efforts aimed at attracting one target audience may deter attendance by other audiences. This implies that organizations and research need to consider the unintended consequences of audience-building projects. Research is required in order to see whether and how this conceptual point is borne out in practice.

- One underexplored question is the extent to which audience declines, and challenges in audience building, are a response to *what* arts organizations are presenting (the art forms), or to aspects of arts organizations themselves, such as *how* arts organizations present the art.

Summary of Findings from the Review of Literature on Financial Health

We found little literature on the financial health of the arts, and even less literature specific to the performing arts. As noted, we therefore also explored aspects of the broader nonprofit financial health literature that might prove relevant for research on performing arts, particularly with respect to definitions and metrics of financial health. Although our literature review focused on publications after 2000, we also discussed William Baumol and William Bowen's classic works on "cost disease" (1965, 1966). While written over fifty years ago, the works continue to exert a significant influence on the more recent discussion of the economics of nonprofit performing arts. The major points to emerge from our review of the literature on financial health are the following:

Organizational financial health is a seemingly simple concept that is, in actuality, quite complicated and difficult to measure.

- The current academic literature has no agreed-upon definitions or measures.
- Howard Tuckman and Cyril Chang (1991) measured risk using four indicators, and the worst performing nonprofits in each measure were deemed "at risk".

- Practitioners have examined capitalization (Nonprofit Finance Fund, 2001), which encourages nonprofits to accumulate savings or reserves rather than spending all resources in the current year.
- Woods Bowman (2011) conceptualized a framework that focuses on organizational capacity and sustainability as measures of fiscal health.
- In all cases, little direct application to performing arts organizations exists. The little there is tends to be fragmented and does not cover long periods of time.
- The 2007-2008 recession seemed to have hurt the finances of performing arts organizations more than other nonprofits (McKeever & Pettijohn, 2014).

The "cost disease" theory states that financial problems arise because the costs for performing arts organizations increase faster than ticket prices. This gap requires other revenue sources—such as philanthropic dollars, contributions, or government grants—to offset operating losses.

- The literature focused on the cost disease finds mixed results. Some empirical analyses find evidence of the cost disease in performing arts organizations (see, for example, Brooks, 2000; McCarthy, Brooks, Lowell & Zakaras, 2001; Last & Wetzel, 2011), while others find no such evidence, question the theory's assumptions, or find evidence of its heterogeneous effects on performing arts organizations (see, for example, Heilbrun & Gray, 2001; Rich, 2012).
- Different-sized performing arts organizations seem affected by the cost disease differently, with small and large arts organizations essentially immunized and medium-sized ones most affected (Rich, 2012).

Audience building is little studied in terms of its relation to finances in the performing arts. Audience building may not yield financial returns, however; it may only generate social returns. If this is the case, performing arts organizations need to know the cost of audience-building activities and secure funding so that the financial health of the organization is not further compromised.

Many important gaps remain in our understanding of performing arts organizations' financial health and the link with audience building.

- Whether particular financial indicators better predict financial health than others in the performing arts domain is unknown.

- The literature also does not analyze how a performing arts organization in financial trouble might turn itself around. This advice is what many performing arts managers seek, and the literature is largely silent on the topic. The cost disease remains an important theory about the economics of the performing arts industry. However, this theory does not account for overhead costs that are not directly linked to performances.

References

Bakhshi, Hasan, and David Throsby. 2012. "New Technologies in Cultural Institutions: Theory, Evidence and Policy Implications", *International Journal of Cultural Policy*, 18(2): 205–222, https://doi.org/10.1080/10286632.2011.587878

Baumol, William J., and William G. Bowen. 1965. "On the Performing Arts: The Anatomy of Their Economic Problems", *The American Economic Review*, 55(1/2): 495–502.

Baumol, William J., and William G. Bowen. 1966. *Performing Arts—The Economic Dilemma: A Study of Problems Common to Theater, Opera, Music, and Dance* (New York: Twentieth Century Fund).

Borwick, Doug. 2012. *Building Communities, Not Audiences: The Future of the Arts in the United States* (Winston-Salem, NC: ArtsEngaged).

Bowman, Woods. 2011. *Finance Fundamentals for Nonprofits: Building Capacity and Sustainability* (Hoboken: John Wiley & Sons), https://doi.org/10.1002/9781118385913

Brooks, Arthur C. 2000. "The 'Income Gap' and the Health of Arts Nonprofits: Arguments, Evidence, and Strategies", *Nonprofit Management & Leadership* 10(3): 271-286.

Brown, Alan, and Rebecca Ratzkin. 2013. *New World Symphony: Summary Report: 2010–2013 Concert Format Assessment* (San Francisco: Wolf Brown), http://cuttime.com/wp-content/uploads/2013/11/nws-final-assessment-report-on-new-concert-formats.pdf

Brown, Alan S., and Jennifer L. Novak-Leonard. 2011. *Getting in on the Act: How Arts Groups Are Creating Opportunities for Active Participation* (San Francisco: The James Irvine Foundation), https://irvine-dot-org.s3.amazonaws.com/documents/12/attachments/GettingInOntheAct2014_DEC3.pdf

Conner, Lynne. 2013. *Audience Engagement and the Role of Arts Talk in the Digital Era* (New York: Palgrave Macmillan), https://doi.org/10.1057/9781137023926

Glow, Hilary. 2013. "Challenging Cultural Authority: A Case Study in Participative Audience", in *The Audience Experience: A Critical Analysis of Audiences in the Performing Arts*, ed. by Jennifer Radbourne, Hilary Glow, and Katya Johanson (Bristol: Intellect), pp. 37–48.

Grams, Diane. 2008. "Building Arts Participation through Transactions, Relationships, or Both", in *Entering Cultural Communities: Diversity and Change in the Nonprofit Arts*, ed. by Diane Grams and Betty Farrell (New Brunswick: Rutgers University Press), pp. 13–37.

Harlow, Bob. 2014. *The Road to Results: Effective Practices for Building Arts Audiences* (New York: The Wallace Foundation), http://www.wallacefoundation.org/knowledge-center/Documents/The-Road-to-Results-Effective-Practices-for-Building-Arts-Audiences.pdf

Heilbrun, James, and Charles M. Gray. 2001. *The Economics of Art and Culture, 2nd edition* (New York: Cambridge University Press).

Kushner, Roland J., and Randy Cohen. 2016. *National Arts Index 2016: An Annual Measure of the Vitality of Arts and Culture in the United States: 2002–2013* (Washington, DC: Americans for the Arts), http://www.americansforthearts.org/sites/default/files/2016%20NAI%20%20Final%20Report%20%202-23-16.pdf

Last, Anne-Kathrin, and Heike Wetzel. 2011. "Baumol's Cost Disease, Efficiency, and Productivity in the Performing Arts: An Analysis of German Public Theaters", *Journal of Cultural Economics*, 35(3): 185-201.

McCarthy, Kevin F., and Kimberly Jinnett. 2001. *A New Framework for Building Participation in the Arts*. (Santa Monica: RAND Corporation), http://www.rand.org/content/dam/rand/pubs/monograph_reports/2005/MR1323.pdf

McCarthy, Kevin, Arthur C. Brooks, Julia Lowell, and Laura Zakaras. 2001. *The Performing Arts: Trends and Their Implications* (Santa Monica: RAND Corporation), http://www.rand.org/pubs/research_briefs/RB2504/index1.html

McKeever, Brice S., and Sarah L. Pettijohn. 2014. *The Nonprofit Sector in Brief 2014: Public Charities, Giving, and Volunteering* (Washington, DC: The Urban Institute), http://www.urban.org/research/publication/nonprofit-sector-brief-public-charities-giving-and-volunteering-2014

National Endowment for the Arts. 2010. *Audience 2.0: How Technology Influences Arts Participation* (Washington, DC: National Endowment for the Arts), https://www.arts.gov/sites/default/files/New-Media-Report.pdf

National Endowment for the Arts. 2015a. *A Decade of Arts Engagement: Findings from the Survey of Public Participation in the Arts, 2002–2012* (Washington, DC: National Endowment for the Arts), https://www.arts.gov/sites/default/files/2012-sppa-jan2015-rev.pdf

National Endowment for the Arts. 2015b. *When the Going Gets Tough: Barriers and Motivations Affecting Arts Attendance, NEA Research Report 59* (Washington, DC: National Endowment for the Arts), https://www.arts.gov/sites/default/files/when-going-gets-tough-revised2.pdf

Nonprofit Finance Fund. 2001. *Linking Mission and Money: An Introduction to Nonprofit Capitalization* (New York: Nonprofit Finance Fund), http://www.nonprofitfinancefund.org/sites/default/files/docs/2010/Linking_MissionWebVersion.pdf

Nytch, Jeffrey. 2013. "Beyond Marketing: Entrepreneurship, Consumption, and the Quest to Rebuild Audiences for the Performing Arts", *Journal of Marketing Development and Competitiveness*, 7(4): 87–93.

Ostrower, Francie. 2008. "Multiple Motives, Multiple Experiences", in *Engaging Art: The Next Great Transformation of America's Cultural Life*, ed. by Steven J. Tepper and Bill Ivey (New York: Routledge Taylor and Francis Group), pp. 85–102.

Ostrower, Francie. 2020. *Data and Deliberation: How Some Arts Organizations are Using Data to Understand Their Audiences* (Austin: University of Texas), https://www.wallacefoundation.org/knowledge-center/Documents/Data-and-Deliberation.pdf

Ostrower, Francie and Thad Calabrese. 2019. *Audience Building and Financial Health in the Nonprofit Performing Arts: Current Literature and Unanswered Questions* (Austin: University of Texas). https://www.wallacefoundation.org/knowledge-center/pages/audience-building-and-financial-health-nonprofit-performing-arts.aspx

Preece, Stephen Bruce. 2011. "Coming Soon to a Live Theater Near You: Performing Arts Trailers as Paratexts", *International Journal of Nonprofit and Voluntary Sector Marketing*, 16(1): 23–35, https://doi.org/10.1002/nvsm.392

Pulh, Mathilde, Séverine Marteaux, and Rémi Mencarelli. 2008. "Positioning Strategies of Cultural Institutions: A Renewal of the Offer in the Face of Shifting Consumer Trends", *International Journal of Arts Management*, 10(3): 4–20.

Rabkin, Nick, and E.C. Hedberg. 2011. *Arts Education in America: What the Declines Mean for Arts Participation* (Washington, DC: National Endowment for the Arts), https://www.arts.gov/sites/default/files/2008-SPPA-ArtsLearning.pdf

Reidy, Brent. 2014. *Why 'Where'? Because 'Who': Arts Venues, Spaces, and Tradition* (San Francisco: The James Irvine Foundation), https://

irvine-dot-org.s3.amazonaws.com/documents/161/attachments/WhyWhereBecauseWho_2014DEC3.pdf

Rich, J. Dennis. 2012. "Baumol's Disease in America", *Megatrend Review*, 9(1): 97–105.

Stallings, Stephanie, and Bronwyn Mauldin. 2016. "Public Engagement in the Arts: A Review of Recent Literature", *Los Angeles County Arts Commission*, https://www.lacountyarts.org/sites/default/files/pdfs/lacac_pubenglitrev.pdf

Stern, Mark J. 2011. *Age and Arts Participation: A Case Against Demographic Destiny* (Washington, DC: National Endowment for the Arts), https://www.arts.gov/sites/default/files/2008-SPPA-Age.pdf

Tepper, Steven J. 2008. "The Next Great Transformation: Leveraging Policy and Research to Advance Cultural Vitality", in *Engaging Art: The Next Great Transformation of America's Cultural Life*, edited by Steven J. Tepper and Bill Ivey (New York: Routledge Taylor and Francis Group), pp. 363–386.

Turrini, Alex, Isabella Soscia, and Andrea Maulini. 2012. "Web Communication Can Help Theaters Attract and Keep Younger Audiences", *International Journal of Cultural Policy*, 18(4): 474–485, https://doi.org/10.1080/10286632.2011.625420

Tuckman, Howard P., and Cyril F. Chang. 1991. "A Methodology for Measuring the Financial Vulnerability of Charitable Nonprofit Organizations", *Nonprofit and Voluntary Sector Quarterly*, 20(4): 445–460, https://doi.org/10.1177/089976409102000407

Walker, Christopher, and Kay Sherwood. 2003. *Participation in Arts and Culture: The Importance of Community Venues* (Washington, DC: The Urban Institute), http://www.urban.org/sites/default/files/publication/58971/310795-Participation-in-Arts-and-Culture.PDF

Walmsley, Ben. 2016. "From Arts Marketing to Audience Enrichment: How Digital Engagement Can Deepen and Democratize Artistic Exchange with Audiences", *Poetics*, 58: 66–78, https://doi.org/10.1016/j.poetic.2016.07.001

Wiggins, Jennifer. 2004. "Motivation, Ability and Opportunity to Participate: A Reconceptualization of the RAND Model of Audience Development", *International Journal of Arts Management*, 7(1): 22–33.

Zakaras, Laura, and Julia F. Lowell. 2008. *Cultivating Demand for the Arts: Arts Learning, Arts Engagement, and State Arts Policy* (Santa Monica: RAND Corporation), https://www.rand.org/content/dam/rand/pubs/monographs/2008/RAND_MG640.pdf

9. Are Labor and Management (Finally) Working Together to Save the Day?

The COVID-19 Crisis in Orchestras

Matthew VanBesien

Pausing to revise this essay in the midst of the 2020 global COVID-19 pandemic presents a very interesting opportunity for reflection. At present, many professional orchestras and opera companies in America have temporarily reduced or suspended operations, and have fully or partially furloughed musicians, artists, stage crews, and administrative teams. At the same time, many companies are indeed staying active and keeping their employees on the organization's payroll, some even fully. They have been able to do so in part because of federal PPP assistance (an unprecedented moment in emergency funding for arts non-profits), and because musicians and managements at many orchestras are working together to adapt to and weather this moment. The weeks and months ahead in the 2020-21 season—and potentially into 2021-22 and beyond—look uncertain at best, and at worst, catastrophic, at least for some. That said, all is not lost in the orchestral world. This article was originally conceived during a more "normal" time. While many would argue that there has scarcely been any "normality" in the performing arts since the global recession of 2007-09, our current moment and experience with COVID-19, accompanied by economic impacts and by social, racial, and political unrest, may in fact ensure that there will be no return to a normal time for the arts in the future. MVB, October 16, 2020.

Introduction

"Our labor unions are not narrow, self-seeking groups. They have raised wages, shortened hours, and provided supplemental benefits. Through collective bargaining and grievance procedures, they have brought justice and democracy to the shop floor."[1] These words were spoken by then-presidential candidate John F. Kennedy in the summer of 1960 to leaders of the AFL-CIO as he was receiving their endorsement for president. It would be two years later that President Kennedy would issue an executive order allowing collective bargaining for workers in federal government, something prohibited up until that point. Two years after that, the New York Philharmonic ratified its first year-round, fifty-two-week, contract for its musicians, described in *The New York Times* as "the first time that an entire symphony orchestra in the United States will operate on a 52-week basis" (Strongin, 1964: 41). While Kennedy was considered a champion of organized labor, and presided over a White House overtly supportive of the performing arts, one wonders if he himself understood that the unionized workforce in America would reach its apex in the 1960s and the early 1970s, only to begin a slow and steady decline in the decades to come (Hamilton Project Report, August 2019).

From this author's vantage point, there may be no more vexing aspect of the professional orchestral sector than historical labor-management dynamics. Yet in this crucial moment of 2020, there appears to be reflection and even inflection—an opportunity for a new paradigm amidst a severe crisis. Orchestras, opera companies, and all the performing arts are wrestling not only with catastrophic disruption of the global pandemic, but also with long-standing issues in engaging and growing new audiences, structural and systemic financial challenges in many major orchestral and opera companies, the long-delayed identification of structural racism and under-representation of musicians of color within the sector, and the sector's slow and often mixed success in embracing digital media and technology, to say nothing of these companies' ongoing desires to further ensure artistic quality and cultural vibrancy at their institutions.

---

1   Papers of John F. Kennedy (1960).

It is within this challenging context that the current labor-management structure and all its related dynamics deserve attention, honest debate, and evolution towards a far more collaborative and transparent model in order to address the daunting challenges ahead. Some might argue this work and resultant progress is already manifesting itself in 2020.

Anyone who has been privileged to work within the field must recognize all the gains organized labor unions have helped provide for musicians and artists over the past century. Professional musicians deserve and need to be able to have representation and to bargain collectively. I myself began my career as a professional French horn player in the Louisiana Philharmonic Orchestra, and was a member of the AFM [American Federation of Musicians] for nearly fifteen years before transitioning to management. We must also recognize that the labor management construct and the resultant dynamics have not always served either party optimally. Labor and management have often become mired in technical, contractual struggles and disagreements at the expense of identifying and addressing larger, systemic issues facing orchestras. This has often resulted in negative PR and public sentiments, difficult organizational cultures, challenging dynamics with philanthropic donors, and in the most severe cases, utter organizational dysfunction and/or dissolution. Even the most calcified stakeholder in either the labor or management camps would concede that some kind of re-assessment and evolutionary moment within the current labor-management structure is likely overdue.

The question that might now be raised in any examination of the orchestra sector is: "How is this all really working, and is our current and historical model actually the best we need going forward—for the musicians themselves, the art form and its future, and the organizations that employ them?" While the current labor-management construct has been in effect for many years and began to truly advance the plight of musicians in the second half of the twentieth century—I'm personally betting that few in our industry would honestly say they feel it has, at least historically, been adaptive to shifting conditions in the marketplace or engendered trust and honest, constructive dialogue amongst stakeholders. The long-standing argument in this space has always been that the orchestral contract model just needs much more flexibility, which is indeed true, but this author would argue that the historical labor-management construct itself, and how it has played out in organizational culture and dynamics, is an equally culpable factor.

COVID-19 Crisis—Orchestras Respond

The Metropolitan Opera provides an arresting example of the economic carnage of COVID-19, considering the drastic steps taken by the company's leadership after only 48 hours into NYC's lockdown, and also how little transparency and consultation appears to have been provided to their musicians, choristers, and stagehands in March 2020 and onward throughout the summer. All the aforementioned stakeholder groups have been furloughed without salary since early March (the company has continued to fund health insurance), and the cancellation of the Met's entire 2020-21 season suggests that this may not change until sometime in mid to late 2021.

Attentive observers of the opera and performing arts world can recognize, over the last ten to fifteen years, the Met's serious financial issues—some structural and systemic, and some conceivably as a result of the shifting of the company's resources towards expanding digital platforms to develop a global audience base, and towards more lavish, built-for-HD productions that require very significant investment. As with so many other facets of the arts, the pandemic now lays bare these systemic challenges, while it also exacerbates and accelerates nearer-term issues a company like the Metropolitan Opera faces. Adaptive leadership, collaboration, transparency, clear communications, and a shared understanding of the key problems and possible paths forward, seem in short supply.

Also striking is some reporting and commentary from the ICSOM newsletter, *Senza Sordino*, for August 2020. In the August newsletter, Chairperson Meredith Snow begins her report by stating, "We find ourselves in a very tight spot. I doubt there has ever been a time… that our orchestras have been in a more precarious situation" (Snow, 2020). Snow goes on to frame the struggle of the arts within the current pandemic, social, racial, and political crisis facing the country, while also acknowledging the opportunity within the crisis to "see where we are headed" stating that, "This is a moment for our nation to do better. It is a moment for us to do better."

Paul Austin, ICSOM President and musician in the Grand Rapids Symphony, feels that even since the global recession in 2007-09, there are more examples of "trusting and harmonious" (Austin, 2020) relationships between labor and managements at major US orchestras than before, that ICSOM is working diligently to encourage a culture of transparency and mutual respect, and, further, that work and commitment from both sides is now benefitting orchestras greatly as they work to weather the challenges of 2020.

Meredith Snow and Paul Austin's words stand in some contrast to the recounting of another situation within the ICSOM newsletter, that of the travails of the New York Philharmonic's early response and attempts to more freely utilize digital media at the onset of the pandemic in March. While all performing arts companies and artists quickly scrambled to provide online content and maintain connectivity with audiences in the early months of COVID-19, the ICSOM bulletin[2] recounts a rather unsavory moment in which, according to the AFM and ICSOM account, management at the New York Philharmonic employed the threat of enacting force-majeure and furloughing musicians to secure unlimited, unpaid use of archival digital content.[3] Fast-forward eleven months, and indications from both musicians and management point now to a more evolved, collaborative relationship based on greater and consistent transparency. Austin also acknowledges that indeed there are still orchestras where the labor-management dynamic is highly adversarial, but many more are committing to "building bridges" (Austin, 2020), whenever possible.[4]

At the other end of the spectrum from the New York organizations above, three other American orchestras—the Philadelphia Orchestra, Houston Symphony, and Grand Rapids Symphony—all appear to be navigating the pandemic crisis more adaptively and successfully, keeping their musicians employed, active, and at least partially compensated, and signaling to their respective communities how they

---

2 See https://www.icsom.org/senzasordino/issues/august-2020/.
3 For more on questions of force-majeure during a pandemic, see Dressman, 2020.
4 As this article was being finalized, the New York Philharmonic announced the full cancellation of the 2020-21 season on October 13, 2020 and the musicians agreed to years of salary cuts: (Jacobs, 2020).

are working together through challenges to engage, entertain, and keep inspiring their audiences.

The Philadelphia Orchestra Association has continued to employ its musicians throughout 2020 and into 2021, though at a reduced salary rate, and has forged ahead with regular digital concert offerings with their Music Director Yannick Nézet-Séguin (who is also the Music Director of the Metropolitan Opera), along with other guest conductors and soloists. While acknowledging the serious challenges of the moment, Philadelphia Orchestra President Matias Tarnopolsky sees the current, collaborative approach taken by both the orchestra's musicians and the management as a furthering of real "change in the paradigm" to a "culture of 'we'." Tarnopolsky goes on to assert that "the institutions who play this moment right, help bring their institutions together, ultimately have the opportunity to fulfill their missions and live up to their responsibility to preserve the music" (Tarnopolsky, 2020).

Tarnopolsky, who began his tenure in August 2018 on the heels of an extended period of financial pressure (including a 2011 bankruptcy) and labor unease, felt from the start it was important for the orchestra to communicate a "warm, open embrace of the community." Working in close partnership with Nézet-Séguin, the two fast-tracked a collaborative approach with the orchestra, board, and staff to become a more unified organization, well before the onset of Covid-19. "We wanted one organization, focused on the community, not just on ourselves," says Tarnopolsky, who stressed that this important work further galvanized the organization once the pandemic set in.

The orchestra CEO relays a story on March 12, 2020, when the initial pandemic lockdown was imminent, and amidst planned concerts both in Philadelphia and at Carnegie Hall in the coming days. "It was really automatic," as he tells it, the musicians and management springing collectively into action, arranging television cameras in preparation to broadcast that evening's concert to Philadelphia audiences and worldwide. Normally the machinations of broadcasted concerts take several weeks (if not months) of preparation; however, the working relationship which they'd already strived toward help pave the way for immediate, decisive, and collaborative action.

As Tarnopolsky looks to the future, he acknowledges all the challenges, but is grateful that, "science that has gotten us through so much of what we've tried to do up to this point." He cites as guiding principles their commitment to the people of their organization, protecting the integrity of their musicians and the ensemble, and to helping the people of Philadelphia throughout the pandemic. "The digital stage is here to stay, as are the important partnerships and collaborations this difficult time has fostered. It's also incumbent on all of us to nurture this new paradigm, a new way of working as we emerge from this pandemic."

Likewise in Houston, at the Houston Symphony, musicians continue to be employed, and live concerts with greatly reduced in-person audiences resumed in Jones Hall in late summer. John Mangum, Houston Symphony CEO, credits their ability to seek out shared solutions to a shift in the company's mindset about negotiating. "Our contract is a living, breathing thing," cites Mangum, and he acknowledges that negotiations happen on a "very regular basis," not merely upon the conclusion of each multi-year agreement. Mangum stressed how the musicians in Houston are "engaged, connected, and interested in real time success" (Mangum, 2020).

Brinton Averil Smith, Principal Cellist with the Houston Symphony (and previously a member of the New York Philharmonic), credits consistent communication, transparency, and shared goals as key factors in Houston's ability to navigate this and other challenges. The positive culture in Houston is "a long time coming," says Smith. "Historically, our orchestra had a very adversarial relationship with management, and even at times with the board and donor community. We've been on a much more positive trajectory for about 15 years, working with each successive leadership team and making a conscious decision to build a more collaborative culture, one plank at a time."

Smith adds that while the Houston Symphony was "one of the first [orchestras] out of the gate to negotiate a pay decrease during Covid, we were also one of the first out of the gate to begin performing live, in-person concerts in our hall starting July 4, 2020." He acknowledges the situation feels like an "existential moment" at times, and there were indeed some tough moments when the orchestra first considered starting concerts again, especially amidst a case count spike in metro Houston. But with regular testing and good safety protocols, the orchestra's musicians and CEO Mangum came to the conclusion, according to Smith, that "we can't go out in normal times and tell our community that music and what we do is essential, then disappear for the next 18 months."

Paul Austin in Grand Rapids also weighed in on how the Grand Rapids Symphony has specifically responded during this crisis, noting immediately in our discussion how they had benefitted from the orchestra's "solid leadership in Mary Tuuk (CEO) and Aaron Doty (GM)." The orchestra is not only still fully employed, but was only recently asked to consider a 5% pay reduction, which was voted on and accepted. Austin notes that management made it clear that from the beginning of the COVID-19 crisis, they would resist "the easy way out" (Austin, 2020), and not place a large burden on the musicians through furloughing and salary reduction, and he feels this approach has yielded very positive results and goodwill within their organization.

Challenges Ahead

Outside of the COVID-19 crisis there are, and will continue to be, real challenges in the orchestra sector, from which a more fundamental question (at least for this author) emerges about the labor-management construct itself, and how musicians and managements will choose to work together (or not) in the coming years. In addition to periodic labor-management relations issues and flare-ups, usually emanating as a result of severe financial challenges, some key issues are as follows:

- Significant changes in audiences, and the public's "consumption" of and support for all of the performing arts, along with rapidly changing buying patterns for ticket sales, both subscriptions and single tickets
- Lingering questions of cultural relevance as to whether these major musical institutions can ever truly be, "representative" of their communities with regard to diversity, inclusion, equity, and social justice
- Philanthropy and sponsorship continuing to make up an ever-growing part of these companies' budgets, bringing the volatility of fundraising as yet another variable in the financial equation
- Healthcare and benefits costs escalating at a pace far faster than other expenses and revenue streams, mirroring the greater health care landscape

- Legacy pension and retirement plans exerting significant financial pressure on organizations, while creating risk to, if not significantly jeopardizing, musicians' retirement benefits altogether (especially for those in multi-employer plans such as the AFM-EP, the union's multi-employer pension fund)
- A decline in the ability to leverage and monetize the various forms of media, recordings, and broadcast activities as organizations and their musicians (and notably the leadership of AFM and orchestra managements) struggle to find common ground
- The near-complete loss of the dominant position classical public radio once held in many US markets

There are also remaining cultural aspects of the traditional, adversarial labor-management construct about which we should have some honesty:

- While collective bargaining is a necessary factor in having unionized musicians, the reality (with some exceptions) is that these isolated negotiating periods, which are usually every two to four years, can result in high levels of added stress, animosity and mistrust across all constituencies
- There are significant temporal, strategic, and emotional drains on the musicians, professional staff, board members, and music directors/chief conductors involved; most managers, and perhaps musicians, would freely admit that combative, adversarial collective bargaining is one of the least enjoyable aspects of leading or performing in any major orchestra
- Alternative methods for collective bargaining (e.g. Interest Based Bargaining) have neither been embraced nor recognized in any consistent way within the sector
- Significant bargaining issues in work rules surrounding conditions of recording, broadcast, and digital media as orchestras wrestle with ways to "deliver" their respective art forms to rapidly changing public tastes and attitudes.

Conclusions and More Questions

My own experience in orchestral management work has been that a vast majority of orchestras and opera companies' managements and boards actually *do* want to employ excellent musicians and artists, secure their services by paying competitive salaries, provide comprehensive benefit plans, and create a positive, safe, respectful, and artistically satisfying work environment. Musicians also share in the desire for organizational success (and this seems even more prevalent today), offering their talents in expanded ways on and off stage.

When you consider the value proposition for both sides of management (board/staff) and labor (musicians), one begins to see quickly how these sometimes adversarial groups could actually develop a much more evolved, collaborative model. Musicians have shown intense dedication and made enormous sacrifices in their own lives, professional work, and education to attain these highly coveted performing roles, and are also keen to bring their energy, ideas, and perspectives to the table. While laypeople on most non-profit arts boards (they receive no compensation and are, in fact, normally required to make sizable annual and capital contributions), and those who are part of professional management and staff (again, with lower salaries than comparable positions in the for-profit sector and a high degree of financial—and sometimes labor—volatility), do have the privilege of working in a field about which they have real passion, the hours, stress, and professional demands on them are not insignificant. Each of the stakeholder groups described above have made conscious decisions to play a role in the orchestral world, and are clearly prepared to continue to be invested in it, so it seems only logical, given each side's commitment, that solutions must be found.

As these organizations strive to keep moving forward in the time of this pandemic and immense challenges, a flood of other questions emerges:

- What examples from other industries, sectors, or countries can be investigated to help inform a path forward? Or, can the orchestral sector actually become a best-case example itself?

- What kind of evolved labor-management construct would the musicians themselves like to see in the future? What

- might ICSOM's role be as both a convening body and a potential industry-specific representation model for the future?
- Is AFM willing to devote real, constructive energy to the orchestral sector and represent their musicians in their current challenges, or at least to empower ICSOM and the artists themselves to take the lead even more?
- Lastly, can the issues of financial pressure, rising health-insurance markets, deteriorating pensions and retirement plans, digital media, diversity, equity, and inclusion, all combined now with COVID-19 and 2020, finally bring about opportunities for increased, honest dialogue on both local and national levels?

Despite all the significant questions and challenges enumerated above, there are some palpable reasons for optimism. While audience loyalty is experiencing seismic change, consumption of live performance remained strong pre-COVID across a good part of the industry, with greater numbers of unique attendees. There also appeared to be a growing appetite for more creative and innovative programming, environments, and contexts in which to experience live performance, and artists and ensembles willing to operate outside the normal parameters and delivery methods of classical orchestral and opera performances. New ensembles with different artistic and operating models (e.g., International Contemporary Ensemble, The Knights) have emerged in North America, demonstrating artistic vibrancy while employing a more cooperative structure, rebuffing the long-held labor-management-board operating model and dynamics of more traditional peer organizations.

If there is indeed a way to cut through the usual rhetoric then perhaps there are new directions and an evolved labor-management construct that can be developed and that will advance the musicians' cause and commitment to music, moving the art form itself forward and helping organizations to weather COVID-19 and emerge as stronger, more successful, and effective advocates for the orchestra in our country. To be sure, managements, boards and musicians all need to acknowledge current and past transgressions, but more importantly now commit themselves to a new relationship based on transparency, shared progress, collaboration, and a unified passion for the advancement of music as an art form in society. In my own career, I have often referred to a group of highly talented musicians coming together as an orchestra as a "very right thing" in a world too often populated by "wrong things." I only hope I continue to be correct about this in the future.

References

Austin, Paul. 2020. Interview by the author, 10 October 2020.

Averil Smith, Brinton. 2021. Interview by the author, February 2021.

Dressman, James A. III. 2020. "The Effect of Force Majeure Clauses during a Global Pandemic", *DBL Law*, 1 April, https://www.dbllaw.com/the-effect-of-force-majeure-clauses-during-a-global-pandemic/

Hamilton Project Report. August 2019. https://www.hamiltonproject.org/blog/the_hamilton_project_2019_a_year_in_figures

Jacobs, Julia. 2020. "New York Philharmonic Musicians Agree to Years of Pandemic Pay Cuts", *The New York Times*, 7 December, https://www.nytimes.com/2020/12/07/arts/music/new-york-philharmonic-pay-cuts.html

Mangum, John. 2020. Interview by the author, October 2020.

Papers of John F. Kennedy. 1960. Pre-Presidential Papers. Senate Files. Speeches and the Press. Speech Files, 1953-1960. New York State AFL-CIO, 30 August 1960. JFKSEN-0910-024. John F. Kennedy Presidential Library and Museum. https://www.jfklibrary.org/asset-viewer/archives/JFKSEN/0910/JFKSEN-0910-024

Skolnick, Rochelle and Deborah Newmark. 2020. "Electronic Media for a COVID Season", *Senza Sordino*, 58.3 (August), 4–7. https://www.icsom.org/senzasordino/2020/08/electronic-media-for-a-covid-season/

Snow, Meredith. 2020. "Lessons for the 21st Century", *Senza Sordino*, 58.3 (August), 2–3. https://www.icsom.org/senzasordino/2020/08/lessons-for-the-21st-century/

Strongin, Theodore. 1964. "Philharmonic and Musicians Agree on Year-Round Contract", *The New York Times*, 1 May, https://www.nytimes.com/1964/05/01/archives/philharmonic-and-musicians-agree-on-yearround-contract.html

Tarnopolsky, Matias. 2020. Interview by the author, October 2020; February 2021.

10. Diversity, Equity, Inclusion, and Racial Injustice in the Classical Music Professions:
A Call to Action

Susan Feder[1] *and Anthony McGill*

Introduction
Anthony McGill

I grew up on the South Side of Chicago with a wonderful family of parents, Demarre and Ira, and an older brother, Demarre. My earliest experiences with music came from my parents' love of music and art. We had music playing all the time at home. We also had an art room, as my parents were both visual artists and art teachers in the Chicago Public Schools. They believed music was an important part of a well-rounded education and just one piece of the puzzle to raise successful children. My brother, now Principal Flutist of the Seattle Symphony, fell in love with music and started practicing hours and hours a day before I ever played an instrument. I wanted to be just like him, so when it was time to pick up an instrument, I jumped at the chance to play a wind

---

1   The views, thoughts, and opinions expressed in this chapter belong solely to the author, and not to the author's employer, organization, committee, or other group or individual. The author wishes to express appreciation to Liz S. Alsina, Afa S. Dworkin, Dr. Aaron Flagg, and Jesse Rosen for their input into various versions of this chapter.

© Susan Feder and Anthony McGill, CC BY-NC-ND 4.0   https://doi.org/10.11647/OBP.0242.10

instrument. The saxophone was my first choice, but it was too big for me, so I eventually settled on the clarinet.

My early years were well supported by a community of mentors, parents, and teachers who gave me the base I needed to thrive as a young musician. One of my earliest musical experiences was as a member of an ensemble of young Black classical musicians from Chicago called the Chicago Teen Ensemble. This ensemble was led by my first music teacher, Barry Elmore. We toured around a lot of the churches on the South Side of Chicago and performed arrangements of famous classical works. These early experiences of having older musician peers and friends that looked like me made me feel welcome in music and contributed to my self-confidence as a young clarinet player. I also attended the Merit School of Music, where I was surrounded by a diverse group of young people who were also interested in music. This community gave me a sense of pride that encouraged my love of music and growth as a person. Merit gave me scholarships to music camps and introduced me to famous teachers. Eventually, I joined the Chicago Youth Symphony Orchestra and continued on this serious musical path. A few years later, I left home to attend the Interlochen School of the Arts. From there I went on to the Curtis Institute of Music, the Cincinnati Symphony Orchestra, the Metropolitan Opera Orchestra, and then to my current seat as the Principal Clarinetist of the New York Philharmonic.

I had plenty of love and support throughout my career, but I also had huge obstacles to overcome. Being Black and from the South Side of Chicago came with its share of preconceived notions about who I was, and I frequently felt like I had to prove myself in order to survive. There were many times I had to put blinders on and pretend that comments didn't hurt, or that I didn't understand the underlying message behind certain statements. I had to ignore many racially charged words from peers and adults in order to stay focused on my goals. These issues have not disappeared as I've achieved higher levels of success. They've continued to occur throughout my career and at every stage of my life. I've had to deal with being asked why I was attempting to enter music buildings because I didn't look like I belonged there. I had a person tell me after a Carnegie Hall solo appearance that I sounded as though I were playing jazz in a lounge bar and that it was inappropriate for the style of the composer. I've had people ask me why I chose classical music, as if it were a field that is not designed for people like me. I've heard board members tell jokes that are insensitive at best and racist at worst.

In addition to these few examples, there is the feeling that one cannot speak up about these issues lest people think you are angry or disgruntled for made-up reasons. The burden people of color have to deal with while trying to achieve the greatest heights in the field, under intense pressure, is a heavy one to bear.

We must do better in order for there to be progress. We need to have transparent discussions and training surrounding issues of bias, racism, and exclusion in classical music. In addition, we need to examine the history of racism in our country in order to understand how this has contributed to the current state of the field. After this work, we should continue to strategize about what actions to take in order to move the needle regarding representation onstage, backstage, in boardrooms, and in administrations. Without proper knowledge and support, all of the necessary attention to pathways, mentorship, education, etc., will not allow all participants to thrive and engage in an inclusive, welcoming industry. I hope that with honest, immediate action, we will begin to see necessary change in our industry.

A Call to Action
Susan Feder

> The conversation of diversity in classical music is still relatively new, but it's one in which more organizations have been engaging for the past several years. The conversation of racism in classical music is a little different, though. Not only does it require us to take a second look at ourselves, but also so much of the music that's become ubiquitous to the genre.
>
> —Garrett McQueen, bassoonist and radio host (2020)

The absence of Black and Latinx musicians in the classical music professions in the United States is deeply rooted in intertwined issues of access and structural racism. Regarding access, the challenges center on how to level the playing field so that talented young musicians of color, from an early age, have the same opportunities in instruction and mentorship as white and East Asian students who often come from more comfortable socio-economic circumstances. These are issues that can be addressed with financial resources. The second issue is far harder to solve. Once students pass through the formidable hoops of formal training, what will it take for arts institutions to overcome the structural racism, microaggressions, and unconscious bias that in combination have made it overwhelmingly difficult for most musicians of color[2] to win auditions, feel welcome, achieve tenure, or be cast, hired, and programmed at the institutions in which they seek to work?

This chapter will take a brief look at the historical circumstances that have amplified racial injustice, current attempts to create systemic and scalable training pathways for BIPOC musicians, and the ongoing barriers to improving levels of participation. Evidently, it has taken the dual challenges of the COVID-19 pandemic and the national outrage following the May 2020 murder of George Floyd to unleash a long overdue reckoning towards implementing positive change. Chafing against pandemic shelter-in-place orders, and with the ascendency of social media as a dominant form of communication, the structures that have upheld racism and systemic oppression in the United States have come under greater scrutiny than at any time since the Civil Rights era.[3] Even as classical music institutions remain physically shuttered, they cannot ignore the zeitgeist without risk of descending into irrelevance. While arts and culture organizations have overwhelmingly responded with statements of support for Black Lives Matter, now is the time to put actions in place to accelerate the pace of change.

As the largest employer of classically trained musicians in the United States, American orchestras bear a particular responsibility, and will be the focus of this chapter.[4] A disturbing review of

---

2 For purposes of convenience, this paper will henceforth refer to people of color collectively using the acronym BIPOC (Black, Indigenous, People of Color), but will focus on Black and Latinx people.

3 As just one marker, books on race comprised eight of the top ten nonfiction books on the 19 July 2020 *The New York Times* Book Review. Articles pertinent to racism and concert music include Brodeur (2020), Tommasini (2020), and Flagg (2020).

4 This is not to say that opera fares significantly better. While some singers of color have achieved the highest levels of success onstage in so-called "color-blind" casting, creative teams, administrators, and board members remain overwhelmingly white

discriminatory practices in the summer 2020 issue of the League of American Orchestras' *Symphony* magazine, by the arts administrator, educator, and trumpeter Dr. Aaron A. Flagg, reminds us that "the history of discrimination in America's classical music field, particularly in orchestras, is not discussed or studied or commonly known, because it is painful, embarrassing, and contrary to how we want to view ourselves" (Flagg, 2020: 36). Flagg cites an "ignored and uncelebrated history of minority artistry in classical music (by composers, conductors, performers, and managers); ignorance of the history of discrimination and racism against classical musicians of African-American and Latinx heritage by the field; and a culture in the field that is indifferent to the inequity, racial bias, and microaggressions within it" (30). He also reflects on the role of musicians' unions, providing a history of their segregation, which "like that of other industries in the late nineteenth century, came with the social prejudices of the time, which discouraged solidarity among racially diverse musicians. Black musicians generally could not join white unions and were treated as competitors in the marketplace" (33). Instead, they formed their own unions, but in the process were largely disenfranchised from job notices, rehearsal facilities in union halls, and job protections until the 1970s, when they were fully integrated into the American Federation of Musicians. Flagg observes that Black musicians only began to be hired in major orchestras beginning in the late 1940s, and even into the 1960s only in rare instances.

Today, although the US Census Bureau estimates that Black and Latinx people make up nearly 32% of the US population, the percentage of them in US orchestras stubbornly hovers below 4% (although it is somewhat higher in smaller budget orchestras than the larger ones; see League of American Orchestras, 2016). This rate has not improved significantly in more than a generation, despite the rise of important

---

(Barone, 2020). Barone's *Times* article links to a gut-wrenching conversation among six leading American Black opera singers: https://www.facebook.com/LAOpera/videos/396366341279710

organizations and initiatives devoted to intensive pre-professional training for BIPOC musicians[5] and prominent performing ensembles.[6]

Equally concerning has been the minimal impact of fellowship programs. Since 1976, some twenty-three US orchestras have hosted such programs for BIPOC musicians. As an enduring strategy for the individuals they served, orchestral fellowships have been demonstrably effective. But they have been insufficient in scope to achieve a critical mass of professional BIPOC musicians. Even more discouraging, those orchestras that hosted fellowship programs over this forty-plus year period evince little evidence that they are any more diverse today than those that did not (League of American Orchestras, 2016). The culture of orchestras has not changed, whether with regard to the consistency of BIPOC conductors and soloists onstage, more regular programming of music by Black and Latinx composers, or more BIPOC leaders in all levels of administrative roles and on orchestra boards. Taken together, such changes would help reassure BIPOC musicians that they indeed belong in this profession. Moreover, all too often, those who have achieved positions are expected to function in the uncomfortable, unreasonable, and untenable positions of being spokespeople for their race when engaging with communities of color, at donor events, during educational activities, or in internal discussions regarding diversity, equity, inclusion (DEI), and racism.

Why then encourage BIPOC musicians toward careers in orchestras, one might well ask? There are many compelling reasons:

- As noted above, up until the 2020 COVID-19 pandemic, orchestras offered **stable employment** with salaries and benefits to large numbers of artists and will presumably do so again in the coming years;

---

5   These include the Sphinx Organization (founded in 1996), Boston's Project Step (founded by the Boston Symphony Orchestra in 1982), the Music Advancement Program at The Juilliard School (1991), and the Atlanta Symphony's Talent Development Program (1994).

6   Among them are the Gateways Music Festival (1993), a biennial gathering of professional musicians of African descent now held in collaboration with the Eastman School of Music in Rochester, NY; Sphinx's Symphony Orchestra (1998) and Virtuosi (2008); the Harlem Chamber Players (2008); the Black Pearl Chamber Orchestra (2008); the Colour of Music Festival (2013); and, in the UK, Chineke! Orchestra (2015).

- For well over a decade, orchestras have begun to **reframe their missions as serving their communities** through the power of great music in addition to aspiring to perform concerts at the highest levels of excellence. They need **diverse perspectives** to do so effectively, especially in light of demographic shifts across US urban centers;

- As they elevate community service, orchestras will need to **hire more entrepreneurial musicians**. Already, some orchestras are considering skills such as teaching artistry, curatorial curiosity, chamber ensemble playing, and public speaking as crucial criteria for employment, after an audition is won but before a job is offered. Such orchestral positions should be more attractive to a generation of musicians who seek variety in their careers;

- Those orchestras that have diversified their programming (both in terms of repertoire and concert formats) and moved away from a tradition of fixed subscription models, have **successfully attracted younger, more diverse audiences**, countering the commonly held perceptions of orchestras that they are exclusively by, for, and about white people; serve an aging and elite audience that can afford expensive tickets, or have a "broken business model";

- In recent years, and in unprecedented numbers, orchestras have begun to regard **DEI as core values across their institutions**. Many are now making intentional efforts to come to grips with racist pasts, improve BIPOC participation in their staffs, boards, and programming, and cultivate more inclusive and nurturing environments, even as the diversification of musician hiring remains complicated by the "blind audition" process (see Tommasini, 2020);

- **Amplifying Voices**, an initiative by New Music USA in partnership with the Sphinx Organization launched in January 2020, is fostering transformation of the classical canon through co-commissions and collective action toward **more equitable representation of composers in classical**

music. To date, twenty-four orchestras have committed to increased programming of works by composers of color during forthcoming seasons.

All this notwithstanding, the fact remains that attaining permanent orchestral employment is a challenge for **all** musicians, regardless of race or ethnicity: the supply of talent far exceeds demand. And although there are more than 1,200 professional orchestras in the US, with rosters as large as 100 musicians, players tend to receive tenure within a year or two of joining an orchestra. Openings thus remain rare and extremely competitive. Still, in the years just prior to the pandemic, many of the orchestras that had reduced the size of their permanent rosters after the 2008 recession through retirement and attrition had stabilized their financial positions sufficiently to begin replenishing their permanent musician ranks. Even now, in the wake of pandemic-related furloughs and layoffs, some long-tenured musicians may opt to retire and claim their pensions, creating opportunities for generational turnover once orchestras resume performing. The pace of hiring may slow temporarily, but pick up again in the next few years.

Another less visible factor regarding employment opportunities: at any given performance, the number of musicians substituting for permanent players can be upwards of 10% of the roster. More intentional recruitment of BIPOC musicians as subs would provide them with intensive professional orchestral experience. Even if temporary employment is less attractive than more traditional forms of job security, musicians at all levels of achievement are accustomed to operating in a "gig economy," combining teaching, administration, and orchestral, solo, and chamber performances as synergistic elements of their careers.

Skeptics might ask if there is a sufficient pipeline of BIPOC musicians to populate American orchestras? And if not, what are the pathways to opening the spigots? While statistics on BIPOC enrollment in higher education are sobering (see Fig. 1), the racial/ethnic breakdown of younger students enrolled in early-access programs at community music schools is startlingly different. Indeed, as a result of the missions and locations of community schools—often in urban centers and in neighborhoods close to their targeted populations—enrollment percentages for African-American, Latinx, and Asian-American students actually **exceed** those of the US population overall (see Fig. 2).

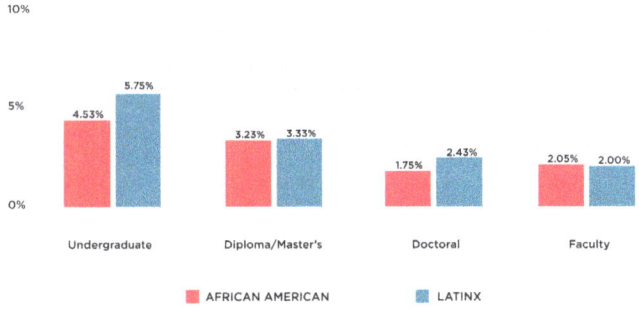

Fig. 1 African American and Latinx representation in higher education music programs. Data drawn from National Association of Schools of Music (NASM) 2015-16 Heads Report. © NYU Global Institute for Advanced Study. CC-BY-NC-ND.

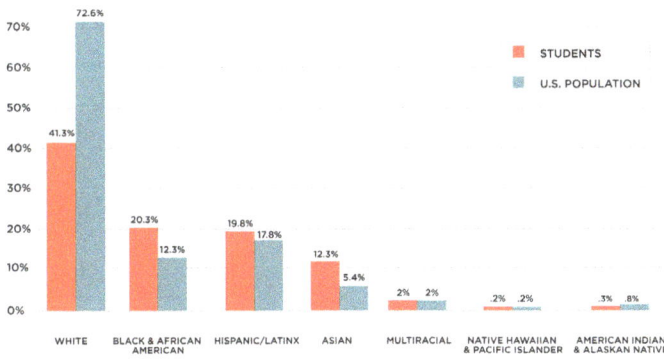

Fig. 2 BIPOC musicians in community music schools. Data drawn from US Census Bureau, 2011 American Community Survey; National Guild for Community Arts Education Racial/Ethnic Percentages of Students Within Membership Organizations. © NYU Global Institute for Advanced Study. CC-BY-NC-ND.

Thus, a strong foundation grounds the prospects for creating more effective pathways for BIPOC musicians. Despite formidable social and economic barriers, academic pressures, and competition from sports and other extracurricular activities as students enter middle and high school, might attrition rates be staunched by earlier and more intentional interventions? A supportive ecology would include such elements as access to private instruction, ensemble playing, fine instruments, college counselling for students and their families, and strong mentoring.

Effectuating systemic change requires collaboration to build, scale, and sustain pathways to careers in classical music. Beyond early access, steps along the pathways include: intensive pre-college preparatory training; scholarships to leading summer programs and music schools, especially those with proximate orchestras willing to offer mentorship; access to concert tickets; mock-audition preparation; and, as greater numbers of BIPOC musicians graduate from college or conservatory, an expansion of early-career fellowship programs and substitute opportunities at orchestras. Systemic change would also require a large and long-term philanthropic investment in young musicians who hail from lower socio-economic backgrounds and cannot afford the considerable expense of such preparation. Given that training must commence at an early age, and continue for years thereafter, it may take a full generation to see significant and sustained impact. But that cannot be an excuse not to make more concerted efforts to improve the status quo. And, progress should be evident relatively quickly by intentionally tracking the career paths of BIPOC musicians who are already in conservatories and fellowship programs through such aggregators as the Strategic National Arts Alumni Project (SNAAP), a national arts data and research organization.

What would success look like? Anthony McGill's own career path, described in the introduction to this chapter, is instructive. Other African-American and Latinx musicians have attained prominence, holding tenured positions at major American orchestras: Judy Dines, flutist with the Houston Symphony; Rafael Figueroa, Principal Cello, Metropolitan Opera Orchestra; Alexander Laing, Principal Clarinet, Phoenix Symphony; Demarre McGill, Principal Flute at the Seattle Symphony; Sonora Slocum, Principal Flute, Milwaukee Symphony; Weston Sprott, trombonist at the Metropolitan Opera Orchestra; and

Titus Underwood, Principal Oboe, Nashville Symphony. Still others are making their way as soloists and chamber artists, among them flutist and composer Valerie Coleman, violinists Kelly Hall-Tompkins and Elena Urioste, composer-violinist Daniel Bernard Roumain, and cellists Gabriel Cabezas and Christine Lamprea. Many of these artists are also active teachers, mentors, and leaders in field conversations around DEI, justice, and racism. Music directors of American orchestras now include Giancarlo Guerrero (Nashville Symphony), Miguel Harth-Bedoya (Fort Worth Symphony), Michael Morgan (Oakland Symphony), Andres Orozco-Strada (Houston Symphony), Carlos Miguel Prieto (Louisiana Philharmonic), Thomas Wilkins (Omaha Symphony, outgoing), and, most prominently, Gustavo Dudamel (Los Angeles Philharmonic). But the fact that these musician leaders can still be named in a single paragraph speaks volumes about how far the field has to go.

Even if the career path of a musician of color does not end up at the New York Philharmonic, Metropolitan Opera or comparable institution, one could nonetheless track some early indicators of success:

- retention in precollege programs;
- acceptance into music programs at institutions of higher education;
- numbers of applicants for auditions;
- numbers of fellowships and job placements; and
- setting of recruitment targets of racially diverse pools of applicants.

And while the primary goal of more intentional pathways training would be to increase the numbers of musicians onstage at American orchestras and other professional music institutions, success can take many forms. Secondary goals include building future audiences of diverse communities of adults who have received intensive exposure to music as children, and increasing the number of BIPOC musicians who might seek careers in arts administration or music education, or who might themselves become future patrons or board members of arts organizations. Intensive training and support from committed adult advocates also teaches skills of self-discipline and persistence in supportive environments, attributes that make young people highly attractive college candidates regardless of the major they eventually choose. Finally, there is a social benefit for all music students, regardless of race or economic status, in learning to perform as members of ensembles with a diverse group of peers.

There are some encouraging signs of progress. In December 2015, the League of American Orchestras and The Andrew W. Mellon Foundation co-hosted a convening of administrative leaders in professional and youth orchestras, higher education, and community music schools, alongside a number of BIPOC artists. The meeting was designed to lay the groundwork for action to improve pathways for BIPOC musicians. Arising from those initial discussions, a number of interventions have commenced. These include:

- the **National Alliance for Audition Support** (NAAS), an unprecedented national collaboration administered by the Sphinx Organization in partnership with the New World Symphony and the League of American Orchestras, and with the financial support of nearly eighty orchestras. In its first two years NAAS has provided customized mentoring, audition preparation, audition previews, and travel support to more than nearly 150 artists, 24 of whom have won orchestral positions and another 12 substitute roles;

- collaborative **"pathways" programs** administered by arts organizations in Baltimore, Boston, Chicago, Cincinnati, Los Angeles, Nashville, Philadelphia, and Washington, DC;

- **fellowships** serving multiple musicians at the Cincinnati Symphony, Los Angeles Philharmonic, LA Chamber Orchestra, Detroit Symphony, Houston Symphony, Minnesota Orchestra, and Orpheus Chamber Orchestra among others;

- participation by some thirty-five orchestras in the League of American Orchestras' **Catalyst Fund**, which provides support for orchestras committed to taking the time necessary to undertake comprehensive DEI assessment, training, and action to change organizational culture within their institutions;

- Intentional recruitment of BIPOC musicians at **leading colleges and conservatories** of music;

- Active involvement of **union representatives** from the American Federation of Musicians, the International Conference of Symphony and Opera Musicians, and the Regional Orchestra Players Association at the annual conferences of Sphinx and the League of American Orchestras;

- Cultivation of Black and Latinx representation among C-Suite and other **administrative leadership roles**. Since 2018, Sphinx's **LEAD (Leaders in Excellence Arts and Diversity)** has enrolled nineteen Black and Latinx administrative leaders, six of whom quickly attained promotion or senior level placement in performing arts institutions, where they can help effectuate change. A number of orchestras, including the Minnesota Orchestra, New Jersey, and New World Symphonies, serve as partners by hosting learning retreats and co-curating the curricular aspects of the program, while also creating direct networking and recruitment mechanisms.

- For orchestras or any other entity interested in gaining access to qualified musicians to engage, NAAS maintains a **national network** of sought-after Black and Latinx orchestral musicians, many of whom have experience working with orchestras of the highest level. And for ensembles wishing to broaden their programming, there are a **number of databases**, including: Music by Black Composers; Institute for Composer Diversity; Chamber Music America (2018); Harth-Bedoya and Jaime (2015); and CelloBello (2017).

But to what extent are our cultural institutions themselves willing to be more proactive? Mentorship programs work. What if every major orchestra committed to taking a **group** of talented early-career musicians under their wings? Would their boards, which are still predominantly white, endorse this financial obligation? How soon will the board makeups become more diverse and inclusive? Are musicians and their unions prepared to alter their collective bargaining agreements to reimagine the circumstances surrounding auditions, tenure, and promotion, to make the processes more transparent, objective, and inclusive of considerations beyond sublime artistry? To what extent do the internal cultures of classical music organizations allow for mistreatment to be acknowledged and acted upon? Are opera administrators willing to cast singers in leading roles, without regard to their race, as has been the case for many years in theater? And when will these artists be conducted or directed by people of color? What will it take for cultural organizations to commit to programming music by BIPOC composers outside of Black History month, Cinco de Mayo, and Chinese New Year celebrations, as well as commissioning BIPOC composers with regularity?

BIPOC musicians have other viable career options, including in popular music, and may find decades of hostile behavior increasingly difficult to overlook. Unless performing arts organizations first diversify onstage and through their programming of diverse repertoire, and commit to a more inclusive internal culture, it will be harder to attract BIPOC musicians to career and volunteer choices as administrators and board members than at other types of institutions with demonstrated commitments to DEI.

Intentionality matters. Take the example of the service organization Chamber Music America (CMA). In 2017, recognizing that African/Black, Latinx, Asian/South Asian, Arab/Middle Eastern, and Native American (ALAANA), women, and gender non-conforming composers had historically been under-represented in its *Classical Commissioning Program*, CMA altered the program's goals. Through intentional recruitment and the panel review process CMA aimed going forward to award a majority of its grants to applicants who apply with ALAANA, women, and gender non-conforming composers. Within three years it had achieved the goal. Or consider the Cleveland Institute of Music. Each year it publicly shares a report card on its progress in improving diversity. From 2015 to 2020 it aggressively recruited BIPOC musicians and increased representation within the student body from 2% to 15%.

The challenges for improving pathways for BIPOC musicians remain formidable, and exponentially more so since the COVID-19 pandemic has halted in-person training and employment opportunities. But with the epidemic of racism also foregrounded in 2020, and with such strong unprecedented momentum among orchestras and educational institutions, the forward-facing efforts simply must continue unabated. To be effective, however, efforts will need to go well beyond the numerous well-intentioned statements of solidarity against racial injustice and in support of Black Lives Matter, which have flooded from arts and cultural institutions across the sector in the weeks since Floyd's death. As the US population continues inexorably to become more diverse, the need for orchestras and other music institutions to overcome their own complacency, understand the extent of systemic racial inequities in the classical music field, acknowledge their complicity in past practices, and improve the stagnant participation rates of BIPOC musicians has become more than a generally recognized moral imperative. It is an existential crisis. Our cultural institutions simply must do so if they wish to survive, thrive, serve, and engage with their communities further into the twenty-first century.

References

Barone, Joshua. 2020. "Opera Can No Longer Ignore Its Race Problem", *The New York Times*, 16 July, https://www.nytimes.com/2020/07/16/arts/music/opera-race-representation.html?action=click&module=RelatedLinks&pgtype=Article

Brodeur, Michael Andor. 2020. "That Sound You're Hearing is Classical Music's Long Overdue Reckoning with Racism", *The Washington Post*, 16 July, https://www.washingtonpost.com/lifestyle/style/that-sound-youre-hearing-is-classical-musics-long-overdue-reckoning-with-racism/2020/07/15/1b883e76-c49c-11ea-b037-f9711f89ee46_story.html

Chamber Music America. 2018. *The Composers Equity Project. A Database of ALAANA, Women, and Gender Non-Conforming Composers*, https://www.chamber-music.org/pdf/2018-Composers-Equity-Project.pdf

CelloBello. 2017. *The Sphinx Catalog of Latin American Cello Works*, https://www.cellobello.org/latin-american-cello-works/

Flagg, Aaron. 2020. "Anti-Black Discrimination in American Orchestras", *League of American Orchestras Symphony Magazine*, Summer, pp. 30–37, https://americanorchestras.org/images/stories/symphony_magazine/summer_2020/Anti-Black-Discrimination-in-American-Orchestras.pdf

Harth-Bedoya, Miguel, and Andrés F. Jaime. 2015. *Latin Orchestral Music: An Online Catalog*, http://www.latinorchestralmusic.com/

Institute for Composer Diversity (ICD), https://www.composerdiversity.com/

League of American Orchestras, with Nick Rabkin and Monica Hairston O'Connell. 2016. *Forty Years of Fellowships: A Study of Orchestras' Efforts to Include African American and Latino Musicians* (New York: League of American Orchestras), https://www.issuelab.org/resources/25841/25841.pdf

McQueen, Garrett. 2020. "The Power (and Complicity) of Classical Music", *Classical MPR*, 5 June, https://www.classicalmpr.org/story/2020/06/05/the-power-and-complicity-of-classical-music

Music by Black Composers (MBC). *Living Composers Directory*, https://www.musicbyblackcomposers.org/resources/living-composers-directory/

Tommasini, Anthony. 2020. "To Make Orchestras More Diverse, End Blind Auditions", *The New York Times*, 16 July, https://www.nytimes.com/2020/07/16/arts/music/blind-auditions-orchestras-race.html?action=click&module=RelatedLinks&pgtype=Article

11. The Interface between Classical Music and Technology

Laurent Bayle[1] *and Catherine Provenzano*

In March 2020, when music and performance institutions across the world emptied their halls, canceled their programs, and closed their doors for the foreseeable future, it was anyone's guess what would crop up in the void. What we have seen, heard, and maybe watched "live" are various innovative attempts, within the constraints of our biological circumstances and media infrastructure, to provide some sense of continuity to an art world completely interrupted. The MET's At-Home Gala, the offerings of individual artists from their homes, the coffers of video archives freely opened—all awkward-to-melancholic-to-desperate expressive outlets during separation—are dangled carrots of eventual reunion.

Before the reunions happen, our attempts at musical gathering in this liminal space might be the driver of improved technologies, or tech newly entrained to the values and needs of this moment.[2] For one, we like to hear each other, and so far our mainstream live video technologies only have basic functionality around the complexity of sound, in particular of sound that is comprised of more than one input (e.g., a

---

1   The views, thoughts, and opinions expressed in this chapter belong solely to the author, and not to the author's employer, organization, committee, or other group or individual.

2   For one small example, the videoconferencing tool Zoom is set to release a "zero latency" version in September 2020, specifically to respond to the sonic shortcomings of the platform.

piano and a voice; a violin, and a guitar, and a bass).[3] While most people are longing to exit the livestream format and get back together again, this concentrated moment of livestreamed musical performance might nonetheless drive improved tech-sonics of the live-by-video concert and pedagogical world. We are hearing, in this forced scenario, what is not working, and what we are missing. And those are chances to drive our technological soundscape toward new ideals and demands. But we are also given an almost perfect experimental environment in which to ask, what are the effective mechanisms of liveness, learning, synchronicity, togetherness?[4]

This lays bare a tension that arises in the remainder of this essay—for all the rapid developments of technological innovations that make things "easier," "better," or "more accessible," at what point and pace does the residue of those growth spurts become slick with loss? What are we left with when technologies stand alone, six feet, or six thousand miles, apart? In other words, there is a longing for in these moments of estrangement—in our educational, social, and creative realms—for something a livestreamed concert or a remote learning environment might never provide. To be sure, the capacities we currently have thanks to our digital tools have been lifelines in this moment, and even opened some remote (to indulge the pun) creative spaces for artists, learners, and institutions. Yet perhaps it has never been so easy to argue the value of gathering, to explicate nearness and community as drives and values many of us share. While our livestreams and our digital archives and our mechanisms of staying digitally connected have been invaluable tools of continuity during this time of estrangement, and will likely get much more use in a post-COVID world, it is easier than ever to realize their status as complimentary, rather than complete.

Classical music and technology have been intertwined in many ways and for a long time. Instrument makers, acousticians, computer scientists, architects and printing presses have all worked to harness

---

3   See, for example, Renee Fleming's performance during the MET's At-Home Gala, which Anthony Tommasini of *The New York Times* described as full of the "flawed balances" characteristic of live audio-visuals streamed from home (Tommasini, 2020).

4   Musicologist María Zuazu has recently written about the imperfect and at times generative "temporal co-presence" that "Quarantine concerts" evoke (Zuazu, 2020).

the materials and techniques used to make music and present it to audiences. As meetings of science, industry, material, and practical application, the label "technology" might apply equally to a tuning fork as a tape machine. Yet over the last two decades, the "digital revolution" has had great impact on our perception of space, time, knowledge, and sound, all factors that condition approaches to music. To talk about the interface between classical music and technology today is to talk about the interface between classical music and digital culture.

Some might hold the position that digital technologies detract from this "enduring" musical practice, lumping it in with media that otherwise, and not always happily, dominate daily life (Balio, 2014). Others tout the real-world experimentation, convenience, access, growth, and quality that the use of digital technologies in classical music settings has catalyzed (Schienen, 2012). While it might be assumed classical music's long history allows it to absent itself from the issues currently raised by new technologies, the classical music community does necessarily respond to them, in one way or another, and certainly not always with consensus. For every collection of classical music listeners who commit to analog formats and high-quality audio, there are just as many who celebrate the abundant access of digital streaming services. For every ensemble that emphasizes live concert hall performance, there is another who sees a future in the digital video archive or simulcast. And for every group of composers who explores the potentials of traditional instruments (and not always traditionally), there is another who writes in Logic or for lightbulbs.

We do not wish to give the impression that these issues have resulted in a chasm, with ideologues divided on each side; rather, they have created a cacophony, whose noisiness might productively point to what's next. "Technology" is not a teleology; on the contrary the current moment in classical music and in culture writ large speaks to how much technology and its enlistment in creative practices, access, circulation, and aesthetics is up for meaningful debate.

This chapter aims to take on the particularities of the possibilities and challenges that emerge out of the meeting of classical music practices and digital culture more broadly. It addresses some of the implications of digital media on classical music creation, transmission, and education while touching on related questions of access, performance, archiving, and listening. In closing we suggests some avenues for further thought and practice, and address these themes in relation to what has been revealed in the world-under-pandemic moment in which we currently live and work.

Musical Creation

From a strictly musical point of view, technology has evolved so quickly that in many cases it outpaces our contemporary understanding. At the same time, many institutions seem to have maintained a nineteenth-century approach to the enjoyment of music. They follow a model that aims to mostly select productions from among one of the twenty most famous operas of the repertoire, or to connect concerto and symphony in a single program. Meanwhile, from the 1950s on, many composers have expanded upon these conceptions, or taken up new methods. Much composition explores, sometimes in a very radical way, the electro-acoustic possibilities of venues and often these traditional "music temples" are not equipped to match such ambitions: many major international concert halls are still unable to program some of the works of John Cage, Iannis Xenakis, Annea Lockwood, Luciano Berio, Karlheinz Stockhausen, Kaija Saariaho, or Pierre Boulez, even though some of these masterpieces combining instrumental compositions and synthetic sounds were completed nearly forty or fifty years ago.

Recent forays into new programming have suggested to us what the future might bring: major technical advancements that will improve our abilities to amplify and spatialize sound. This will allow us to easily improve the control of sound in concert halls in order to, for example, increase or reduce reverberation in real time, or program works composed specifically with sound spatialization in mind (see, e.g., Malham & Myatt, 1995; Peters, Braasch, & McAdams, 2011). Such systems will meet many musicians' demands to incorporate, in a piece or a concert, electronic sounds and modified voices, as well as other artistic media. In ten or twenty years' time, these new devices will likely be incorporated into both new concert halls and older, already established ones.

There are recent examples, too, of works that challenge the traditional boundaries of the concert hall and engage new technologically-enabled performance practices. "Invisible Cities: An Opera for Headphones," composed by Christopher Cerrone and commissioned by The Industry and L.A. Dance Project is one example. The opera was performed in Los Angeles' Union Station in October and November of 2013—while the quotidian life of the train station continued around it—as a sold-out ticketed audience participated. Or, very recently, the International Contemporary Ensemble's performance of Ashley Fure's "The Force of Things: An Opera for Objects" (2017) was delivered at the Gelsey Kirkland Arts Center in Brooklyn, NY in 2018 as part of Lincoln Center's Mostly Mozart Festival. The work garnered critical praise and what audiences described as a profound, disturbing, and memorable musical experience.

There are of course myriad examples that could be added to this list, but the question remains for those committed to or interested in more traditional repertoire of what, if anything, digital technology has to offer music composed with different materials and techniques in mind. Yet music, including that which might be called "classical," is no stranger to technological revolution, and in fact even the most narrowly- or conservatively-defined classical music benefitted from innovations in instrument building, print technologies, concert hall acoustics, and early recording.[5] Music was also one of the first artistic disciplines to integrate acoustic, electronic, and analog techniques in an experimental way. We contend that classical music might well benefit from digital technologies today.

Transmission

Music was one of the first industries to be transformed by the unexpected expansion of peer-to-peer networks, file sharing, and, within the last ten years, streaming. New devices and audio formats seem to have facilitated a democratization of listening, even if these fundamental mutations force us to be both prudent in our judgment and extremely

---

5   See, for example, Emily Thompson's important and exhaustive 2002 book, *The Soundscape of Modernity*. For earlier examples of the intersections of science, technology, and music, see Jackson, 2006.

engaged. Today, the rise of Creative Commons,[6] as a part of a new sharing ecosystem, for example, offers us the promise of an immense amount of knowledge, information, and creativity. Is this a new Library of Alexandria, or just a huge disorganized aggregate of texts and media? It is up to us to choose, to classify, to comment on, and to find a common or shared sense out of this abundance.

Music streaming services like Spotify, Apple Music, and Amazon can feel similarly labyrinthine and vast, and veiled in the opacities of corporate control. These services have obvious drawbacks. First, the economic model of these platforms compensates artists exceedingly poorly, at the rate of about 0.0006 dollars per stream, a fact that even those musics more suited to repeat listening and better-funded through ancillary revenue (like pop) have sought to address and improve.[7] Second, as many audiophiles have noticed, the quality of streamed audio leaves much to be desired.[8] Third, the cataloging systems for streaming services like Spotify and Apple Music bury the pertinent information a classical music listener might seek, like the names of solo artists, the date of a performance, the conductor, the movement, or any number of other descriptors that allow one to choose a specific recording. Instead, the data is reduced to "artist" and "album," making it at times difficult to find and access particular recordings.[9] Furthermore, "classical" is the only genre for which artists who upload their music to iTunes and

---

6   Creative Commons is a non-profit organization that aims to organize, distribute, and make accessible "creative and academic works" that have historically existed behind paywalls in private organizations. See https://creativecommons.org/about/

7   Recently, Spotify founder and CEO Daniel Ek responded to ongoing outcry by artists about Spotify's poor artist compensation by suggesting that artists simply need to update their mode of creation to one of "continuous engagement with their fans. It is about putting the work in, about the storytelling around the album, and about keeping a continuous dialogue with your fans" (Dredge, 2020). Artists and some critics responded with vocal objection to this construction, but it is yet to be seen whether that will make much of a difference in the streaming giant's business model.

8   Spotify streams audio at 160 kbps (kilobits per second) in its standard version, about half the quality of an Mp3. The pay-only service Tidal offers "lossless compression" streaming, which is about equivalent to that of a CD. Other streaming services vary in their kbps, with most topping out at 320 kbps, or the equivalent of a standard Mp3, and less than the "definition" of CD audio.

9   Using the "Search" tool on Spotify, for instance, will yield tiered results, with "Popular" individual tracks, followed by "Merch" (merchandise), followed by "Albums." Combined-term searches have the tendency to take the user far afield from the content they seek.

Amazon streaming services are required to list a record label under which their music is released.[10] This not only creates a barrier that does not exist in other genres, it excludes new creators by adding an unnecessary gatekeeper.

Yet streaming services have their advantages, too, in particular that they give access to a great store of recordings, which is utterly unprecedented. This can be of great use not only to curious individuals, but also to teachers who are given the opportunity to assign readily-available listening to students and share listening experiences in the classroom environment, researchers looking to evaluate a large amount of material or closely listen to one rare recording, or institutions who might aggregate publicly-available playlists around a season's theme, or a conductor's or performer's previous work.

Perhaps most encouragingly, "streaming" is not confined to large commercial platforms; in the past ten years, there has been an initiative to digitize audio collections that might never find themselves as a Tidal or Amazon search result. There is the Naxos Music Library, the Library of Congress's National Jukebox, the Alexander Street video and audio streaming archive, all of which are staples in many private research libraries and some public libraries. Large institutions like Carnegie Hall, the New York Philharmonic, and the Library of Congress Digital Collections (to name just a few US-based organizations) have received generous grants to create digital archives to stabilize older analog recordings and make them available to future generations. This is of course no replacement for live performance, but these no-pay services could have some effect on providing context, history and intrigue to new listeners, and will likely reshape for researchers what it means to do "archival" research.

In this spirit, contemporary ensembles have innovated approaches to digital archives that can catalog a season's program for future viewing, highlight new composers and works, and provide new audiences an introduction to a group's or institution's approaches to performance. One sophisticated example is DigitICE, the digital video archive of the International Contemporary Ensemble, which allows the user to search by composer, season, location, concert hall, performer, and instrument.

---

10   As of 2018.

It is a place to browse a decade of performances, or search out exemplary new repertoire for bassoon, hammered dulcimer, electronics and so on. It is hosted on an integrated webpage that places this archive alongside ways to view upcoming events and buy tickets, see upcoming educational workshops, and read about participating artists, all of which encourage participation and engagement "out of the box".

Of course, real-world engagement is the aim, but it must be acknowledged that before concert-goers visit any performance space, they most often make first contact with institutions' and artists' digital platforms, whether they are archives or simple, ticket-issuing webpages. These are places where visitors are able to discover the program of the season, watch videos of previous performances, and possibly buy tickets for concerts or other activities. As such, web design for these platforms is a worthy (and relatively inexpensive) investment. Based on the fact that there is rarely a professional or fledgling ensemble or institution without an Instagram and Twitter account, Facebook page, and YouTube, or Vimeo channel, we also recognize the ways social media "branding" has come to seem like a prerequisite for representation and audience engagement. We might lament this reality if it does not extend far beyond things such as the likes, shares, and views usually used to calculate value in digital space. While the specifics of social media strategy are not our focus here, we do contend that there are novel possibilities for how participation in this part of the mediascape might cultivate excitement around places, performers, and ensembles, and translate into real-world encounters.

Another shift in transmission that digital technology has facilitated is the recording and broadcasting of live concerts on apps and websites. Although we think this is a positive move, it has not sufficiently opened doors in ways some institutions had hoped. For example, The Berliner Philharmoniker launched its "Digital Concert Hall" over ten years ago, which allows customers an unlimited access to all live concerts and archives. Approximately 22,000 paying users are registered, including 75% non-German viewers. This result is, without a doubt, inferior to what was initially projected. The high subscription cost of this business model is surely the cause of these disappointing results.[11]

---

11   In 2020, the subscription cost was 134 euros ($151) for a twelve-month ticket.

These examples show the scale of the challenge musical institutions face. It is however certain that digital media are a key to facilitating and encouraging access: access to youth, openness towards artistic disciplines and techniques, and an eye on and towards the international. However, in the current moment a working business model is almost impossible to find. Many concert halls have recorded their concerts and offered them in open access on their websites. From a long-term perspective, this approach could be beneficial. Thus, the Cité de la musique Philharmonie has now over three thousand five hundred hours of video and audio recordings, which are about to become an important database for educational tools as well as the subject of specific agreements with private internet operators worldwide.[12]

Education

Concerning classical music education, our efforts and investments only fully make sense if we are able to clearly define our priorities. Pedagogy across disciplines is grappling with how to present, test, and train material in light of new tools and shifting realities of classroom equipment, attention, and educational expectations. Music is no different, and as noted elsewhere in this report, there are several levels on which musical education has changed in recent years, and not necessarily in relation to digital technologies. For our part, we focus on some possibilities of digital educational tools for children, researchers, and audiences.

Digital educational activities are best, of course, if they coexist with more traditionally embodied activities. Children and teenagers might discover the beauty of woodwind and brass instruments, learn to sing and dance, collaborate in person to perform and compose, while *at the same time engaging* digital pedagogical tools offering rewarding tactile and intellectual experiences, complimenting instead of replacing more traditional approaches. With that in mind, we should focus and look at digital tools as cognitive possibilities: such technologies can empower

---

12 The full collection may be accessed at the multimedia library of the Philharmonie de Paris, as well as through an internet network for French public libraries and high schools. A collection of 100 hours of video may also be accessed via the platform "Philharmonielive". For more information see https://bit.ly/2TgqIGG and https://pad.philharmoniedeparis.fr/comment-ca-marche.aspx.

the young musician, giving her/him/them both the means to progress and to develop her/his/their curiosity.

Music creation and mixing apps that one can manipulate without any prior knowledge of theory provide interesting examples for children. Some of them are designed so well that they come close to being true artistic objects. We are referring, for instance, to the cost-free app *Toc & Roll*, which enables children to compose songs using a multitude of sounds. New digital tools might also promote the creation of an innovative educational discourse on music, which will be key in maintaining a fascination for classical music over generations. An interesting example is the app for iPad made by Esa-Pekka Salonen and the Philharmonia Orchestra, named *The Orchestra*, which enables the user to listen to a piece while reading a scrolling score and watching the movements of the conductor.

For researchers, Digital Score archives at places like the Morgan Library & Museum in New York, the International Music Score Library Project based in Canada, or the Loeb Music Library at Harvard University make available a host of rare manuscripts, public domain works, and lesser-known compositions that can be studied, analyzed, or played without or prior to visits to the institutions that house them. They also make it possible to share these works in the classroom, and open students up to works that might fall outside of narrowed and reduced canons of works. On the business research side, digital data analytics services can help us understand how new audiences are constituted, what they are interested in, and thus adapt our discourses in accordance. Data analysis and services related to ticket sales are evolving towards counseling and guiding more and more "independent" visitors, precisely the kind of visitor classical music has most precipitously lost over the last thirty years.

For audiences, institutions might harness their web platforms to offer interactive content around a piece, a season, or a performance. Program notes and pre-concert talks can be useful in clueing audiences in to details about a work they might not otherwise know, yet these institutional standbys might at times feel a bit stale to new audiences. Player, composer, and conductor testimonials, "behind the scenes" looks into rehearsals, and short video documentaries that provide historical context for works from 1450 or 1980 are some of the ways to deepen audience engagement pre-concert. These kinds of materials might easily be included and sent along with a digitally-purchased ticket.

We must combine our knowledge of pedagogy, entertainment, design and programming, and find ways to connect these new tools to the artists, the orchestras as well as to concert halls. Presumably, we should bring artists and spectators closer, gather energies and talents, and contribute to the education of younger generations. If we want to share classical art with the largest and most diversified audience, we must try to redefine all the elements that make up the mass of experiences and knowledge that will then enable us to generate new ties with music lovers.

Conclusion

That people love various kinds of music and in various ways is evident in every corner of daily life; but no fan, practitioner, or institution of any genre is entitled to the fandom and participation of "new" or "diversified" audiences. Technologies that present things differently in order to make them more readily available, and offer context, education, and possibilities for artistic innovation, do not themselves guarantee that new audiences will be bitten by the classical music bug. They do, however take seriously contemporary realities of saturated and diffracted art markets; the way standard repertoires may appear opaque or alienating to newcomers; and the desire for musical experience to speak to quality as well as relevance, accessibility, and personal and communal significance.

The degree of hopefulness around digital technologies presented here is not an uncritical one. "Digital" does not flatly translate into the more complicated ambitions of "education," "engagement," or "access". Meeting these aims requires a level of media facility among the community that allows individuals and groups to critically assess, navigate, and make use of things like digital archives, streaming audio, and digital educational and data analysis tools. Not all of these things are equally useful or well-designed, but without some degree of media literacy it is difficult to tell the difference, and even more difficult perhaps to suggest improvements to these relatively young technologies that might serve classical music makers, programmers, and listeners.

Of course, engaging with and building new structures for technology in music is not an end in itself. Yet arguments that stabilize "classical" by asserting its perennial quality[13] are unsurprisingly baffled by how to grapple with an ever-changing technological landscape. While these times seem overwhelmed by disagreement and change, it is worth remembering that very similar questions have been asked before (see, e.g., Dolan, 2013; Jackson, 2006; Bijsterveldt & Pinch, 2003). The challenge is how to avoid nostalgia for norms without falling into the fetish of the new, or newly mediated. In other words, we should approach with as much caution the discourses that claim classical music as transcendent and universalizing as those similar discourses that attribute those ideals to technology.

Nonetheless, we contend that digital culture *is* the culture in which classical music is currently embedded, and in which it might thrive in a real-world context. As we see it, a robust classical music future requires neither a wholesale adoption of new media, nor a protectionist rejection of what these media might offer. Instead, it requires a community committed to confronting a changing world, and finding a home for the art it prizes within it.

Coda: Black Lives Matter
Catherine Provenzano

In June 2020, after the police killings of Breonna Taylor in Louisville, KY and George Floyd in Minneapolis, MN, and with the momentum of recent memory (Sandra Bland, in 2015; Michael Brown, in 2014; and Tamir Rice, in 2014; to name just a fraction of similar tragedies) and the centuries of oppression behind them, millions of people took to the streets with calls for a restructuring that have reverberated through just about every institution in the United States, and beyond. This is a time of accountability and opportunity, and there is no need to go back to a "normal" that, for so many, never appealed, or never worked.

---

13 To quote the "independent, non-partisan, and nonprofit think tank dedicated to classical music," Future Symphony, classical music is "eternal and transcendent," and "stands outside of time, and looks lovingly from its vantage point across the wide panoply of history".

This moment also takes to task the ideals of community engagement, education and accessibility, the responsibility for which we so often pass off to new technological interfaces and tools, as though these are going to fix the problems of racial oppression and economic injustice that permeate the classical world. This is not to say that artists and institutions have not engaged technology in profound creative ways, or to diminish the fact that artists of color so often make up the vanguard of technical and technological experimentation and practice in musical forms. It is simply to emphasize that no digital tool is going to change the white-dominated and deeply classist lineage and current reality of the North American classical music world. At least in North America, and to varying extents in other places, classical music has been bolstered by its proximity to, even its very index of, governmental and financial power, class status, and cultural capital, to use Pierre Bourdieu's famous term. In the US, this power and status has in many historical instances been built upon the explicit exclusion and othering of Black people. What we are seeing now is that the "technological savior" narratives that are both upheld and papered over by the new offerings of technological advancement (e.g., "This new tool might help Black and Brown children become interested in classical music!" or, "Now that we have made concerts available online, more people from all walks of life will feel comfortable in our concert halls!", to exaggerate somewhat) are no longer going to work.

But what will work? Anti-racism, a term many have learned over the last few months, means a commitment to active restructuring, space building, accountability, resource allocation, and policy change that is far from the passive "non-racist" laurel-resting that stops, contentedly, at representation without enacting any real change for individuals and communities. Lest this seem like too high of a mountain to climb, the insight on how to move forward is everywhere, offered (not just, but especially) by Black artists and administrators (see Woolfe & Barone, 2020; and Lewis, 2020), by the members of our institutions we tend to take care of the least, like staff, teachers, custodial, and tech support workers. There are organizations such as Chineke! Foundation in the UK, and the Sphinx Organization in the US, which work to redress the imbalances in opportunity and education that have accumulated in classical music spaces and practices.¹⁴ And the art is everywhere, too, we simply haven't programmed it (see Lewis, 2020; and the Black Music History Library). Anti-racist work happens at every single level, from there interpersonal to the institutional. But it bears stating that it is not the sole responsibility of people of color in our musical communities to educate those of more power and privilege on these issues—that requires a voluntary willingness and commitment from individuals ready educate themselves. What if, in that spirit, we heard what our colleagues have to say? Heard, and took seriously, those alienated by the current institutional structures and workings? Heard, and took seriously the artworks of those the classical world has thus far tokenized at best and ignored at worst? The good news is, these hearings draw on a skill and a value that brought most of us here in the first place—a desire to listen.

References

Alexander Street, https://alexanderstreet.com/

Balio, Andrew. 2014. "Saving Classical Music: A Return to Tradition", *The Imaginative Conservative*, 8 October, http://www.theimaginativeconservative.org/2014/10/saving-classical-music.html

Bijsterveldt, Karin, and Trevor Pinch. 2003. "'Should One Applaud?': Breaches and Boundaries in the Reception of New Technology in Music", *Technology and Culture*, 44(3): 536–559, https://doi.org/10.1353/tech.2003.0126

Black Music History Library, https://blackmusiclibrary.com/Library

Bourdieu, P. 1977. "Cultural Reproduction and Social Reproduction", in *Power and Ideology in Education*, ed. by J. Karabel and A. H. Halsey (New York: Oxford University Press), pp. 487–511.

Carnegie Hall Digital Archive, https://www.carnegiehall.org/About/History/Archives/Archival-Collections

Chineke! Foundation, https://www.chineke.org/

Digital Concert Hall, https://www.digitalconcerthall.com/en/home

---

14   Chineke! Foundation, https://www.chineke.org/. It is also worth watching founder Chi-chi Nwanoku's introduction to the Foundation https://www.youtube.com/watch?time_continue=212&v=oepETzk0YLU&feature=emb_title ("Introduction the Chineke! Foundation", 3:32, posted online by Chineke! Foundation, Youtube, 28 April 2017).

DigitICE, https://www.iceorg.org/digitice

Dolan, Emily. 2013. *The Orchestral Revolution: Haydn and the Technologies of Timbre* (Cambridge: Cambridge University Press, 2013), https://doi.org/10.1017/cbo9781139235976

Dredge, Stuart. 2020. "Spotify CEO Talks Covid-19, Artist Incomes and Podcasting (Interview)", *Music Ally*, 30 July, https://musically.com/2020/07/30/spotify-ceo-talks-covid-19-artist-incomes-and-podcasting-interview/

Future Symphony, https://www.futuresymphony.org/about/

International Music Score Library Project, https://imslp.org/

Jackson, Myles. 2006. *Harmonious Triads: Physicists, Musicians, and Instrument Makers in Nineteenth-Century Germany* (Cambridge, MA: MIT Press).

Lewis, George E. 2020. "Lifting the Cone of Silence from Black Composers", *The New York Times*, 3 July, https://www.nytimes.com/2020/07/03/arts/music/black-composers-classical-music.html

Library of Congress Digital Collections, https://www.loc.gov/collections/

Library of Congress National Jukebox, http://www.loc.gov/jukebox/

Loeb Music Library, https://library.harvard.edu/collections/digital-scores-and-libretti?_collection=scores

Malham, David G., and Anthony Myatt. 1995. "3-D Sound Spatialization using Ambisonic Techniques", *Computer Music Journal*, 19(4): 58–70, https://doi.org/10.2307/3680991

Morgan Library & Museum, https://www.themorgan.org/collection/music-manuscripts-and-printed-music

Naxos Music Library, https://www.naxosmusiclibrary.com/home.asp?rurl=%2Fdefault%2Easp

New York Philharmonic Digital Archive, https://archives.nyphil.org/

Peters, Nils, Jonas Braasch, and Stephen McAdams. 2011. "Sound Spatialization across Disciplines using Virtual Microphone Control (ViMiC)", *Journal of Interdisciplinary Music Studies*, 5(2): 167–190.

Schienen, Richard. 2012. "How Digital Technology is Impacting Classical Music: Three Voices", *The Mercury News*, 28 March, https://www.mercurynews.com/2012/03/28/how-digital-technology-is-impacting-classical-music-three-voices/

Sphinx Organization, http://www.sphinxmusic.org/

Thompson, Emily. 2002. *The Soundscape of Modernity: Architectural Acoustics and the Culture of Listening in America, 1900–1933* (Cambridge, MA: MIT Press).

Tomassini, Anthony. 2020. "The Met Opera's At-Home Gala: Informal Yet Profoundly Moving", *The New York Times*, 26 April, https://www.nytimes.com/2020/04/26/arts/music/metropolitan-opera-at-home-gala.html

Woolfe, Zachary, and Joshua Barone. 2020. "Black Artists on How to Change Classical Music", *The New York Times*, 16 July, https://www.nytimes.com/2020/07/16/arts/music/black-classical-music-opera.html?action=click&module=RelatedLinks&pgtype=Article

Zuazu, María. 2020. "Aliveness: Technologies of Gathering in Times of COVID", *FlashArt*, 30 June, https://flash---art.com/2020/06/listening-in-4-technologies-of-gathering-maria-zuazu/

PART II

12. Expanding Audiences in Miami: The New World Symphony's New Audiences Initiative

Howard Herring and Craig Hall

Introduction

The New World Symphony (NWS) is a hybrid educational and artistic institution, an orchestral academy that prepares graduates for leadership positions in orchestras and ensembles. Unique in American music, it is also a research and development facility. The program is built around eighty-seven Fellows, each fulfilling a three-year course of study and performance. They are at the center of a dynamic educational experience that annually includes seventy performances, 200 community engagement events, and robust leadership training. NWS advances its mission in a Frank Gehry-designed campus that is at the intersection of music, education, architecture, and digital technology. 1,200 applicants seek thirty annual openings. An undergraduate degree is required for acceptance. Most Fellows hold a master's degree. NWS is committed to a diverse community. On average, 15–18% of the orchestra are players of color. The number of alumni stands at 1,150, with 90% of these actively involved in classical music and making a difference in the field.

From this platform, NWS pursues a New Audience Initiative, an acquisition system that can be useful for professional orchestras and presenters of classical music.

A Start-Up Mentality

"Whoever thought a start-up could change the way people feel about classical music?" is the opening sentence of a LinkedIn post by Michael Moritz, venture capitalist and partner of Sequoia Capital (Moritz, 2013). Moritz's observation sets the context for New World Symphony's search for new audiences. In his statement, two important understandings are revealed. Start-up implies inventing a solution to a difficult problem. And those who oversee this invention are concerned with how people *feel* about classical music. People who have known this music for a lifetime, people who have yet to encounter its magic, and everyone in between.

Led by founding artistic director Michael Tilson Thomas (MTT) and in the company of Fellows who will become classical music leaders, the New World Symphony has been pursuing new audiences since its inception.

Early Days

In 1980, the US Census asked a question for the first time—"Have you attended at least one classical music concert in the last year?" In that year, 13% of American adults said yes (US Census Bureau, 1980). By 2017, only 8.6% answered in the affirmative (National Endowment for the Arts, 2017). The decline was steady in that thirty-seven-year period. In the 1990s, music lovers and orchestra professionals became concerned about the diminishing audience. This prompted a variety of responses, including the Knight Foundation's creation of the Magic of Music program.[1]

The Magic of Music Program

In 1994, the New World Symphony was invited to join fifteen professional orchestras in the Magic of Music program. The Magic of Music program initially created a $5.4 million, five-year initiative to

---

[1] The Knight Foundation is a national foundation which invests in journalism, the arts, and in the success of cities where brothers, John S. and James L. Knight once published newspapers. The goal of the Knight Foundation is to foster informed and engaged communities (Knight Foundation, a).

encourage orchestras to be more entrepreneurial with their audience building initiatives. In 1999, the foundation approved a second phase spanning from 2000–2005 and expanded the funding of the program to a total of $13 million (Knight Foundation, b). With the encouragement of generous funding from the Knight Foundation, the New World Symphony launched a series of audience engagement experiments. The work was led by Michael Tilson Thomas, the staff, and Fellows of NWS. A review of findings reveals the importance of this work.

The first phase of the Magic of Music project can be summarized as follows:

- Repertoire from the Western canon does not attract new audiences even when played at the highest levels of excellence.
- Bringing prospects to their first concert experience is only the beginning of the development of a relationship.
- Serious audience development requires fundamental change in the understandings and behaviors of all orchestral constituents.
- Performances outside the concert hall have high value in attracting prospective audiences.

In the second phase of the Magic of Music, a market study reoriented all participants (Knight Foundation, 2002). Findings included:

- The prospective audience is much larger than most orchestra leaders believe.
- Beyond live, traditional performances, there are multiple distribution channels that connect listeners to the music in meaningful ways.
- A significant number of prospective audience members did not find the concert hall to be the preferred venue for a classical music experience.
- Affinity for classical music did not translate into attendance at concerts.
- 74% of ticket-buyers played an instrument or sang in a chorus at some point in their life (Wolf, 2006: 32).

In the program's final report, *The Search for Shining Eyes,* issued in 2006, the Knight Foundation's leadership chose to turn away from stopgap funding and focus on transformational change that would lead to a reversal of the declining audience trend. In an environment of experimentation and with the Knight Foundation's Magic of Music funding, the New World Symphony began to explore contextualized presentations, informal concerts in non-traditional venues, the use of ultra-high-speed Internet in bringing composers into the concert experience, and theatrical lighting and effects.

Throughout his career, Michael Tilson Thomas has demonstrated the power of contextualized presentations for the benefit of all members of the audience. NWS Fellows, eager to share their music-making with the broader public, were ideal Magic of Music participants. As an institution, NWS understands itself as a laboratory for generating new ideas about the way music is taught, presented, and experienced. Over the course of the ten years of the Magic of Music program, NWS began to capitalize on its unique skills and structure. Research results from Magic of Music formed the foundation for a second, more intense effort funded by the Andrew W. Mellon Foundation.

The Magic of Music initiative coincided with the period of program articulation and architectural design for the New World Center, NWS's new campus. Beginning in 2002, Michael Tilson Thomas and senior staff started to reimagine the educational and artistic future of the New World Symphony. NWS's mission is to train graduates of music schools for leadership in classical music. That mission was the basis for imagining a dynamic, unique, and Fellow-centric educational program that prepares graduates for an unpredictable future. In turn, the program guided Frank Gehry and his team in the design of the New World Center.

As design led to construction, NWS crafted a vision statement: NWS envisions a strong and secure future for classical music and will reimagine, reaffirm, express, and share its traditions with as many people as possible. From the conclusion of the Magic of Music program in 2005, the forces that guided NWS's physical transformation have driven the institutional emphasis on the pursuit of new audiences.

The New Audience Initiative

Beginning in 2008, and with funding from the Andrew W. Mellon Foundation, NWS developed a sequential system for audience acquisition based on the following steps:

- Identify a prospective audience based on age, affinity, geographic proximity, lifestyle choices, and similar factors.
- Design an experience that would attract individuals from this group.
- Place classical music at the center of this experience.
- Describe and market the experience to the target prospects.
- Execute the experience including a performance of the chosen symphonic repertoire at the highest level of artistic excellence.
- Survey the audience.
- Analyze the survey results.
- Compare analysis with intuitive judgement.
- Reimagine the experience.
- Repeat the cycle.

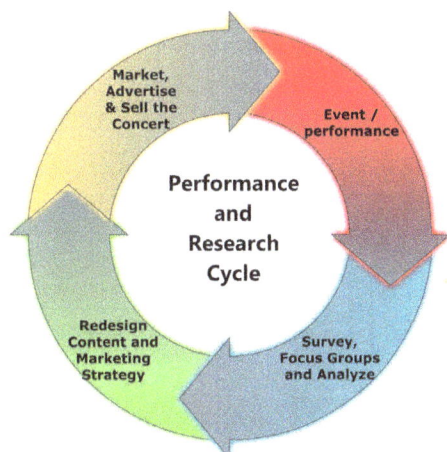

Fig. 1 New World Symphony's performance and research cycle for audience acquisition and engagement. Graphic by Howard Herring and Craig Hall (2012), © 2012, New World Symphony, Inc. All rights reserved.

In the first years, three prospective audiences were identified.

- Curious twenty-somethings with varying exposure to classical music. This group included the Friends of New World Symphony, a philanthropic membership organization for young adult patrons looking for a social and networking vehicle. This group previously had little connection to classical music (New World Symphony, b).
- Casual strollers on Lincoln Road, the pedestrian mall in front of NWS's original performance home, the Lincoln Theatre.
- Residents who are attracted to the Miami Beach club scene.

NWS designed specific performance experiences for these groups and established a research program with WolfBrown to assess the efficacy of each experience.[2]

- For the curious, younger, and newer prospects, *Symphony with a Splash*—a two-part event with a reception followed by an hour of contextualized performance. Author, narrator, and filmmaker Jamie Bernstein developed and delivered the scripts.
- For the Lincoln Road pedestrians, a thirty-minute *Mini-Concert*—priced at $2.50 and scheduled at 7:30pm, 8:30pm, and 9:30pm.
- For the club goers, *Pulse—Late Night at the New World Symphony*—a 9:00pm to 1:00am event with DJ-spun electronic music alternating with orchestral sets.

Results for Each Alternate Format

Symphony with a Splash/Encounters put the emphasis on the reception with music to follow. Via survey results, the audience was quick to say they wanted the music first. The order was reversed, and the experience renamed *Encounters*. From inception, 25% of the audience was new to the

---

2 WolfBrown is a consultancy and works with funders, nonprofit institutions and public agencies on research, planning, resource development, and capacity building.

organization's database. This was more than double NWS's standard of 10–12% for traditional concerts. Yet, 75% of the audience were returning patrons. Based on survey results, NWS learned that contextualization of the music was important to both the new and returning audience members.

Encounters served a second purpose, to engage members of the Friends of the New World Symphony. *Encounters* was a natural and popular way for them to be drawn into the music and better understand the mission and vision of NWS. Audience survey and focus group results made it clear that contextualization and informal relationships between Friends and Fellows led Friends members to unexpected musical transformations and more energetic advocacy.

The survey results for the audience of *Encounters* included the following:

- 25% of attendees were new to the database.

- 95% of first-time attendees said the concert had a positive influence on returning to a future NWS concert.

- Informational and theatrical elements enhanced the event for infrequent attendees of classical music.

- Focus groups with first-timers showed a preference for this type of event over traditional concerts.

Fig. 2 Jamie Bernstein narrates during an *Encounters* concert performed by the New World Symphony orchestra at the New World Center. This video as well as the graphics and animations featured as performance elements within the video were created in the Knight New Media Center at the New World Center campus in Miami Beach, FL. Knight Foundation and New World Symphony: Reimagining classical music in the digital age. © 2020, New World Symphony, Inc. All rights reserved. Duration: 1:35.

To watch an excerpt from an *Encounters* concert, featuring Jamie Bernstein narrating her script, scan the QR code or follow this link: https://vimeo.com/432672314

Mini-Concerts were thirty-minute events offered on Friday and Saturday nights at 7:30pm, 8:30pm, and 9:30pm. Tickets were offered for only $2.50. The offering was designed to lower an individual's required investment of time and money. After a short introduction delivered by a Fellow, the orchestra played one musical work. There was often a simple video image to set the mood. Before 2011, when these concerts were staged in the Lincoln Theatre, there was immediate proximity to Lincoln Road Mall patrons who were spending the evening dining, shopping, and people-watching. A street team of New World marketing staff and Fellows engaged those who were casually strolling in front of the Lincoln Theatre, often convincing them on the spot to come in for a classical music experience.

In 2011, when New World Symphony made the move from the Lincoln Theatre to the New World Center just one block north of Lincoln Road, it lost the direct relationship to pedestrians. Without access to this prospective audience, attendance faltered. Knowing the value of *Mini-Concerts* to first-time attendees, NWS reinvented the strategy. Its new focus became affinity groups including yoga enthusiasts, cyclists, and running clubs. The yoga audience proved to be loyal and curious. Currently, New World Symphony offers yoga experiences with and without music. These events have helped NWS attract major sponsorship by local health care organizations.

A summary of the *Mini-Concerts* audience survey results told us:

- This audience is significantly new and slightly younger than traditional audiences with 45% new to the database and 44% under fifty-five years of age.
- 88% reported a strong emotional response.
- 33% of the audience stayed for a second performance. (Each scheduled performance featured a different musical work.)
- 91% said they were more likely to attend a future NWS concert as a result of the experience.

Fig. 3 NWS Fellow, Grace An, gives an introduction during a *Mini-Concert* (2012). New World Center, Miami Beach, FL. Photo courtesy of New World Symphony. © 2012, New World Symphony, Inc. All rights reserved.

Pulse—Late Night at the New World Symphony targets younger prospective concert attendees who are attracted to the club-style entertainments of Miami Beach. The experience begins at 9:00pm with a DJ spinning in the performance hall. As the crowd gathers, the energy in the performance hall increases. At 9:45pm, NWS offers its first classical set, twenty to thirty minutes of edgy, often contemporary music. The evening goes back to the DJ in anticipation of the second and final orchestra set at 10:45pm. At 11:30pm, the DJ continues to spin in the performance hall while NWS offers chamber music in the quiet of the hundred-seat SunTrust Pavilion, a separate room typically used for chamber performances within the New World Center.

Throughout *Pulse*, lighting and video elements are coordinated with the music. The NWS video team finds *Pulse* to be fertile ground for mixed-media experimentation.

Fig. 4 NWS Conducting Fellow, Joshua Gersen, leads *Pulse—Late Night at the New World Symphony*. The proximity of the audience to performers and the freedom to take photos (red circles) and enjoy drinks in the concert space (yellow circles) contribute to the interactivity of the event. Knight New Media Center environments invite social media sharing of *Pulse* using mobile phones and other digital devices. Photo by Rui Dias-Aidos (2013), New World Center, Miami Beach, FL. © 2013, New World Symphony, Inc. All rights reserved.

Pulse occurs twice per season. Audience survey results show the following:

- After eight years, it continues to be one of the hottest tickets in Miami. Dynamic pricing—which increases the ticket cost as the date of the event approaches—carries the $25 ticket price to $60.
- 40% of the audience is new to the database.

- The median age of attendees is thirty-eight.
- Focus group participants have requested additional classical music sets and want to engage with the music afterward. Set lists provide them with the information they need to search and download the music they have heard.
- When asked to define the experience, audience members are unable to find a single word that would encompass the many facets of the experience.
- *Pulse* audiences engage in a wide variety of activities at the event, highlighting the participatory nature of the experience.

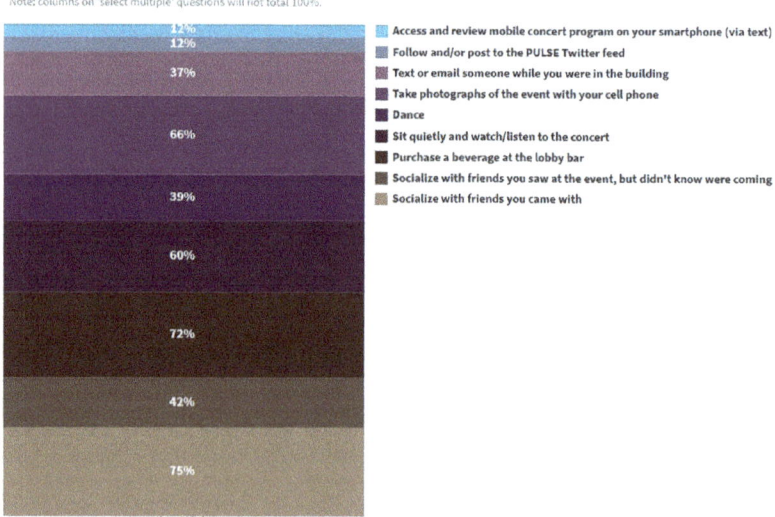

Fig. 5 The chart indicates the variety of activities in which audiences engage throughout *Pulse—Late Night at the New World Symphony*. The audience experience at *Pulse* is participatory—much more than traditional concerts—and is highly customizable to the preference of each audience member. Research and results compiled by WolfBrown in partnership with New World Symphony. © WolfBrown dashboard, www.intrinsicimpact.org. All rights reserved.

Fig. 6 Luke Kritzeck, Director of Lighting at NWS, describes the technical production and audience experience of *Pulse—Late Night at the New World Symphony*. This video as well as the video projections and lighting treatments featured within this video were created in the Knight New Media Center. Knight Foundation and New World Symphony: Reimagining classical music in the digital age. © 2020, New World Symphony, Inc. All rights reserved. Duration: 1:49.

To watch this video online scan the QR code or follow this link: https://vimeo.com/432597241

WALLCAST® Concerts

Fig. 7 *WALLCAST®* concert outside the New World Center. *WALLCAST®* concerts are produced in the Knight New Media Center at the New World Center campus. Photo by Rui Dias-Aidos (2013), New World Center and SoundScape Park, Miami Beach, FL. © 2013, New World Symphony, Inc. All rights reserved.

The NWS vision statement is the philosophical underpinning of the *WALLCAST®* concert phenomenon: "the New World Symphony envisions a strong and secure future for classical music and will reimagine, reaffirm, express, and share its traditions with as many people as possible" (New World Symphony, a). The design of the performance hall/outdoor simulcasting system was driven by the desire for sharing traditions with as many people as possible. Ten robotic cameras and an immersive microphone distribution allow the NWS audio/video staff to capture concerts at an unparalleled level of sophistication. The resulting audio/video is transmitted to a 7,000 square foot projection surface on the primary façade of the New World Center. A Meyer Constellation sound system synchronizes with the video to produce a three-dimensional sonic environment. The audience gathers in SoundScape Park, a 2.5-acre public park designed in conjunction with the New World Center. *WALLCAST*® concerts are free to the public and attract 1,500 to 3,500 people per event. NWS simulcasts between ten to twelve *WALLCAST*® concerts per year. After ten years, *WALLCAST*® concerts have become a cultural center in South Florida. They have created yet another NWS audience.

Several performing arts organizations around the US are planning outdoor simulcasting based on the *WALLCAST*® model. They include the Kennedy Center for the Performing Arts, the University of Michigan, the Kentucky Performing Arts Center, the Germantown Performing Arts Center in Memphis, TN, and Oklahoma State University.

The *WALLCAST*® concert audience is defined in the following ways:

- 75% have never purchased a ticket to a New World Symphony concert.
- 70% are under the age of sixty-five, compared to 19% for traditional concerts indoors.
- 80% attend in groups of five or more people.
- 56% are infrequent attendees of classical music events, attending two or fewer classical concerts in the past year.
- 34% self-report their ethnicity as African American, Hispanic, or racially mixed compared to 11% for traditional indoor concerts.
- The top three reported motivations for attending are:
    - Experiencing music in a relaxed and social environment,
    - Spending quality time with family and friends, and
    - Enjoying Miami Beach's public SoundScape Park.

Fig. 8 Clyde Scott, Director of Video Production at NWS, gives an overview of aspects of a *WALLCAST®* concert, from the technology used to produce the simulcast to the experience of the audience in the park. This video as well as the *WALLCAST®* production featured in this video were produced in the Knight New Media Center. Knight Foundation and New World Symphony: Reimagining classical music in the digital age. © 2020, New World Symphony, Inc. All rights reserved. Duration: 2:49.

To watch the video online scan the QR code or follow this link: https://vimeo.com/432751918

Audience Development— Current Observations

Most major American orchestras serve a small percentage of the populations of their metropolitan areas. According to the Magic of Music research, on average only 3–4% of a city's residents attend symphonic performances (Wolf, 2006: 32). A primary assumption of NWS's New Audience Initiative is that alternate performance formats can be effective in attracting new concert goers, expanding the reach of live performance. The following graph indicates results to date (see Fig. 9).

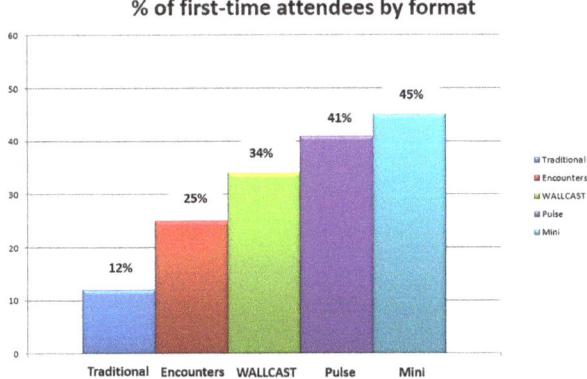

Fig. 9 Percent of first-time attendees by concert format at New World Symphony. Graphic by Craig Hall (2015). © 2015, New World Symphony, Inc. All rights reserved.

The market study done during the second phase of the Knight Foundation's Magic of Music research indicated that far more people had a relationship with classical music than were buying tickets (Knight Foundation, 2002: 7). NWS has proof of this concept. 75% of the *WALLCAST®* concert audience has never purchased a ticket to an NWS concert. Over the past twelve years, NWS has used alternate formats to create 15,877 new accounts for patrons with whom it had not previously had a relationship. 30% of these accounts have purchased tickets for a second NWS performance. This begs a fundamental question. How can NWS specifically, or American orchestras in general, transition prospective audiences from reluctant to curious to attending? Taking one more critical step, the audience can only grow if the first-timers return. NWS has promising statistics.

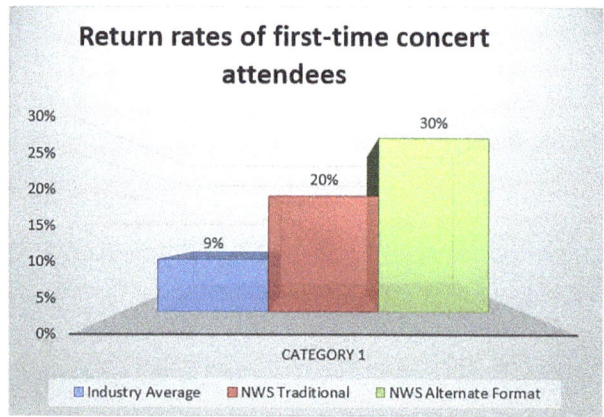

Fig. 10 First-time attendees to alternate performance formats at NWS return at a higher rate than first-time attendees to traditional concerts at NWS. Graphic by Craig Hall (2018). © 2018, New World Symphony, Inc. All rights reserved.

Tracking of ticket purchases indicates that first-timers are most likely to return to the format that drew them initially. While the hope was that first-timers might begin to explore other alternate formats and/or traditional presentations, NWS now realizes the value of multiple audiences. There are five conclusions that could be helpful:

- NWS has seven distinct audiences based on the experiences; traditional, chamber music, family, new music, contextualized, *Pulse*, and *WALLCAST®* concerts. Of these seven, only the first two attract an average (10–12%) number of new attendees. There is little crossover between these audiences.

- Orchestras must be one step ahead of their audiences, identifying prospective groups then designing experiences to attract and engage them.
- The center point of each alternate format must be an excellent performance of serious music.
- Listening carefully to prospective audiences is essential to the acquisition process.
- Engaging new audiences is costly and requires a long-term institutional commitment. However, ignoring the need for new audiences is far more costly in the long run.

Next Steps at the New World Symphony

Encounters to *Double Take*

As mentioned earlier in the text, *Encounters* was a one-hour contextualized concert followed by a reception for musicians and audience members. Over the years, Fellows—guided by MTT—have become more involved in the design and execution. These themed concerts have proven productive in gathering new audiences. An NWS concert called *Heard It Through the Grapevine* was based on the association of wine and music and was led by cello Fellow Hilary Glen and a master sommelier. Another Fellow-led concert, *Fiesta Cubana*, was for the Cuban Americans of Miami with visual art, folk and dance music, and orchestral music sharing the focus. *Dimensions* and *Mixtape* gave Fellows a chance to speak directly and personally about their associations with specific pieces of music.

The most recent format, *Double Take*, goes one step further, with the Fellows becoming even more sophisticated with their contextualization of the repertoire, drawing parallels to personal experiences. These formats are traditional-length concerts. The post-concert interaction remains in place and is essential to the success of the format. In the

2018/19 season, NWS targeted family audiences with *Face Off—A Battle of the Instruments*.

Fig. 11 Blake-Anthony Johnson, NWS Cello Fellow, introduces the symphony's performance of Debussy's *Prelude to the Afternoon of a Faun* drawing on his personal experience with the music to contextualize the piece for the audience. This video was created in the Knight New Media Center. Knight Foundation and New World Symphony: Reimagining classical music in the digital age. © 2020, New World Symphony, Inc. All rights reserved. Duration: 15:15.

To watch the video online scan the QR code or follow this link: https://vimeo.com/432973486

As Fellows have taken on greater responsibility in creating the concert experience and contextualizing the music, the number of new audience members at each performance has increased slightly, from 25% to 30%. And the return rate of those first-timers has thus far mirrored that of traditional audiences at 21%. Return rates increase as time passes.

Now the expectation is that a third of the audience for *Double Take* will be attending their first New World Symphony concert. The challenge is to discover the reason for this increase.

Pulse—Don't Argue with Success

Pulse continues to bring first-timers. It is unlike any other NWS performance, so it is a greater challenge to direct *Pulse* attendees to other formats. However, it is a brand-defining format for NWS in Miami and the national orchestra community. As a model for others, it is a raucous call for innovation. Even with this success, it is not too soon to evolve this format to keep it fresh.

NWS Goes to the Community

During the 2017/18 season, NWS staged two significant community-based initiatives, Project 305 and a week of Community Concerts. Funded by a major grant from the Knight Foundation, Project 305 asked residents of South Florida to capture and upload audio and video samples of *their* Miami. Working with Artistic Director Michael Tilson Thomas, composer Ted Hearne and filmmaker Jon David Kane brought this material together in a symphonic documentary called *Miami in Movements*.

Originally designed for performance using the five-screen capabilities of the New World Center, it is being edited into a cinemascope version and a one-screen version. The new *Miami in Movements* will be shown in a variety of community venues with introduction and discussion led by NWS staff and Fellows. These events will be a catalyst for conversations about the future of Miami.

At the world-premiere performance of *Miami in Movements*, 37% of the audience were attending New World Symphony for the first time.

Fig. 12 Project artists, contributors, and NWS staff members describe Project 305 and the culmination of the project in Ted Hearne and Jon David Kane's symphonic documentary, Miami in Movements. Project 305 was supported by the Knight Foundation. This video was created in the Knight New Media Center. Knight Foundation and New World Symphony: Reimagining classical music in the digital age. © 2017, Ted Hearne and Jon David Kane, Miami in Movements. © 2020, New World Symphony, Inc. All rights reserved. Duration: 7:23.

To watch the video online scan the QR code or follow this link: https://vimeo.com/276349368

Community Concerts—twenty-one in all—were staged by small ensembles of NWS Fellows over the course of the 2017/18 season. Farm workers, the transgender community, and visitors to the Everglades were three of the audiences that exemplify efforts by NWS to go beyond the traditional in pursuit of new listeners. The initiative was repeated in the 2018/19 season. Concerts in remote locations make it difficult to bring audiences to the New World Center. However, the connection between Fellows and audiences in last year's experiment indicates that this strategy is worth further exploration.

Fig. 13 Explore NWS's 2018 Community Concerts conceived and created by NWS musicians in an interactive video highlighting four projects. This video was produced in the Knight New Media Center. Knight Foundation and New World Symphony: Reimagining classical music in the digital age. Video features 'Suite Antique' by John Rutter © Oxford University Press 1981. Licensed by Oxford University Press. All rights reserved. © 2020, New World Symphony, Inc. All rights reserved.

To watch the video online scan the QR code or follow this link: https://video.eko.com/v/zRwyvA?autoplay=true

Alternative Concert Formats and the Knight New Media Center

Early audience experiments were driven by the Knight Foundation's Magic of Music grant program. That work was a prelude to the digital expansion of engagement enabled by endowment and subsequent operating support that created the Knight New Media Center. Contextualization for *Encounters* and Fellow-driven projects uses the five projection sails of the New World Center's performance hall as teaching tools to augment the spoken delivery of information. For *Pulse*, lighting and video combine with music for a hyper-sensate artistic experience. WALLCAST® concert technology and program design are democratizing classical music in Miami and beyond as the idea takes hold in other US cities. Project 305, *Miami in Movements* was a journey in which the sonic and visual essence of Miami met one another in an artistic form that integrated crowd-based musical ideas with performative video. The New World Symphony and Knight Foundation are strong partners in this work, believing that the reach of digital expression will increase the size of the audience for classical music as well as the intrinsic value of performances for individuals in these audiences. The New World Symphony is especially grateful to Alberto Ibargüen, President and CEO of Knight Foundation, for his encouragement and insight.

Partnerships—New World Experiments at Scale

NWS new-audience experiments were formed within the environment created by the Magic of Music program. As the only educational institution in the research cohort, NWS was building an audience engagement system outside the parameters of the eleven professional orchestras in the program. During the Mellon-funded phase of the work, NWS realized the need to build models in conjunction with orchestras that would test them at a professional scale. *Encounters, Pulse, Mini-Concerts,* and later *WALLCAST*® concerts became the prototypes. The primary orchestras of Atlanta, Charlotte, Detroit, Indianapolis, and Kansas City were NWS partners. In each case, they applied NWS principles to their unique market. They identified a prospective audience, built an attractive experience, remained true to the classical music repertoire and excellence of performance, and listened carefully to their new audiences. Along the way, they discovered inventive ways to deploy their musicians, on the stage and in the community. Of greatest importance, they won new audiences and new donors using sustainable formats.[3]

Next Steps—Return Strategy for the Future

Across the country, professional orchestras are pursuing new audiences, attracting them to concerts, then convincing them to return. There are two important distinctions between that work and the NWS New Audience Initiative. The first is the singular nature of each alternate format experience. First impressions are important. An individual uses the first experience as a reference when deciding whether to return to a second NWS performance. Knowing this to be true, NWS makes a significant investment in each alternate format program. The NWS companion strategy is to get beyond marketing ploys when inviting first-timers to return. An accurate and evocative description of the initial concert experience, delivered in a personal and direct way, can be successful. This is the context for the Return Strategy.

---

3   Additional information from these orchestras' audience research can be found at https://www.nws.edu/PartnerResearch

- Returning audiences rarely stray from the format that initially brought them to NWS. "Killer offers"—free drinks and inexpensive tickets—are used to capture the attention of first-timers.

- NWS Fellows are in touch with first-time ticket-buyers by email and phone. A personal invitation has high value.

- Special events including social experiences can be a particularly promising tool in reengagement.

- First-time subscribers receive special attention from the NWS family—Fellows, trustees, and staff. Informal receptions are scheduled for them throughout the year.

NWS monitors the number of returning ticket-buyers. Currently, 30% of first-time ticket-buyers have returned for a second NWS experience. The challenge will be to increase this percentage over time.

Conclusion—A Thoughtful Approach to Sharing with as Many People as Possible

Historically, musicians and orchestra leaders, staff, and volunteers have assumed that classical music is relevant to society based on their lifelong commitment to the art form. Yet attendance is diminishing, and media coverage is being reduced. It is possible that there is a crisis of relevance.

Based on the results of the New Audience Initiative, committed ensembles can take structured steps toward increasing their relevance and reversing downward attendance trends.[4] If 75% of ticket-buyers report studying an instrument or singing, one obvious strategy is to include as many children as possible in school music programs. For adults who have not studied music, orchestras must build bridges, creating experiences that are comfortable and inviting. These experiences can be developed within a methodical process that integrates audience study with the intuition of the orchestra leaders. It is essential to preserve the integrity of the music and the excellence

---

4   NWS shares its New Audience Initiative findings broadly and without charge at https://www.nws.edu/research

of performance no matter what the design of the experiences. Each experience, defined as an alternate performance format, can attract a distinct new audience.

NWS experiments indicate that audiences rarely migrate between formats, making loyalty to formats a strong indicator of audience development opportunities. Multiple formats will establish multiple audiences, increasing the size of the overall orchestral community. A larger audience can increase an orchestra's revenue and establish greater relevance in the community.

Bibliography

Knight Foundation. (a). "About", *Knight Foundation*, https://knightfoundation.org/about/

Knight Foundation. (b). "Magic of Music Final Report: The Search for Shining Eyes", *Knight Foundation*, https://knightfoundation.org/reports/magic-music-final-report-search-shining-eyes/

Knight Foundation. 2002. *Classical Music Consumer Segmentation Study* (Ann Arbor, MI: Inter-University Consortium for Political and Social Research), https://doi.org/10.3886/ICPSR35535.v1

Moritz, Michael. 2013. "The Miami Startup Striking the Right Note", *LinkedIn*, 1 May, https://www.linkedin.com/pulse/20130501121220-25760-the-miami-startup-striking-the-right-note/

National Endowment for the Arts. 2017. "The 2017 Survey of Public Participation in the Arts (2017)", *National Endowment for the Arts*, https://www.arts.gov/artistic-fields/research-analysis/arts-data-profiles/arts-data-profile-18

New World Symphony. (a). "About", *NWS*, https://nws.edu/about/about-nws/

New World Symphony. (b). "Support NWS", *NWS*, https://www.nws.edu/support-nws/friends-of-new-world-symphony/

US Census Bureau. 1980. *1980 Census of Population and Housing*, https://www.census.gov/prod/www/decennial.html#y1980popv1us

Wolf, Thomas. 2006. *The Search for Shining Eyes: Audiences, Leadership and Change in the Symphony Orchestra Field* (Miami: John S. and James L. Knight Foundation), https://knightfoundation.org/wp-content/uploads/2019/06/2006_Magic_of_Music_Final_Report.pdf

WolfBrown. "Expertise", *WolfBrown*, http://wolfbrown.com/expertise

13. Attracting New Audiences at the BBC

Tom Service[1]

This chapter was originally written at the very end of 2018. The COVID-19 pandemic has palpably changed the possibilities for the BBC's performing groups and its festivals, and above all the BBC Proms, in 2020—and no doubt, beyond. However, the strategic direction of the corporation in terms of the ongoing necessity to attract younger audiences has not changed, and, if anything, the avenues that the BBC, and BBC Radio 3 in particular, have developed and explored, which are outlined in this chapter, have only become more urgent over the last eighteen months. The pandemic is a potentially existential threat to all live-music making organizations, but the BBC's ensembles are relatively insulated from financial repercussions by the way they are currently funded through the license fee, so the conclusions presented here as of July 2020 continue to reflect the BBC's strategy.

1. A Pessimistic Prognosis

The problem has always been staring at us, head-on. It's just that we've scarcely acknowledged it. The word "classical" has a congeries of problematic associations that have accreted over centuries and are still employed across contemporary media to define an art form that has self-consciously manufactured the image that this music is better, greater, and more transcendent than we, its humble audiences, will ever be.

---

[1] The views, thoughts, and opinions expressed in this chapter belong solely to the author, and not to the author's employer, organization, committee, or other group or individual.

The "classical"—as aesthetic and as lifestyle—has been commodified, re-packaged, and re-distributed across the physical spaces of concert halls and the digital landscapes where most of the consumption of this music takes place to shore up these associations of artistic exclusivity and social and economic elitism.

The pre-history of how we got here might be sketched as follows: the growth of bourgeois audiences and institutions in the Western world, and the concomitant shrinking of the repertoire to an officially-sponsored canon; made even more "official" because the offices of who chose what and when for admission to the classical music Parnassus have always been deliberately hidden by an ideology claiming that the values of the "great" will always win out over the temporal, so the self-perpetuating diminishment of the canon continues. The increasing expense of keeping the vast institutions of orchestras and opera houses afloat, and the consequent inflation of ticket prices charged for admission, mean that the associations of the "classical" and "this isn't for you" have been allowed to atrophy to the point where no amount of musical education initiatives or well-meaning outreach projects can overturn the one-way tide of elitist-ist reception history.

The "classical" is fighting a battle that it is doomed to lose, and its losses—of listeners, of engagement, of a place in the popular consciousness—are felt especially sharply where they matter the most, in the hearts and minds and above all, the time, of today's generation of under-thirty-five year-olds. If this age group continues not to do what it already isn't doing—going to classical concerts, listening to classical radio stations, learning and playing instruments—classical music's shelf life is short. Will the last orchestra to leave please turn the lights out, when the end finally comes, in around thirty years or so?

Or so a pessimistic cliché of a state of the art form might run. It's a situation that finds support in a culture in which (in the United Kingdom, and elsewhere in the world) classical music is played in the entrance halls of tubes, metros, and undergrounds as cultural crowd control: the idea is to soothe the furrowed brows of commuters, and to ensure that groups of people don't congregate there, such is the unbearable torment of having to put up with a litany of terminally un-hip canned classical tracks, played on an ever-changing loop of background music banality—Berlioz, Beethoven, Mozart, Stravinsky, all reduced to a one-size-fits-all association of classical irrelevance, at best, and malicious social engineering, at worst.

In British culture, the freight of responsibility and opportunity to engage with—and to change—this crisis in the connection between young audiences and classical music is felt by all of its major stakeholders: by its orchestras, opera houses, and above all, by the single biggest employer of orchestral musicians and commissioner of new music in the country, the BBC. Through its exposure of classical music via a variety of platforms—TV, online, and radio stations (especially BBC Radio 3, for whom the author is employed as a presenter)—the BBC is facing the challenges of the future of classical music not only by reflecting and broadcasting what's happening in the country, but shaping what that future might look and sound like, in the scope of its programming, its broadcast schedules, its ever-increasing roster of online content, from podcasts to social media, and its educational initiatives. At the heart of these projects is a fundamental question: how can audiences aged thirty-five and under engage more meaningfully in the BBC's classical output, and by extension, in classical music in general? The answers the corporation has found so far, and its ideas for future lines of development, some of which this chapter outlines, reveal a set of concerns and possible solutions that may offer resonant models for others to learn from.

2. The BBC's Existential Challenge

Before outlining the scope of the challenge that the BBC, and Radio 3 in particular, is addressing, there are some signs that the Cassandran pessimism of our assessment above isn't as watertight as it seems. In a survey carried out by YouGov for the Royal Philharmonic Orchestra, published in 2019, the category of "classical/orchestral" was the most popular genre that young people and students wanted to learn more about and participate in, in addition to its growing popularity across streaming platforms (RPO, 2019: 5, 11).

This does not suggest there can be any complacency around the idea that because just over a quarter of a sample of young people are in some way enthusiastic about classical music that the problem of the culture's relationship with the mainstream is somehow solved.

But these findings could demonstrate that the cultural work that has gone into creating the firewall between the "classical" and the rest of the musical world has not—fortunately—been as successful as our pessimistic prognosis suggests. As well as the popularity of classical music on mood-based playlists and streaming in general, there is the long-overdue acknowledgement of the decades-long history of classical and orchestral styles in the increasingly sophisticated soundtracks to video games. Gaming is an art form that under-thirty-fives spend more time consuming than any other generation in history, which opens up new opportunities for music as a whole, for everything from live concert experiences to broadcasts of music composed for games such as the *Dragon Quest* series to *Final Fantasy* and *The Legend of Zelda*. One important symbol of this representation is the video-game composer Jessica Curry's recent show *High Score* on Classic FM, Radio 3's major commercial competitor—with consistently more than twice as many listeners, over five million as opposed to Radio 3's two million, as an average of recent RAJAR listening figures (RAJAR, 2020). The first series of *High Score* was the most downloaded show in Classic FM's history (BBC Radio 3 subsequently commissioned Curry for a series on their network, *Sound of Gaming*, in 2019 and 2020).

The possible erosion of those associations of the "classical" and the "orchestral" with exclusivism and elitism is one of the most powerful pieces of potential evidence that could secure the future of the "classical" in the decades to come. But it's worth noting that hasn't only come about through the work of the major performing institutions themselves, but from the ground up, from what composers are writing, what gamers and cinema audiences are hearing, the samples that pop artists are using, and the innovations that broadcasters and music streaming services are developing and leading—or beginning to catch up with.

How the BBC might use these possibilities is our question for this chapter, but the conversations around how the BBC deals with the challenges of the classical need to be placed in a wider context about how under-thirty-fives are engaging, or not engaging, with BBC content as a whole. As the landscapes of TV and film become increasingly identified with the rise of streaming and subscription services like Netflix and YouTube, and given how much more time than their elders the under-thirty-fives are known to spend accessing content that does not originate with the BBC, their loyalty and sense of ownership of the BBC's brand is in a state of transition.[2]

As the BBC is financed by a government-agreed Charter (which is next due to be ratified in 2026), and is paid for by the direct imposition of a license fee upon anyone in the country who uses its television services (either through a TV or watching live broadcasts online), the values of trust and the sense that the BBC speaks to the British people in a unique way could be under threat unlike ever before if its future audiences no longer identify its content as inherently more valuable, its news more trustworthy, its dramas and music programming more enticing, than its competitors. The decline in rates of engagement shows that just such a moment may be ahead, were it not for the launch of projects designed specifically to appeal to the under-thirty-fives.

At the end of 2018, the BBC launched BBC Sounds, an app in which all of its audio content has been made available, from live radio to podcasts to programmes that are available in perpetuity for audiences based in the UK, and music shows limited to a thirty-day catch up period, thanks to rights agreements with record companies and the music industry. BBC Sounds was designed to replace the successful iPlayer Radio app, where this content was previously accessible, which closed in September 2019.

Curated playlists—such as the classical-based "Mindful Mix" playlist that was the most downloaded collection when the Sounds app launched at the end of November 2018, proving more popular than playlists of genres of pop and rock, according to the BBC's internal assessments —are central to the way that Sounds seeks to occupy territory that comparable playlists on Spotify have proved successful in introducing and owning. On Spotify, mood-based or lifestyle-based playlists, organised not by genre but by emotional or temporal states (a random handful of Spotify playlists, at the same time BBC Sounds launched, included: "Classical Lullabies," "Relaxing Classical," "Morning Classical," "Late-Night Synths and Strings") are downloaded and streamed tens of millions of times.

Identifying this trend, the BBC seeks to own a piece of that increasingly popular digital space. It has competitors not only in the internationally available streaming services, but in the shape of the Global Player app,

---

2 For the BBC's assessment of the challenge of these changes, see Hall (2018).

launched shortly after BBC Sounds. Global is one of the main commercial competitors for the BBC Radio in the UK, and the app repackages the content of Classic FM into playlists (as well as the output of Global's other stations, such as LBC, Heart, and Capital). The BBC's strategic decision was to make the most of their curatorial distinctiveness, given the fact that, unlike Spotify, which has access to its music in perpetuity, their rights to the music they play is dependent upon those tracks having been broadcast on their network in the last thirty days. If the BBC can't compete with permanent access to the whole history of recorded music, in their presenters and the long-running successes of their programmes, they do have a trusted curatorial expertise, a resource that Sounds plans to mine. It is early days for BBC Sounds, but the future of the BBC as a major player in the increasingly crowded marketplaces of digital and streamed music is staked on its success.

Yet despite the innovations around downloadable playlists, the way that individual programmes are turned into podcasts online after their broadcast, and the realities of gradually declining audiences for the live broadcasts themselves, it remains the case for BBC radio in general and for Radio 3 in particular that the majority of its listeners are still found for linear, real-time listening. The necessity of launching Sounds comes as an answer to a potential future in which audiences for radio as a whole continue to age and dwindle (a version of the same audience problem that classical music cultures all over the world face). Given that Radio 3's audience is the smallest and oldest of any of the major BBC networks, this is a special challenge for its future.

3. The BBC's Response: Radio 3

Among other initiatives, Alan Davey, Controller of Radio 3 since 2015, has launched an approach to format and content that is promoted as "Slow Radio". Developing ideas that were first explored on Slow TV shows—single shots of canal boats on trips lasting for a whole day of broadcasting, long-form visualizations of the natural world, etc.—Slow Radio presents extended radiophonic meditations, performances, and experiences. These include programmes such as the writer Horatio Clare embarking on journeys by foot in Herefordshire (*Sound Walk*), or retracing Bach's pilgrimage to visit Buxtehude in Lübeck (*Bach

Walks). These programmes are conceived and presented as whole-night broadcasts of the sounds of nature along the walk, interwoven with Clare's occasional commentary, and the sounds of his feet and body in the landscape, along with a playlist of appropriate and quirkily surprising pieces of music. For Davey, the point about Slow Radio is to associate Radio 3 with a species of listening that's an increasingly rare commodity in today's world, and the marketing and messaging about Slow Radio highlights this idea: Slow Radio is "an antidote to today's frenzied world. Step back, let go, immerse yourself: it's time to go slow," as the strapline on the Slow Radio portal on the Radio 3 website describes it.

It's an approach that is designed to brand Radio 3 as a place associated with broadcast innovation, and to act as a gateway into a more intense way of listening. It's not only the long-form broadcasts, since the Slow Radio ethos is now heard in regular appearances of unfiltered sounds of nature in shorter segments—birdsong, landscape, weather—as part of the regular programming of other strands, from Breakfast to the network's contemporary music show. "Listening to these sounds," Davey says, "is a way of getting people used to the idea of listening to longer pieces of classical music" (Davey, 2018a).

Some of Slow Radio's messaging puts it in line with the practices of mood-based playlists: there's a connection, at least in principle, between the idea of an "antidote to today's frenzied world," and something like Spotify's "Peaceful Choral Music" playlist; their soundworlds are completely different, but the idea of classical as a place to escape the stresses and traumas of daily life is common to both.

But while Slow Radio and Mindfulness playlists have proved successful in terms of BBC Sounds and of Radio 3's brand identity, Davey acknowledges that there could be a problematic future if classical music is only connected with a type of listening, or with emotional and lifestyle characteristics, which are heavily associated with the relaxing, the soporific, or the somnolent. Mind you, that very somnolence can be a positive, in terms of public profile and broadcast possibility: Max Richter's *Sleep* was first broadcast on Radio 3 in 2015 from midnight on the 28th of September, a Guinness World Record-beating program in terms of the length of a single piece and performance, and music designed by its composer to allow its listeners to drift in and out of consciousness: eight hours of music created to be simultaneously listened to and not listened to. Davey feels that the balance between Radio 3's playlists (every day on the drivetime *In Tune* show, a half-hour long, music-only mixtape is broadcast, often themed around single ideas, moods, or emotions) and the uniquely challenging and in-depth content it also presents—its new music, its discussion programmes, its concerts—means that Mindfulness and Slow Radio can both be gateway experiences that can lead to deeper relationship with classical music and its repertoires. Having experienced the slow and mindful, having been encouraged to listen, Radio 3 wants its listeners—and its younger audience in particular—to discover the shocking, the new, and the visceral, to experience classical music as something that makes you listen intently as opposed to creating a background noise of mood-enhancement.

That marks a clear strategic difference between Radio 3's priorities and those of its main commercial competitor, Classic FM, and the streaming services that BBC Sounds is designed to complement. Where the essential rationale behind those networks, their on-demand playlists, and their social media presence, is to maximize the number of listeners, clicks, and engagement with content in order to satisfy the needs of advertisers and the market, Radio 3's playlists, its increasing roster of podcasts, and its own online resources have a superficially similar but radically distinctive policy. The BBC and Radio 3's endgame is about deepening the journeys of discovery that any listener can embark upon. These are geared not towards a mass diversity of sameness—the goal of recommended playlists on Spotify and elsewhere—but towards a series of fractal connections that will lead you towards musics and repertoires you may not have known before. That should mean exploring corners of the musical universe—new music, musical cultures from all over the world, early music, less familiar orchestral repertoire—that the BBC represents in ways that none of its competitors can, thanks to the license fee. The principle makes sense: the question of how these journeys are brought to individual listeners through the operation of the music- and audio-recommending algorithms of BBC Sounds will be proven in the years to come.

4. Radio 3's Performance Possibilities

But Radio 3's possibilities and opportunities extend beyond the broadcast, the podcast, or the playlist. The ensembles directly employed and created by the BBC (its five orchestras: the BBC Symphony, BBC Philharmonic, BBC Scottish Symphony, BBC National Orchestra of Wales, BBC Concert Orchestra, as well as the BBC Singers, Britain's only professional full-time professional chamber choir) represent the single largest roster of orchestral musicians whose music-making is overseen by a single corporation in the UK. Their live and pre-recorded concerts are vital to the audiences in their home concert halls from Glasgow to Cardiff and to the broadcast schedules of Radio 3 as network. In addition, the BBC Orchestras perform more BBC Proms concerts at the Royal Albert Hall than any other groups. Across live concerts and broadcasts, they are the most frequently heard orchestras in the country (although Radio 3 also has broadcast partnerships with all of the country's major orchestras) and have the greatest potential to offer new visions of how an orchestra might relate to all of its listeners, from concert halls to on-line. Thanks to the BBC's funding arrangements, there is a chance for the BBC to go further than other ensembles in terms of experimentation not only with programming (collectively, the BBC orchestras perform more commissions and a higher proportion of new music than comparable ensembles) but also with formats, function, and future opportunities.

These individual projects include the BBC Philharmonic's Red Brick Sessions, taking the orchestra to sites associated with the industrial past of the North-West of England, putting the orchestra in disused warehouses and factories, creating site-specific experiences in which a piece is opened up and explained in the first half through presented discussion and exploration before being played complete in the second. Another of the Philharmonic's initiatives, Philharmonic Lab, encourages audience interaction through technology, and the orchestra wants listeners to keep their phones switched on during performances to download live program notes that change and update during the course of the concert.

The BBC has a long history developing the principle of explanation of musical works through long-running programs such as *Discovering Music* on Radio 3, but today's world offers new ways of achieving a similar engagement through different means. As well as the BBC's own programmes, recent collaborations between Aurora Orchestra and the Proms, in the 2015, 2016, and 2017 seasons, featured memorized performances that were preceded by on-stage explorations of symphonies by Mozart, Beethoven, and Shostakovich. The Proms has proved a catalyst in recent seasons in taking concerts out of the Royal Albert Hall to regional venues and locations such as a car-park in Peckham on South East London. In Peckham, the Multi-Story Orchestra's concerts for the communities of Peckham, including groups of schoolchildren not only in the audience but performing as part of the Prom, reached exponentially more listeners thanks to their broadcasts as part of the 2016 and 2017 seasons, with concerts that included works by Steve Reich and John Adams. That's another way in which the BBC catalyzes work designed to engage younger audiences, by working in partnership with innovative, project-based orchestras like Aurora and Multi-Story to enhance the reach and power of their concerts across broadcast on-air and on-line.

The BBC's most ambitious music education project is its ongoing Ten Pieces project, which began in 2014, in which films, audio, and online resources about a wide range of short pieces of classical music—such as excerpts from Holst's *The Planets* and Verdi's *Requiem*, as well as new works by Kerry Andrew and Gabriel Prokofiev—are made available to every primary school in the country, for pupils aged 7–14 and their teachers (corresponding to Key Stages 1–3 in the educational system of England, and the First and Second Level in the Scottish education system, the period in which music is a statutory part of the National Curriculum). Ten Pieces' multi-dimensional realizations have left a permanent legacy of content that allows teachers to introduce these experiences to their classrooms through freely available lesson plans and other resources. The project was the result of a series of partnerships that connected the BBC's music and education offers with national institutions like the Association of British Orchestras and the Associated Board of the Royal Schools of Music, and the Music Hubs who deliver music education across the country. Ten Pieces also took over individual Proms concerts, and lavishly produced films of the pieces, performed by BBC Orchestras, were shown in cinemas. While Ten Pieces is a classical music-focused, the participation of programmes and presenters from the BBC's internationally popular CBeebies channel ensured a high level of visibility and take-up from schools all over the country, and its resources are updated and available in perpetuity.

But the most ambitious opportunity for the BBC Orchestras in the future is the chance to re-site the BBC Symphony Orchestra in a new home in East London, on the former site of the 2012 Olympics, at the heart of a suite of studios, replacing the Maida Vale recording studios that have been the home of the orchestra since 1934. As Davey said in a speech given at the end of 2018 (Davey, 2018b), the idea is to reanimate Ernest Fleischmann's concept of the orchestra as a "community of musicians" in ways that live up to that aspiration for the twenty-first century, to make the most of the new sets of possibilities that digital technology can unlock for new audiences and across genres undreamt of when Fleischmann outlined his vision in the 1960s.

The potential program around the building, which would open in the early 2020s, is to be embedded as no BBC orchestra has been before with the needs of the London borough where the studios will be situated, Newham. Schools and schoolchildren will be part of the orchestra's work, to realize Newham Council's stated ambition to embody the ideals of "Every Child a Musician". As Davey says, "This area of east London is one of the poorest, most diverse, and youngest populations in the UK. The aim is to use the move to reinvent the role of a classical music ensemble, working with creative partners including colleagues involved in Rock and Pop and other art forms [...] We would be able to invite schools in for learning sessions with musicians in the studio itself—something we can't do with our current facility—and also to experience rehearsals and bespoke concerts from smaller ensembles as well as the main ensembles. Added to this will be work in schools, with ensembles playing there, and using the BBC's Ten Pieces and digital resources as a backbone" (Davey, 2018b). Collaborations with the creative partners who will also be in the new studios—Sadlers Wells Dance Company, the London College of Fashion, the Victoria and Albert Museum, and University College London—offer another creative horizon for new engagements with younger audiences, all built around a central notion of how the BBC's salaried musicians can be useful to their immediate communities of schoolchildren, Music Hubs, and audiences, alongside their concerts, broadcasts, and Proms.

5. The BBC's Part in the Future of Classical Music

To summarise the BBC's current position: this work is being carried out in at least three main ways. Firstly, the BBC is competing with the largest commercial providers of playlists and streaming content on their terms, to make sure the BBC's voice and distinctively adventurous ambitions for the development of listening are reaching the largest number of under-thirty-fives as possible, through the BBC Sounds app, the inclusion of Slow Radio as part of Radio 3's schedules, the development of bespoke podcasts, and the offering of further journeys of discovery based on the BBC's uniquely diverse archive. Secondly, the BBC is developing new formats of programmes, broadcasts, and concerts, to serve equally their audiences online and those attending and experiencing their orchestras in concert halls from factories in the North-West of England, new locations in the East End of London to the Royal Albert Hall. And thirdly, there is the BBC's ongoing commitment to educational projects, from the largest scale of Ten Pieces and its national reach, to the smallest but arguably most profound scale of individual encounters with musicians in the communities that the orchestras and ensembles serve.

For all their innovation, none of these BBC projects is happening in isolation in the UK, as orchestras all over the country continue to promote the education and outreach projects the country has pioneered and developed over the last forty years. However, as the biggest employer and sponsor of orchestral culture in the country, and as the public service broadcaster of classical music and its cultures, the BBC's projects have the greatest potential impact in creating the participative engagement with classical music that is the most meaningful way of securing the art form's future.

The BBC has assessed the state of the challenge, as the foundation of BBC Sounds shows and as the aspiration for a new model orchestra in the East of London demonstrates. The answers these and other schemes provide will not only be a passive reflector of the future place of orchestral and classical music in the cultural life of the UK, but will continue to shape it. There has never been a time when more is at stake, or when there is so much opportunity. The next decade of the BBC's classical music output is, arguably, the most significant in its history in the ongoing story of the corporation's relationship with and promotion of the art-form.

At the BBC, the clichéd pessimism that opened this chapter has been replaced by a clear-sighted analysis of the problems that a diminishing and aging audience presents. The optimism will come once it is clearer how the BBC's projects are bearing fruit in the deeper engagement and participation of younger generations in classical music. That result will be crucial for the UK's musical life.

References

Davey, Alan. 2018a. Conversation with the Author.

Davey, Alan. 2018b. Speech to the Danish Composers' Society, Christiansborg, 29 November (unpublished).

Hall, Tony. 2018. "Tony Hall's Speech to the Royal Television Society", *BBC Media Centre*, 18 September, https://www.bbc.co.uk/mediacentre/speeches/2018/tony-hall-rts

RAJAR. 2020. "Quarterly Listening: All Individuals 15+ for Period Ending March 2020", *Rajar*, https://www.rajar.co.uk/listening/quarterly_listening.php

RPO. 2019. "A New Era for Orchestral Music: A Report by the Royal Philharmonic Orchestra, 2018 edition", *Royal Philharmonic Orchestra*, https://www.rpo.co.uk/images/pdf/Press/RPO-report-Spring-2019.pdf

14. Contemporary Classical Music: A Komodo Dragon?
New Opportunities Exemplified by a Concert Series in South Korea

Unsuk Chin and Maris Gothoni[1]

Composer and professor Joshua Fineberg, in his thought-provoking analysis of the state of the reception of classical music, prophesizes that composers will find themselves in the situation of the Komodo dragon, facing likely extinction if no societal consensus about the value of their existence is being restored (2006: 142–143). Fineberg diagnoses a changing environment to which contemporary classical music may not be adaptable in the mid-term future.

At first glance, such a pessimistic claim seems puzzling. There exists undoubtedly no shortage of classical music events. YouTube, Spotify, and other such companies make the world flat, and, as for the circuit of live performing arts, at least the global jet set can theoretically experience a variety of musical styles, genres, and approaches unheard-of in previous times.

And yet, something has changed. The notion that society should support forms of art that possibly only a small minority will engage with is currently losing traction (Fineberg, 2006: 10–14). Market-think and the omnipresence of quickly changing modern mass media alter

---

1 Both authors were active in curating the new music series of the Seoul Philharmonic Orchestra (SPO), Unsuk Chin as Artistic Director and Maris Gothoni as Artistic Programme Planner.

expectations and contexts radically. There exists an unprecedented amount of available information due to the Internet revolution. Theoretically, this could contribute to inspire wonder in a manner similar to ancient cabinets of curiosities (Gehl, 2009) and help to spotlight niche players who would otherwise not get a chance to be heard. Such a democratic dream may bear some fruit here and there, but does not always hold true since the monetization of user-generated content has created new hierarchies, not to mention the establishment of veritable digital "disinformation architectures" (Pomerantsev, 2019). At worst, this unaccustomed explosion of "information" leads to a state of overload, with no control over quality and lots of "alternative facts": social media algorithms are very poor educators, as recent political upheavals have proven, and certainly not adequate curators for the arts. Just because there is an oversupply of content in this ecosystem, does not in the least guarantee biodiversity.

The problem, of course, starts with a decline in general music education. Children's aesthetic tastes form at an early age, and their innate curiosity and instinctive understanding for the arts atrophies if it is not being trained, and if one is instead left uncritically exposed to options providing instant gratification. Some universities appear to seek music students who are not able to read sheet music, a notion of inclusion that can take on rather myopic forms and could very easily lead to the further erosion of general musical culture and skills (Pace, 2017). Ironically, the effect of this relativism can be non-democratic, actually fostering social division. This is especially true when people who have had the benefit of such a musical education decide that current students don't need it; or when children with affluent parents get an early music education while others do not. It is not that classical music is (or has to be) elitist: it becomes so if people are deprived of making an informed choice about whether they would like to occupy themselves with it or not.[2] It is an exclusion that happens not by way of decree, but when there

---

2   The popular sociologist notion of elitist traditional culture used as a device of class distinction has, by and large, become obsolete ever since homogenized popular culture has become the dominant culture and ever since forms of counterculture have been commercially exploited. See Johnson (2002: 112, 122) and Heath & Potter (2004). We do not advocate the notion of "Western" classical music as superior to other kinds of music. However, we decry the widespread uncritical exposure to the commercial logic of a homogenized global music industry which degrades music

is tacit consent that school curricula have mainly to serve the purposes of efficiency and economy, and that, in music, a basic general education worthy of its name, is not required. All of this is based on the premise that the arts—unlike the humanities or, in particular, mathematics and the natural sciences—are merely a matter of taste, resisting any claims of objectivity. This premise, like many clichés, may contain a grain of truth, but is nonetheless a fatal oversimplification. There is insufficient space to discuss this complex topic further here,[3] except to remark that it is rather difficult to develop one's personal tastes if the act of choosing is merely being left to the "pseudodemocracy of the marketplace" (Johnson, 2002: 25). It too often happens that the (in principle) well-meaning notion of pluralism inadvertently leads one to become an uninformed and docile aide of the market, which is, in fact, the opposite of free choice. A common phenomenon is a cul-de-sac situation where both a number of educational institutions and arts enterprises try to imitate market-think methods, a race that is usually doomed in the same way as the contest between the hare and the victorious hedgehog in the classic tale by the Brothers Grimm.

Proclamations of the decline of culture are probably as old as mankind, and—in hindsight—usually turn out to be examples of tunnel-vision. Besides, promulgating news of doom and gloom, let alone scapegoating, is hardly ever a helpful approach. One can keep lamenting the state of school music education, and may conclude that, as long as it remains as it is, providing access to classical music is piecemeal work. Even if this may be true, would it not be more productive to listen to those who look for pragmatic solutions, who place trust both in the common audience and in the communicative power of complex art? In one of his case studies, the late neurologist Oliver Sacks described a man who acquired an obsessive musicophilia after he had been struck by lightning (Sacks, 2007). Such a wondrous "conversion" is an extreme case. Still, it is reasonable to assume that there exist "late bloomers," audiences that can be won over with creative ideas and new approaches even though they may not have had previous exposure to classical music.

---

    into a mere commodity. This is a tendency that works at the expense of musical biodiversity equally in the realm of non-Western musical traditions, "Western" classical music, independent rock, and jazz, among other musical forms.

3   For a more substantial discussion of the topic, see Johnson (2002: 10–33).

Yet, irrefutable seismic changes have occurred during the last decades, and their full impact still remains to be seen. Arguably, the change has been especially palpable in Europe, since the arts have traditionally relied on state support there. As early as the 1990s, key orchestras that had been, up until then, untouchable—to mention one example—began to merge, be radically cut, or abolished. This is a tendency that started in Italy, the United Kingdom, Belgium, the Netherlands, France, and Poland (Goertz, 2004: 20), and that has also reached German-speaking countries.[4] The problem here is not that changes take place, a phenomenon which is—to a degree—inevitable, but that classical music is highly vulnerable as "the infrastructure it requires is so massive and so expensive" (Fineberg, 2006: 148). The problem is hardly that this music would vanish altogether, but rather that the consensus of the importance of supporting it is being questioned, which can lead to a silent erosion from within.

In a way, the COVID-19 crisis could be likened to a macabre litmus test which mercilessly exposes the level of importance our societies attribute to non-functional and not immediately accessible art. At best, it might—despite all the tragedy it causes—re-awaken the appetite for what classical music can offer: as a source of intellectual and emotional stimulation, a health product whose effect can be profound even though it cannot be easily measured, and a powerful refuge of contemplation in our age of profitability, efficiency, information overkill, and consumerism. At worst, it could mark a landslide for the fragile infrastructures of classical music. Whatever comes out of the crisis—and it is impossible to generalize on a global scale as funding systems and approaches are different—we already sense that it could be at the cost of diversity, due to economic reasons. The situation is especially worrying

---

4   A case in point is the fusion of the two orchestras of the Südwestrundfunk (SWR) broadcasting company in 2016. The fusion was especially problematic since both orchestras had distinct profiles and served different purposes. The SWR Baden-Baden Freiburg Symphony Orchestra, led by leading lights of modernism such as conductors Michael Gielen and François-Xavier Roth, used to be Germany's flagship orchestra for modern music. The SWR Stuttgart Radio Symphony Orchestra, on the other hand, used to be pioneering in the area of historical performance practice due to its long-time association with Sir Roger Norrington. One can expect further changes to happen with broadcasting orchestras, which have traditionally been a supporting pillar of (not only) experimental contemporary music in Central Europe.

for small- or medium-scale free-sector music ensembles which have been the great success story of the last fifty years. Free ensembles with their modular organizational structures have been an indispensable thorn in the side of large-scale established institutions,[5] and there is no doubt that a functioning musical life needs both sides.

Since this chapter focuses on contemporary classical music, a few words about the situation of the composer today are necessary.

In many ways, the life of a composer has improved during the course of the last centuries, with the present degree of performances and working conditions being, in principle, of probably unprecedented quality, composers being potentially recognized by a very diverse group of listeners, and, of course, a staggering availability of music from all epochs (Tiensuu, 2000). Nor do the usually non-existent financial prospects scare aspiring composers from entering the profession and trying their luck (Fineberg, 2006: XIII). (Any jury member of an international composition competition can testify to this.) Many musical institutions, even previously rather inflexible "dinosaurs," have become much more accommodating to new music and experiments, often due to the significant input of a new generation of conductors for whom the challenges of new scores are as natural a part of their repertoire as the Classical-Romantic canon.[6] And the idealistic entrepreneurship of numerous ensembles, soloists, and auteurs in the world of contemporary music deserves high praise.

At the same time, one can argue that the ideal of a composer largely independent from Court, Church, or the marketplace—writing music that is often not immediately appreciated, but the support of which is seen as valuable from a long-term perspective—is in peril. Market-think

---

[5] A prominent pattern is as follows: the historical performance practice movement transformed from a fringe phenomenon to a predominant one, setting the tone also in symphony orchestras. The innovations of the free sector are not only stylistic, but have also led to new modes and a kind of utopia of collaboration, education, communication, and even marketing.

[6] Simon Rattle, Alan Gilbert, and Esa-Pekka Salonen are merely a few obvious examples. Here, the influence of a trailblazer such as Pierre Boulez has been pivotal. Ensemble intercontemporain, founded by Boulez, became a potent breeding ground for talent, with former and present Music Directors including names such as Peter Eötvös, Kent Nagano, David Robertson, Jonathan Nott, Susanna Mälkki, and Matthias Pintscher, all of whom are in high demand with symphony orchestras nowadays.

has also permeated the spheres of contemporary classical music. The reality, then, is multifaceted and complex—in many ways. Old certainties crumble: the turf wars between tradition and the avant-garde[7] cannot have a place in a world where classical music faces major challenges because of the rapid change of society and technology, and where the prejudice that classical music is merely a substitutable commodity and a tiny minority's pastime has gained ground (Chin, 2015).

The new disorder also creates opportunities. While music education is dwindling in countries where it has had a particularly strong foothold—such as Germany—many Asian and Latin American countries are experiencing an impressive surge of musical talent and activities. What is already clear is that collaboration, openness, and cosmopolitanism are more important than ever. Strangely, although music is often—usually in a simplistic way—talked of as a "universal art," the fences here often seem especially thick, when compared with cinema, visual arts, and even literature. Prejudices that imply that an Austrian musician performs the most authentic Schubert, and that an interpretation of Debussy must come from France, are still prevalent. Even in the field of contemporary music the exchange is often surprisingly limited between countries, as well as between the different scenes and sub-scenes of contemporary music.

With all due respect for maintaining precious traditions, art has always thrived when there has been the possibility of cross-fertilization, and advocating identity traps (Sen, 2007) would be a grave misunderstanding of the concept of heritage, especially in our times. The world of contemporary music is an international one, as the list of students at any leading music university or the list of composition competitors testifies: stylistically speaking, it has been split up into different linguae francae, where different schools (which are, in a simplistic manner, associated with catchphrases such as spectralism, musique concrète instrumentale, postserialism, neotraditionalism, etc.) often become more of a hallmark than one's national identity.[8]

---

7   As reflected, for instance, in the previously radical difference between the aesthetics of a specialized contemporary music festival and the more established large-scale institutions.
8   Which is surely an option to be preferred to any retro-nationalistic imitations and other calculated "inventions of tradition" (to borrow Eric Hobsbawm's famous concept), yet often falls short in exploiting the potentially available range of musical material.

What is often lacking here is communication and collaboration, the critical reception of different approaches, and the embrace of diversity. Furthermore, it seems that the music business still thrives on obsolete images: instead of actively promoting interchange and interaction, the finding of the next national celebrity is, consciously or unconsciously, still often the order of the day.

Regardless of old habits and inflexible patterns, the growing diversification is palpable. Whether it comes to symphony orchestras, festivals, or contemporary music, or the classical music circuit in general, there is no single center that has defining power. This creates a situation where that which used to be the periphery can become fertile ground for creative impulses.[9]

This was our hope when we were curating and managing "Ars Nova," the Seoul Philharmonic Orchestra's new music series, for twelve years.[10]

When founding the Ars Nova series, the starting assumption was that the act of choosing repertoire and curating concerts arguably becomes more and more important given the conditions of our time, when it is easy to become disoriented due to the huge range of options available. This is particularly true when it comes to new music about which quality information is not readily available. When "everything" is out there on the net 24/7, and on a global scale, and when listening habits have changed due to the immediate accessibility of masses of recorded music, it becomes more and more crucial to provide orientation and to offer something that can only happen here and now. Spotify and YouTube algorithms can never replace conscious programming policy, and glossy and slick market trends cannot compensate for a deeply satisfying artistic experience.

Music, an art form occurring in time, demands great concentration and receptivity from the listener. Hence, it may be especially challenging

---

9 Of course, this is nothing new. Consider, for example, when the Austro-German tradition entered a period of "supersaturation," as reflected in frequently gigantic orchestral and operatic works—a tendency from which, within that national tradition, only utter abstraction such as dodecaphony seemed to show a way out. Some fresh air was offered by composers from the outskirts (e.g. Bartók, Janáček, Stravinsky, Sibelius), who drew upon unexhausted musical traditions beyond the shackles of high culture.

10 The series existed from 2005–2018. It was founded by Unsuk Chin, when she was appointed SPO's Composer-in-Residence in 2005 at the invitation of the orchestra's Chief Conductor, Maestro Myung-whun Chung.

to find new forms of presentation keeping up pace with the rapid changes of our times without compromising what constitutes its core essence. This also partly relates to the question of whether the etiquette of the classical concert and its other traditions are obsolete and whether they should be combated—an interesting topic that certainly merits discussion (Ross, 2005; Brönnimann, 2014). Most arts institutions are very active in finding new approaches, and many of these initiatives are worthwhile. Yet, none of these initiatives will bear long-term fruit if they don't, first and foremost, serve the artistic purpose of an organization.[11]

In the following section, we will focus on the curatorial work itself and on the experiences gained when working in Seoul. We wish to stress that the following examples may not be adaptable everywhere: the challenges may be international, but each community and organization must find their own ways of addressing the issues at hand.

***

Founding the Ars Nova series (and curating it for twelve years) could be seen as an open-ended experiment. The goal was to provide new aesthetic experiences which would not be straitjacketed by market-think, nor constricted by mere academic discourse. The context—a symphony orchestra in South Korea—provided two particular challenges.

Firstly, a symphony orchestra is not an institution that readily embraces the spirit of experimentation new music calls for, for it is an organization that has its roots in the nineteenth century. While it is a great cultural achievement that has ongoing relevance, it nonetheless carries a certain risk of conservatism, of the mere preservation of existing conventions, and—due to its hierarchical structures—is occasionally in danger of draining the creativity of individual orchestral musicians

---

11 "The last few decades have seen orchestras become involved in an everything-but-the-kitchen-sink range of activities, apparently designed to draw people in. Non-traditional programming, casual concerts, film nights, singles events, education, community outreach, open rehearsals—the list could go on and on. And don't get me wrong—many of these activities are powerful and very worthwhile. The problem has been that as orchestras are involved in more and more areas, it is often not clear why they are doing what they are doing. When you get the sense that something might as well be a stand-alone venture, that it actually does not connect to the core of the organization that is behind it, you might reasonably start to wonder what the point is" (Gilbert, 2015: 7).

which can, at worst, cause frustration and a detached attitude to music-making. To this structurally conditioned risk, there may be no easy answers,[12] although the aforementioned achievements of ensembles and chamber orchestras during the last fifty years have often, by the effect of example, managed to stir up the internal workings of symphony orchestras in a positive way.

The second challenge was to launch this kind of series from scratch in South Korea, a country which has roughly a one-hundred-year-old history with Western classical music, a relationship that has been highly intense, probably partly prompted by the fact that most ties with traditional Korean music were cut during the Japanese occupation in the early-twentieth century. There have been Korean composers of international stature since the 1950s (Isang Yun, living in German exile, was the trailblazer), and a number of brilliant performing musicians, several of whom reside abroad, as well as an enthusiastic audience. Yet, what has been more difficult has been building up an infrastructure with orchestras, ensembles, and festivals with continuous quality and stability. Besides, the concert circuit, generally speaking, remains star-centered and traditional in its expectations.

The installation of a series for new music coincided with radical changes in the structure of the Seoul Philharmonic Orchestra, when it became a foundation on its own: an orchestra that had not even been performing with regularity was catapulted into a very different level when a leading international conductor, Myung-whun Chung, was appointed as its Chief Conductor in 2005 (Park & Schmitt, 2008; see also Stephan, 2012).

What was immediately noticeable was the pressing need to catch up in terms of repertoire and diversity of styles. Here, Korean orchestras and other institutions used to have, and still have, a conservative approach, with a focus on an unquestioned and not infrequently narrow "canon of

---

12   A number of musicians and other arts practitioners, among them Pierre Boulez, Iván Fischer, and Ernest Fleischmann, have envisioned future symphony orchestras as pools (or communities) of musicians and requested structural changes where musicians could lead the more fulfilling experience of a "complete" musician, a change that could also be to the benefit of the audience and to that of composers. Similar ideas have, to varying degrees, been put into practice in several institutions, among them the Berlin Philharmonic and the Los Angeles Philharmonic, but the purest realization of that utopia may be the Budapest Festival Orchestra. See Vermeil (1996: 123–127), Gerstein (2020), and Judy (1996).

musical masterworks". This was noticeable with the music of all epochs, but first and foremost with twentieth- and twenty-first-century music.

Fig. 1 ARS NOVA, Dress rehearsal for the Korean premiere of Pierre Boulez' Notations pour orchestra. © 2008, Seoul Philharmonic Orchestra. CC-BY-NC-ND.

In the twelve years of our association with the Seoul Philharmonic, we counted approximately 200 Korean premieres of works of the twentieth and twenty-first centuries, and this applied not only to Iannis Xenakis, György Ligeti, Pierre Boulez, Karlheinz Stockhausen, and contemporary rarities, but also to classic works such as Claude Debussy, Anton Webern, Charles Ives, Sergei Prokofiev, Dmitri Shostakovich, Igor Stravinsky, Leonard Bernstein, Alberto Ginastera, Olivier Messiaen, and many others.[13] Even national "classics," such as works from the 1960s and 1970s by Isang Yun or Sukhi Kang, had not entered the orchestral repertoire.

The Ars Nova series was a mixture of a festival and a concert series, with two concerts, one for full orchestra and the other one for ensemble (as well as workshops, masterclasses, reading sessions and, occasionally, fringe activities) within a two-week span twice a year. The ensemble concerts were an indispensable part of the series, bearing in mind that a great deal of twentieth- and twenty-first-century masterpieces have been written for non-standard formations.

Conductors included Myung-Whun Chung, Susanna Mälkki, Peter Eötvös, François-Xavier Roth, Pascal Rophé, Thierry Fischer, Stefan

---

13   For a detailed list and full documentation, please see Lee (2017). See also Harders-Wuthenow (2011).

Asbury, Ilan Volkov, Baldur Brönnimann, and others. The idealism of the conductors and the other artists was remarkable: though the repertoire was usually pre-determined by the curators, everyone accepted the heavy workload, even though it could have meant learning ten new scores for a two-week festival.

Commissions were an important part of the series. Starting in 2011, a symphonic work by an international composer was regularly commissioned for the series, among them Pascal Dusapin, Peter Eötvös, Tristan Murail, York Höller, Ivan Fedele, Jukka Tiensuu, Anders Hillborg, and Bernd Richard Deutsch. Equally important was the supporting of Korean contemporary music, with eighteen premieres of commissioned work by composers from different generations. This also presented an opportunity to involve the Korean diaspora (not only a number of remarkable performers but also several accomplished composers live abroad, often without contact with Korea—and vice versa). Talented young composers who had not yet had a chance to have works performed by a symphony orchestra got a chance to have their sketches rehearsed by high-profile conductors such as Susanna Mälkki, François-Xavier Roth, and Ilan Volkov, in reading sessions. There were regular masterclasses and workshops held by the undersigned (Unsuk Chin) as well as by guest composers such as Peter Eötvös, Tristan Murail, Pascal Dusapin, York Höller, Ivan Fedele, Johannes Schöllhorn, and Chris Paul Harman.

New music often requires additional in-depth information. All program notes were written by Habakuk Traber, a Berlin-based musicologist and dramaturg known especially for his pre-concert talks and program notes for the Berlin Philharmonic and the Deutsches Symphonie-Orchester Berlin, and every concert was preceded by an extensive pre-concert talk hosted by Unsuk Chin. The symphony concerts (which took place at Seoul Arts Center, the Lotte Concert Hall, and the LG Arts Center in Seoul) were attended by 800–1200 people, which could be considered a success given the novelty of the concept, but was not always seen as such by local authorities and other commentators, some of whom wondered why it wasn't possible to fill a 2000-seat hall, as it would be with the Chief Conductor's interpretation of a Mahler symphony.

As for programming, it was clear from the outset that the mission could not simply involve presenting another festival for contemporary music, but that cutting-edge works had to be put into specific contexts in order to create a point of orientation for listeners and musicians alike. This was a crucial difference from, say, new music enterprises in Europe, since, in Korea, there is a greater need to inform the audience about the general landscape of modernist twentieth-century music. Yet, virtue could be made out of that necessity, since it requires the curator to think more diversely and to program a wide range of musical styles, and also prohibits succumbing to "premieritis," i.e. the tendency to overemphasize the first performance. Instead, a mixture of music by excellent, but unheard-of composers with lesser-known works and revived "classics" by more established or canonic composers could be attempted. Since most of the repertoire was completely new for the vast majority of audiences, reactions could sometimes be surprising—occasionally, a more recent piece by a living composer received the warmest audience reaction.

The need to find meaningful contexts was exemplified by the first concert in our series which carried the programmatic title "EarlyNew". One of the crucial influences on modernism, starting with von Webern, Ravel, and Stravinsky, was an enormous, heightened curiosity about music that preceded the romanticist aesthetics of genius and expression. We took up this concept two more times, presenting the way J. S. Bach was reflected through the lens of Webern's pointillism; how strongly Stravinsky and Ravel were influenced by pre-Classical music; how Oliver Knussen reworked medieval organa, as well as "meetings" between Betsy Jolas and Orlando di Lassus, Harrison Birtwistle and Johannes Ciconia, Isabel Mundry and Louis Couperin, Sukhi Kang and Antonio Vivaldi, George Benjamin and Nicolas de Grigny, Brett Dean and Carlo Gesualdo, Johannes Schöllhorn and Bach, Georg Friedrich Haas and Franz Schubert, or Bernd Alois Zimmermann, Alfred Schnittke, and Luciano Berio playfully reflecting centuries of musical history.

The message could also be a controversial one. Korean audiences were used to putting Beethoven on a pedestal, and an unusual interpretation or a loving parody—let alone questioning his stature—could be perceived as provocative. A concert titled "A Different Beethoven" presented Mauricio Kagel's avantgarde movie *Ludwig van* from 1970 (which was met with outrage by parts of the audience), Jukka Tiensuu's ironic collage work *Le Tombeau de Beethoven* (1980), P. D. Q. Bach's parody of a moderated performance of the iconic Fifth Symphony (1971),[14] as well as Brett Dean's "environmental" Pastoral Symphony (2000).

Fig. 2 ARS NOVA, Korean premiere of John Cage's Credo in the US. © 2008, Seoul Philharmonic Orchestra. CC-BY-NC-ND.

Differences and diversity were frequently celebrated in many other contexts: an ensemble concert in April 2010 contrasted Roberto Sierra's salsa-infused *Piezas caracteristicas* (1991) with a spatially experimental work by Dai Fujikura, a work employing special techniques by Sun-Young Pahg as well as John Adams's *Chamber Symphony* (1992). A program from October 2011 juxtaposed John Zorn's avant-garde wind quintet, an austere meditation on writings by Walter Benjamin, with a song cycle by Perttu Haapanen which commented musically on how European society has dealt with Otherness and on "madness" in different times, juxtaposing ancient witch hunt documents, Google Search protocols, and poems by Paul Celan.

An important attempt was made to break with conventional concert structure, as exemplified in most symphonic performances by the usual order of overture-concerto-symphony. In our view, an orchestral concert could just as easily start with a work for violin solo and live electronics, or include a work for a percussion ensemble.

---

14 P.D.Q.Bach (alias Peter Schickele), *New Horizons in Music Appreciation: Beethoven's Fifth Symphony* (1971).

Often the connections were hidden, as in an ensemble concert from 1 November 2012, when Peter Eötvös's contemplation on texts by Samuel Beckett was set side by side with Donghoon Shin's Led Zeppelin-influenced work, Ligeti's apocalyptical *Mysteries of the Macabre* (1977), and Luke Bedford's work *By The Screen in the Sun at the Hill* (2009), an almost musico-sociological study about the city of Johannesburg. Another case in point was a concert in October 2006, which juxtaposed—as if in a hall of mirrors—François Couperin with Béla Bartók, George Benjamin, Messiaen, as well as a work of Marko Nikodijevic (which, in turn, was influenced by DJs, Stravinsky, Ligeti, and algorithms), with Michael Daugherty's *Le Tombeau de Liberace* (1996). What may sound chaotic when outlined in this manner was in fact a conceptual programme with different red threads. Modern music, often highly abstract, can also be full of emotional messages, as expressed, for instance by two concerts called "Fairy Tales".

Modernism brought with itself a liberation of sound and of timbre. This was reflected in a number of programs and their titles. A concert featuring viola soloist Richard Youngjae O'Neill with two contemporary viola concertos (by Brett Dean and Chris Paul Harman) placed them alongside cosmically-inspired works by Alexander Scriabin and his contemporaries, so as to create a stark contrast with the viola's austere sound-world. As a further example, a concert on 13 June 2018 was named "Couleurs exotiques," a title also referring to the pivotal inspiration of non-European musical cultures. But modern composers were also obsessed with the emancipation of rhythm and were always looking for new sources of inspiration outside the "civilized" sphere of symphonic high culture. Most explicitly, this was commented upon in two concerts named "Dance," two programs called "Folk Music," and a concert titled "High&Low".

While, in general, the earliest pieces were from the early-twentieth century, it was occasionally necessary to go further back in time. A program called "Carnival" presented Heinrich Biber's proto-avant-gardistic *Battalia* (a macabre battle piece written on the occasion of a Carnival in 1673) alongside the Korean premieres of Francis Poulenc's surrealist *Le Bal Masqué* (1932) and of Anders Hillborg's sinister *Vaporised Tivoli* (2010). Political and satirical dimensions of music, reflected also in the biographies of the composers, were explored in a concert combining the music of Xenakis with the Korean premieres of Shostakovich's suite from his opera *The Nose* (1928) as well as Witold Lutoslawski's Cello Concerto (1970).

Other thematic rubrics included cities and countries that had been central to crucial developments: for instance, Vienna—with a wide-ranging repertoire from Arnold Schönberg to Olga Neuwirth and Georg Friedrich Haas—Paris, American mavericks (such as John Cage, Henry Cowell, Charles Ives, George Antheil, Conlon Nancarrow, Terry Riley, Elliott Carter, and John Zorn), and Hungarian modernism.

Fig. 3 ARS NOVA, video installation of Hugo Verlinde. © Seoul Philharmonic Orchestra. CC-BY-NC-ND.

A recurring topic was the exploration of meeting points between Eastern and Western traditions, and also an attempt to discover connections between the music of different East-Asian countries, which—due mostly to political sensitivities and historical reasons—had not taken place to a large extent. Key composers of the second half of the twentieth century were honored with special themed programmes: Ligeti in March 2007, Messiaen in October 2008, Boulez and Yun in March 2017.

A number of concerts were devoted to certain instruments: such as viola (November 2007) and experimental piano (June 2008 and October 2016, ranging from toy piano to innovations on the piano's strings and music inspired by player piano). Vocal experiments were celebrated in October 2006, October 2010, October 2011, and November 2012. In turn, more unusual instruments were showcased, with special focuses on the accordion (with Stefan Hussong, in May 2012), the trumpet (with Håkan Hardenberger, in April 2013), and the sheng (the Chinese mouth organ, with the instrument's leading virtuoso Wu Wei, in November 2015). The exploration of novel sounds did not stop with standard instruments: good examples were concerts featuring Ligeti's *Poème symphonique* (1962) for 100 metronomes, a performance overseen by children, Cage's *Living Room Music* (1940), and a performance by Stringgraphy, an ensemble from Japan which had constructed a new instrument, a kind of gigantic avant-garde harp constructed after the principle of the tin can telephone.

Fig. 4 ARS NOVA, preparations for the Korean premiere of György Ligeti's 'Poéme symphonique pour 100 metronomes". © 2007, Seoul Philharmonic Orchestra. CC-BY-NC-ND.

And, of course, the super instrument of our time had to be featured (in October 2009): the computer. A collaboration with IRCAM, the Paris-based center for electro-acoustic music, with Susanna Mälkki as conductor, presented central works created at IRCAM alongside a revival of Korean electronic music classics, as well as acoustic works influenced by the techniques and aesthetics of electronic music. Sound and light installations, as well as outreach events involving children, rounded out the picture.

What was the series' legacy? This is always difficult to frame, as many changes happen under the radar and are not readily visible. Of course, there are facts and figures involving such things as the number of repeat visitors, as well as the performers, composers, and organizers who gained inspiration as a result of the events. And this, of course, would be the most important achievement: stimulating curiosity among performers, audiences, composers, as well as arts administrators. The musicians did a remarkable job in all phases of the process, becoming ever more acclimated to the new compositions, and knowledgeable about the individual musical language of modernist composers. This was also true when the process involved a work with lots of special techniques by composers such as Helmut Lachenmann or Beat Furrer. A number of long-time participants in the masterclasses of Ars Nova have made international careers since that time.[15] Other Korean orchestras have introduced Composer-in-Residence schemes and are becoming more active in commissioning new music or offering workshop opportunities for young composers. The series was noted internationally, and its concerts were frequently featured on *The New York Times*'s international classical season picks. Reviewers also remarked that the Seoul Philharmonic had developed a reputation of programming more new music than any other Asian orchestra (Swed, 2012), and the series' tenth anniversary celebration book included contributions from a number of international and local musicians and arts practitioners, among them Kent Nagano, Peter Eötvös, George Benjamin, Alex Ross, and Ivan Hewett (see Lee, 2017). The Ars Nova series was one of the nominated projects for the Classical:NEXT 2018 Innovation Award.[16]

Fig. 5 ARS NOVA, audiovisual installation inspired by Mauricio Kagel's movie 'Ludwig van'. © 2006, Seoul Philharmonic Orchestra. CC-BY-NC-ND.

---

15 Among others, Donghoon Shin and Texu Kim.
16 See https://www.classicalnext.com/previous_editions/2018_edition/program/classicalnext_award/longlist

A European representative of the music industry once asked: "But is there any interest in this kind of music over there?" Yes, there is. We are convinced that audiences outside of Europe are not just hooked into endless Mahler- or Beethoven-cycles, but that part of the future of classical music will doubtlessly be in those countries outside Europe and North America. (Western) classical music has long since ceased to be only European, and if it is to stay alive audiences and practitioners will have to be found away from old centers, discourses, and temples, and further internationalization will be necessary.

Maintaining this series was constantly challenging—and its existence was called into question often enough, with only little guarantee of stability. However, the most important thing is not that a series or an institution survives forever, but that it sets something into motion. It could be likened to a message sent out in a bottle, sent out in the hope that whoever picks it up will draw inspiration and motivation for new innovative ideas and approaches.

References

Brönnimann, Baldur. 2014. "Ten Things We Should Change in Classical Music Concerts", *BIT20*, 17 October, http://bit20.no/blog/2014/10/17/10-things-that-we-should-change-in-classical-music-concerts

Chin, Unsuk. 2015. "Classical Music—Just Give Children the Chance to Love It", *The Guardian*, 21 October, https://www.theguardian.com/music/2015/oct/21/classical-music-just-give-children-the-chance-to-love-it

Fineberg, Joshua. 2006. *Classical Music, Why Bother? Hearing the World of Contemporary Culture through a Composer's Ears* (Abingdon: Routledge).

Gehl, Robert. 2009. "YouTube as Archive: Who Will Curate this Digital Wunderkammer", *International Journal of Cultural Studies*, 12(1): 43–60, https://doi.org/10.1177/1367877908098854

Gerstein, Kirill. 2020. "Iván Fischer: The Future of the Symphony Orchestra— 'Kirill Gerstein invites' @eiserlab HfM Eisler", 1:44:40, posted online by Kirill Gerstein, YouTube, 22 July, https://www.youtube.com/watch?v=iXpf1WevZhg

Gilbert, Alan. 2015. "Orchestras in the 21st Century; a New Paradigm", 15 April, Royal Philharmonic Society Lecture, Milton Court Concert Hall, London, https://royalphilharmonicsociety.org.uk/assets/files/Alan-Gilbert-speech.pdf

Grimm, Jacob, and Wilhelm Grimm. "The Hare and the Hedgehog", *University of Pitttsburgh*, https://www.pitt.edu/~dash/grimm187.html

Goertz, Wolfram. 2004. "Zwischen Arthrose und Spaziergang—Überlegungen zum Zustand der deutschen Orchesterlandschaft", in *Deutsche Orchester zwischen Bilanz und Perspektive*, ed. by Junge Deutsche Philharmonie (Regensburg: ConBrio), pp. 18–74.

Harders-Wuthenow, Frank. 2011. "'Ars Nova'—à sa manière. Unsuk Chins bahnbrechende Konzertreihe beim Seoul Philharmonic Orchestra", in *Im Spiegel der Zeit. Die Komponistin Unsuk Chin*, ed. by Stefan Drees (Mainz: Schott), pp. 205–216.

Heath, Joseph, and Andrew Potter. 2004. *Nation of Rebels. Why Counterculture Became Consumer Culture* (New York: HarperCollins).

Johnson, Julian. *Who Needs Classical Music? Cultural Choice and Musical Values* (Oxford: Oxford University Press).

Judy, Paul R. 1996. "Pure Gold: The Fleischmann-Lipman-Morris Debate of 1987–89", *Harmony*, 2: 55–69, https://iml.esm.rochester.edu/polyphonic-archive/wp-content/uploads/sites/13/2012/02/Pure_Gold_SOI.pdf

Lee, Heekyung, ed. 2017. 현대음악의 즐거움 : 서울시향 '아르스 노바' 10년의 기록, *Ars Nova 2006–2016* (Seoul: Yesol Press).

Pace, Ian. 2017. "Response to Charlotte C. Gill Article on Music and Notation—Full List of Signatories", *Desiring Progress*, 28 March, https://ianpace.wordpress.com/2017/03/30/response-to-charlotte-c-gill-article-on-music-and-notation-full-list-of-signatories/

Park, Hun-Joon, and Bernd Schmitt. 2008. "Seoul Philharmonic Orchestra. How Can the Leader of Seoul Philharmonic Set the Stage for Continued Success?", *Columbia CaseWorks*, 080509, https://www8.gsb.columbia.edu/caseworks/node/278/Seoul%2BPhilharmonic%2BOrchestra

Pomerantsev, Peter. 2019. *This Is Not Propaganda. Adventures in the War against Reality* (New York: Faber & Faber).

Ross, Alex. 2005. "Applause: A *Rest Is Noise* Special Report", *Alex Ross: The Rest Is Noise*, 18 February, https://www.therestisnoise.com/2005/02/applause_a_rest.html

Sacks, Oliver. 2007. "A Bolt from the Blue", *The New Yorker*, 16 July, https://www.newyorker.com/magazine/2007/07/23/a-bolt-from-the-blue

Sen, Amartya. 2007. *Identity and Violence: The Illusion of Identity* (London: Penguin).

Stephan, Ilja. 2012. "Seoul Philharmonic—Musik als Chefsache", *das Orchester*, 1: 32–35, http://www.iljastephan.de/publikationen/presseartikel/64.html

Swed, Mark. 2012. "Young Talent Not Always Orchestrated", *The Los Angeles Times*, 21 April, https://www.latimes.com/archives/la-xpm-2012-apr-20-la-et-seoul-philharmonic-review-20120421-story.html

Tiensuu, Jukka. 2000. "The Future of Music", ed. by Roger Reynolds and Karen Reynolds, SEARCH EVENT I, 16 April, University of California, San Diego, http://www.rogerreynolds.com/futureofmusic/tiensuu.html

Vermeil, Jean. 1996. *Conversations with Boulez. Thoughts on Conducting* (Oregon: Amadeus).

15. The Philharmonie de Paris, the *Démos* Project, and New Directions in Classical Music

Laurent Bayle

Music is often practiced collectively. From this point of view, the orchestra could be perceived as a mirror of society. It sometimes even gives the impression of anticipating certain changes in society, a characteristic which its social history has reflected over the centuries. Today, in our twenty-first-century world, what we call globalization is interrogating musical life in different ways: how can we keep attracting audiences to venues when new technological means allow citizens to enjoy unlimited content remotely? How can audiences be renewed and increased, especially for classical music, when the amount of culture and entertainment on offer is multiplying everywhere, and new forms are emerging that are more suited to the tastes of young people? How can we imagine the financial survival of orchestras in an increasingly liberal world—from an economic perspective at least—which accepts less and less the idea that there can be art forms which are structurally supported by public authorities or by the generosity of patrons? How do we avoid being labeled as an elitist art, engaged only in the satisfaction of a privileged audience? How can we instead establish a dialogue with populations, citizens, families, young people, and children who are totally cut off from cultural offerings which are essentially available in large urban centers?

In this conflicted context, it becomes urgent to invent new models for the dissemination of music in which culture is merely a vector for the personal fulfillment of a few people, but also a force for social cohesion. These new models must be based, in my view, on a more generalist vision allowing us to project our future on the basis of a broader historical perspective.

First of all, our customs divide high and popular culture: the symphonic repertoire, for example, suffers from being almost exclusively played in specific iconic buildings erected in the center of large cities and frequented by rather privileged citizens. This situation could change. By way of example, the Philharmonie de Paris gives more than five hundred concerts a year. The entire history of music is represented on its stage: the Western repertoire of the past, as well as that of today; popular music (from jazz to pop, to today's emerging forms); but also traditional and modern music from other continents (Japan, China, Cambodia, Africa, The Middle East, India, etc.).

Another related problem is that the way we present our music sets the urban against the suburban, and even against areas far from the main urban centers. In Europe, the Philharmonie de Paris is the only major musical complex built in recent decades to have chosen not to settle in the city center or in a well-off neighborhood, but rather in a district that mixes different populations, close to the ring road, near the Parisian suburbs where struggling populations are living.

Furthermore, our musical practices also set the local against the international. While we do need to rely, to some extent, on the prestige of great artists or orchestras from all over the world, a project cannot genuinely resonate if the audience does not feel some kind of local affiinity. This can be provided by involving regional orchestras, or by performances given several times a year that mix professionals and amateurs, and even allow for audience participation. There are many initiatives to be taken in this regard. For instance, most cultural institutions do not consider the fact that children represent a potential relationship with a future audience. Even prestigious institutions should explore the issue of transmission in all its forms: specific events, workshops, exhibitions, etc. To demonstrate the social role that music can play, in 2010 the Philharmonie de Paris launched a children's orchestra project called Démos, which may be defined as follows: a musical and orchestral educational system with a social vocation.

From 2006 onward, our budding Philharmonie project was the subject of much criticism from politicians, senior officials, and music lovers alike. The arguments ranged from the view that classical music was an art of the past, interested only in an elderly elite, to the idea that new generations identify with other, more modern and entertaining musical practices, such as pop or electro; that classical music was the music of the privileged and that young people living in working-class neighborhoods have their own cultural practices, such as rap or hip hop, and, finally, that only young people with very favorable family backgrounds receive real musical training. And the indictment would often conclude with this final sentence: this project is not appropriate, because young people will not recognize themselves in it and music lovers will never venture into a disadvantaged neighborhood.

We considered that some of these attacks, which we regarded as specious, were actually based on observations we had made ourselves, and which could be supported by sociological studies. One of these studies (Dorin, 2012), which focused on symphonic life in Paris, interestingly pointed out that the median age of the classical audience is about sixty, whereas the median age of all those over eighteen in France is close to forty-eight. As a result of this age difference, 50% of the specific classical music audience have no dependent children, and 75% have a higher diploma, compared to 20% of the total French population. More than 50% (and up to 80% among those under twenty-five) have received a musical education, compared to 20% of the total French population. Finally, as regards the financial situation of classical music lovers, the average household income is close to 70,000 euros net per year, compared to 25,000 euros for the total French population.

We chose to use this statistical data constructively by initiating our Démos project, which envisioned setting up orchestras comprising children living in underprivileged areas. We postulated that it is not the music itself that creates barriers, but rather the way it is presented and the customs that have developed around it.

Thus, an educational model that keeps struggling families, and therefore some children, at a distance from the practice of music has been erected. In music schools, music theory is an obligatory stage that precedes the magical discovery of an instrument. But disadvantaged children often lack reference points and the fewer reference points a child has, the more the learning of music theory becomes an obstacle. Afterwards comes the actual practice of music, which is highly individualized, with one teacher, and one pupil. Once again, this context has a tendency to intimidate disadvantaged children, who will be more at ease in a group dynamic.

Our bet was that if children who were cut off from music, or even from any cultural practice, were put in physical contact with classical music, they would be able to identify with it. If they were part of a collective adventure, for example an orchestra, they would want to join the project and blossom. We thus decided to create our first children's orchestras, and to carry out our action in the underprivileged suburbs of the Paris region, in response to the controversy surrounding our project.

Initially, we observed new models already set up abroad to address the same issues, the most successful one being the Venezuelan El Sistema project in South America. However, it was not directly transposable to the French situation. The El Sistema, which brings together several hundred thousand children, imposes a daily orchestral rehearsal. A large proportion of the children do not go to school, and El Sistema therefore takes the place of the educational system as a whole, which would be prohibited in Europe.

However, we have learned a great deal from Venezuela, especially concerning the project's educational dimension: how to teach an instrument collectively; how to approach a score for people without any knowledge of music theory; how a child can at first imitate with great ease the gestures of a professional musician, and then, when he or she has acquired a little confidence, begin to approach the first notions of music theory; or how to prepare the coaches for these new methods, knowing that it is necessary to recruit between fifteen and twenty coaches per orchestra.

We also studied the ways other European cities have been inspired by the South American model. We set up a partnership with the London Symphony Orchestra, which has developed substantial and effective activities for many populations in difficulty (specific communities, sick people or prison inmates, and so on). We have also learned a good deal from the London musicians, who came to train their fellow Parisian colleagues in new teaching methods and provided us with simplified versions of works, so that they could be more easily played by children.

Finally, in 2010, we created four orchestras in the Paris region. We started on the following basis: children would get free training and would receive their instrument (strings, winds, or brass) as a gift; they would make a commitment for a minimum of three years, with the possibility of continuing with us in another form or entering a conservatory; there would be regularity in the process, in the form of two workshops of two hours a week, which is the maximum number of hours permitted for schooled children; workshops would sometimes be organized in social centers close to the children's homes and other times at the Philharmonie; there would be about twenty professional musicians involved with each children's orchestra and social actors responsible for maintaining links with schools, families, and the children's environment; children would not be selected based on the preconceptions of musicians, but completely put in the hands of social actors; these orchestras would offer an unusual definition of what is called classical music, through a program mixing works from the Western repertoire and other parts of the world with commissions to composers or film music; and finally, in June, an annual musical presentation of the resulting work of each orchestra would take place on our main stage, where the world's largest orchestras perform.

After our first experiment with four orchestras of children aged eight to twelve years, we expanded to eight orchestras in 2012. But, as is well known, our country was marred by the tragedy of the Paris attacks in autumn 2015. They affected us deeply as citizens, but also as musicians. More urgently than ever before, we felt the need to defend music against all those attempting to silence diversity of expression.

This is the reason why we decided to root our project more firmly in the underprivileged areas around Paris, and to apply the model in other places with a concentration of social difficulties throughout France. As of today, forty-five orchestras have been created or are in the process of being implemented. Twenty of them are located around Paris and directly managed by the Philharmonie de Paris, while twenty-five have been set up in the other regions of France, through partnerships with local authorities, and also with local musical institutions, such as local orchestras or conservatories.

This project benefits from a permanent evaluation by researchers in cognitive sciences and humanities (specialists in music anthropology, sociology, educational sciences, and social psychology). The studies (Dansilio and Fayette, 2019: 27) show that children's support for the project is very high and that the desire to continue learning music after experiencing these first three years is shared by a vast majority of them. Evaluators (Barbaroux, Dittinger, & Besson, 2019: 18) also noted positive changes in their behavior, and regard the project as an educational tool for learning diligence, concentration, respect for others, socialization, and listening.

By way of conclusion, I would like to emphasize that an initiative like Démos is obviously not enough to single-handedly transform the existing situation. Our world is going through profound changes that notably challenge its order, the actual means of communication, the hierarchy of values, the place of culture and leisure in our society, and the role of education.

Démos seeks to address issues that go beyond itself and lie at the heart of our social challenges, including, among other things: the fight against barriers in cultural practices between audiences, social classes, generations, and territories; the renewal of cultural consumption habits; the promotion of cultural diversity; and the development of arts education for young people. All these questions, which can find answers in the type of field experience we have described, call for a broader political vision capable of guiding the future of our societies.

References

Barbaroux, Mylène, Eva Dittinger, and Besson Mireille. 2019. "Music Training with Démos Program Positively Influences Cognitive Functions in Children from Low Socio-Economic Backgrounds", *PloS ONE*, 14.5: 1–21, https://doi.org/10.1371/journal.pone.0216874

Dansilio, Florencia, and Nicola Fayette. 2019. *Après Démos: enquête sociologique sur les trajectoires des enfants de Démos 1*, CREDA, Paris III, 2019, https://demos.philharmoniedeparis.fr/media/DOCUMENTS/EVALUATIONS/DOCT_2019_Dansilio-Fayette_Apres-demos_Etude.pdf

Dorin, Stéphane. 2012. "Enquête sur les publics des concerts de la musique classique en France", PICRI program of the Région Île de France, and Paris 2030 program of the City of Paris, in partnership with FEVIS.

16. What Classical Music Can Learn from the Plastic Arts

Olivier Berggruen[1]

Over the last few decades, interest in the visual arts has grown dramatically. A few basic facts and figures can attest to this trend (Graw, 2010). The number of museum-goers has reached a record high. The Metropolitan Museum of Art had seven million visitors in 2017, while Tate Modern and the Louvre had over five million visitors. The same applies to visitors to large exhibitions. It is not uncommon for a show to get nearly a million visitors, such as the exhibition in 2016 of the former collection of Sergei Shchukin at the Fondation Louis Vuitton in Paris. In 2017, according to Clare McAndrew (2018: 15), the art market easily surpassed the $63 billion mark. Within the global market economy, this is hardly a significant number. Nonetheless, it is fairly remarkable in comparison to sales generated by content for classical music. Let us not forget the activities and industries generated by the visual arts: namely magazines, periodicals, blogs, fashion projects that are carried out in collaboration with artists; not to mention a whole range of ancillary activities, such as talks, conferences, debates, art fairs, previews, studio visits, etc. Further quantitative evidence speaks to the enduring strength of the visual arts, and the variety of its offerings. In 2017, the art market employed an estimated three million people. That year alone, there were approximately 310,685 businesses operating in the global art, antiques and collectibles market, accounting for 296,540 in the gallery sector and 14,145 in auction houses. It is estimated that the global art trade spent

---

1   I would like to thank Mebrak Tareke for her comments and research.

$19.6 billion on a range of business-related services, supporting a further 363,655 jobs (McAndrew, 2018: 21).

Here I would I would like to offer a very succinct historical perspective about the rapid development of the trade in artifacts in the West (based on Watson, 1992). Until the late eighteenth century, the plastic arts were reserved for a small, wealthy elite. For centuries most artistic practice was nearly exclusively devotional and religious in nature. Painters and sculptors were employed by the church, the state, and various potentates. With the emergence of the merchant classes in Florence and other small states in Italy and the low countries in Northern Europe, private commissions by wealthy individuals became more common. Art for the masses only emerged in the late eighteenth century with the creation of spaces for the public consumption of art, such as the Salons in France and exhibitions at the Royal Academy in London. In the Romantic era, artistic production became less dependent on commissions, and artists such as Eugène Delacroix or Théodore Géricault would initiate and pursue their own projects, often regardless of patrons and commissions. This can also be seen as a rebellion against the constraints imposed by donors and their political or social agenda.

A few decades later, with the building of the National Gallery in London and other similar institutions in Europe and North America, the visual arts became available to the vast majority of people, and often (as in the case of Sir George Beaumont at London's National Gallery) they were imbued with a sense of educational and moral purpose. That being said, with the rise of Modernism and various avant-garde movements on the cusp of the twentieth century, art became a way to rebel against the establishment. There was a fairly widely shared belief that the modern visual arts, as in Fauvism, Cubism, Constructivism, etc., were aimed against the prevailing current, against the status quo. The same could be said of the modern music of the Vienna School in its quest for a radical musical expression.

In the West, the visual arts continued their expansion in the first half of the twentieth century, yet the public was largely drawn from educated elites and programs were subsidized by wealthy donors, such as the founders of the Museum of Modern Art in New York, foremost among them the Rockefeller family. Great art exhibitions of contemporary art such as documenta in Kassel or the Venice Biennale attracted a loyal following, consisting of mostly well-heeled professionals. A seismic shift occurred in 1973 with the Robert Scull auction in which, for the first time, relatively modest prices were replaced by record prices for works by Andy Warhol and others. In today's context, these prices seem modest, but they changed public consciousness. In more general terms, works that were deemed arcane, difficult, and eccentric attracted wide attention.

Since 1973, lobbying for contemporary art has grown more intense. What was once considered marginal or intellectual has permeated pop culture, and this has to do with the joined efforts of large blue chip galleries such as Pace, Gagosian, Hauser & Wirth, Zwirner, etc., as well as the auction houses Sotheby's, Christie's, Phillips, but also Poly Group in China, international art fairs in Basel, Miami, and Hong Kong, and non-commercial art extravaganzas such as biennials and large-scale events (Christo in Central Park or Olafur Eliason at Tate Modern, for instance).

The success and popularity of the visual arts cannot be dissociated from certain economic factors. After all, works of art are physical, tangible objects that can be bought or exchanged, just like other commodities. A piece of music can be downloaded, it can be purchased in various formats, but music hardly has the tangible uniqueness that we associate with artifacts. The trade in works of art gives rise to a vast economy on a global scale, stimulated by aggressive marketing at galleries and auction houses. The network of museums, exhibition spaces (often associated with innovative architecture), galleries, biennials, and art fairs, ensures the popularity of art beyond the circles of wealthy patrons and art professionals. Nowadays, art has become a lifestyle issue, a rarefied, but not overly rarefied, offshoot of pop culture. Museums, once seen as the bastion of the elites, have succeeded in bridging the divide between pop culture and the elites. Jeff Koons and Takashi Murakami can co-exist with Hanne Darboven or Pierre Huyghe.

The museum can be seen as a place of social interaction, as an open-ended secular church—it doesn't require total devotion, but nonetheless it inserts itself in daily life, as do reading, sports, and yoga. Museums and galleries have succeeded in establishing themselves as trendy establishments. As a public forum, a museum serves the community in a variety of ways. The Museum of Fine Arts in Montreal, for example, offers a dedicated art therapy space, one that welcomes as many as 300,000 participants per year, including autistic children, the sick, as well as marginalized groups. There are even consulting rooms staffed with professional doctors within that space. The same museum also has a studio devoted to social interaction in the workplace, in which teachers are encouraged to understand the emotional, political, social impact of works of art. Over the past few years, the number of visitors has doubled. In a similar vein, Tate Modern's extension now boasts a large space called "Tate Exchange" devoted to debates on human interest stories. According to Chris Dercon, Tate Modern's former director who oversaw these changes, "The museum was centred around individual experience. It needs to become the locus of collective exchange" (Dercon, 2019).

Many museums are large institutions which are run like complex organizations. They position themselves as brands. So do Carnegie Hall, the New York Philharmonic, and the Paris Opera. Institutions in the visual arts are good at blending mass-appeal with other, more daring or difficult projects. Tate Modern in London, for example, under the leadership of Nicholas Serota, put up blockbuster exhibitions, such as the recent "Picasso 1932" show (2018), as well as a more demanding ones, such as the Donald Judd retrospective (2004). They will mix high and low art, scholarly exhibitions and blockbusters, educational programs, performances and art-historical lectures.

Music venues could learn from this, in particular in terms of making the experience more inclusive, without sacrificing high standards. The idea is to be more inclusive of a variety of tastes, therefore increasing the overall reach, and to combine these with more focused projects as well. Carnegie Hall, for example, has been successful at mixing performances that have a wide appeal with more targeted projects, such as a composer-in-residence series and the Perspectives series.

Synergy and Collaboration between the Arts

Another crucial question, to my mind, has to do with the gradual divide between contemporary music and visual arts. In the last few years, I have come to the realization that the worlds of music and the visual arts seem to be evolving in different spheres. Perhaps this is because nowadays, society sees artistic disciplines as intrinsically separate—a tendency, which, I feel, has grown over the past few decades. This is very different from the days of Sergei Diaghilev's Ballets Russes, in which dancers, composers, performers, writers, and composers all conspired to create works of art that brought these various forms of artistic expression together. There were also striking parallels in terms of the approach and the overall spirit, as in the irreverent cultivation of parody and the off-centered classicism of Diaghilev's post-World War One productions. Igor Stravinsky's tapestry of clashing tonal orientations and rhythms that disrupt continuity, as a form of discontinuity that endeavors to create more space in the listener's imagination. Often, compositions by Stravinsky from this period manage to juxtapose or to bring together high and low art, ranging from the classical to the vernacular. Here we find echoes of Picasso's cubist method of assemblage and discontinuous surfaces. Or we could evoke the historic collaboration of Merce Cunningham with Jasper Johns and John Cage. That being said, initiatives such as Tauba Auerbach's recent collaborative project with the composer of electronic music Eliane Radigue in Cleveland, or William Kentridge's stage designs for the opera, are noteworthy. There is synergy between the arts, fashion, and architecture; perhaps this is to be expected since it all relates to space and the visual realm. But music can also be the locus of such efforts. Architecture and the auditory experience are also related, as illustrated in the next section.

New Technology

Based on my observations of contemporary art shows, there's a great deal to be said for merging sound art/technology and architecture. We see it with Oliver Beer's sound compositions. Oliver Beer, an artist based in London, is classically trained in composition and the foundation of his practice is in music and sonority. He has done several works which explore the resonance inherent in the shape of objects and artifacts. New works showing Beer's development in his *Two-Dimensional Sculptures* were also on view at the Met Breuer in 2019. Created using objects such as musical instruments, cameras, shotguns, and often imbued with personal history, the artist slices them with surgical precision before immersing them in white gessoed plaques. Only the cut surface of the object remains visible, the objects losing their volume and becoming two-dimensional images of themselves, which gives them new meaning, blurring the boundaries between painting, drawing, sculpture, and sound.

We have to embrace technology, starting with developing social media and social networks, new ways of expanding and engaging communities of like-minded people with common interests. In the long term, it is crucial for classical music platforms to increase connectivity, especially as new generations grow up with technology. This prompts the question of how we receive our music. Much of it is transmitted digitally, whether it is through streaming services, but let's not forget words (podcasts), images transmitted through a variety of platforms, video, etc.

Here the strategy common to art galleries and performing arts centers (music, but also ballet) should emphasize the sense of surprise in terms of content; that is, to make an "old fashioned" experience (i.e., unmediated) fresh and relevant. There are two aspects to this: on the one hand, the live experience, the flesh-and-blood of the concert hall, involving the senses (sounds, but also visual and other sensory aspects in connection with a live performance; the tactility and physical, relational, and spatial aspect of works of art in a gallery), and, on the other hand, digital formats like TV, radio, social media, etc. These two aspects can complement each other; the digital platform can be seen as an extension of live experience. Yet it remains crucial to focus on live events—such moments are unique, with a sense of place and festive atmosphere; the more formal setting offering added weight and solemnity at times.

That being said, it is also worth considering and exploring the full range of sensory aspects elicited by the concert hall experience. The enduring popularity of opera stems from its unique blend of music, singing, dance, acting, stage sets, costumes, etc. We can also evoke trends whereby venues such as the Shed or the Park Avenue Armory in New York have sought to create a musical experience in which space and stage are not just added aspects to the auditory experience, but foundational, as in Hélène Grimaud's collaboration with the Scottish artist Douglas Gordon at the Park Avenue Armory (Water Music). These experiments are now more common, and they push the boundaries on what that concert experience could be.

Innovative and Diverse Programming

New forms of programming reflecting a more contemporary sensibility seem to be an important step forward. Music can only evolve if new content is created. This involves music education, both private and public funding, but it also requires encouraging new music and new compositions. It is incumbent upon music professionals and managers to insist on more contemporary forms of programming. Conservative audiences are resisting this, but to me it seems to be the way forward. That's how barriers can be broken down as well; the future doesn't merely reside in creating crossover appeal (classically trained opera singers singing Broadway songs), but in more innovative programming. Venues should be places of experimentation in a world in which many contemporary musicians embrace larger traditions and propositions than the classical canon. Large museums are good at being inclusive: the same could apply to musical spaces, which offer a range of options for various tastes, from Baroque music to contemporary music, from recitals and small ensembles to large orchestral concerts. At the same time, at the opposite end of the spectrum, there is a future for small, targeted efforts: small museums devoted to one private collection or artist (the Frick Collection in New York, the Noguchi Museum in Long Island City) are thriving, and they can operate on small budgets; similarly small ensembles or musical entities without a permanent space such as the Mahler Chamber Orchestra, the Little Opera company, the Loft Opera or ICE can do the same.

Our view of the legacy of classical music is changing, to include histories that have been sidelined or marginalized. In the wake of World War Two, a new international order emerged, and as networks became increasingly connected through technology, globalism became a much-talked about notion. Today's museums and art institutions give a voice to neglected or forgotten artists. Similarly, musical programming should embrace this diversity, to include composers whose works have been marginalized. One example involves some of the German- and Polish-Jewish composers who faced adverse political circumstances, such as Erich Wolfgang Korngold and Mieczysław Weinberg, ignored for decades and now given their due. Women composers, as diverse as Clara Schumann, Amy Beach, or Germaine Tailleferre, are now finally given greater exposure.

A Holistic Experience: The Concert Hall as a More Fluid Destination

Large museums today are very good at transforming their spaces in such a way as to provide a global experience in which the visual arts are only the core aspect. The architecture, restaurants, workshops, lecture halls, surrounding gardens, sculpture gardens, etc. are some of the attractions which allow visitors and families to spend as much as half a day there, particularly on weekends. What helps, needless to say, is the open-ended aspect of the experience. They can choose between various alternatives and programs, as opposed to the constraints of a concert which starts at a set time. Ticket holders are rushing to get a drink before the concert, or during the intermission. Perhaps there are ways to make the spaces and opportunities for socializing more friendly and inviting. Even the format could be changed; the traditional two-part structure with one intermission needs to be re-considered.

To conclude, if there are three things that we can discern about the future of music, it's that there is an urgent need for the entire experience to be more inclusive, to narrow the yawning gap between the visual arts and music, and that technology will play a pivotal role in heightening the ways in which we experience music, especially when it comes to drawing in new audiences. I have not tackled issues of music education in this paper; these warrant a separate discussion, and are addressed by a rising number of dedicated scholars and musicians (see also Chapters 3 and 4 in this volume).

References

Dercon, Chris. 2019. Communication with Author.

Graw, Isabelle. 2010. *High Price: Art between the Market and Celebrity Culture* (Berlin: Sternberg Press).

McAndrew, Clare. 2018. *The Art Market 2018. An Art Basel and UBS Report* (Basel: Art Basel & UBS) https://d2u3kfwd92fzu7.cloudfront.net/Art%20Basel%20and%20UBS_The%20Art%20Market_2018.pdf

Watson, Peter. 1992. *From Manet to Manhattan: The Rise of the Modern Art Market* (New York: Random House).

Index

Academy of Ancient Music 4
Adams, John 152, 169
Adès, Thomas 5
Africa xliii, 23, 43, 178
Ali-Zadeh, Franghiz 43
Alkhamis-Kanoo, Huda xxix
Amazon 108–109
American Federation of Musicians (AFM) 77, 83, 85, 91, 99
Andrew, Kerry 152
Andrew W. Mellon Foundation 98, 124–125, 139
Antheil, George 171
Apple Music 108
Asbury, Stefan 42, 167
Asia xxxvi, 43, 90, 95, 100, 162, 171, 173
Association for the Advancement of Creative Musicians 43
Atlanta Symphony 92
  Talent Development Program 92
audience building xli, 61, 63, 64, 65, 66, 67, 68, 69, 70, 76, 109, 112, 113, 121, 122, 123, 124, 125, 133, 135, 139, 141, 143, 153, 177, 190. *See also* New World Symphony: New Audience Initiative
Auerbach, Tauba 187
Auner, Joseph 2
Aurora Orchestra 152
Austin, Paul 79, 82
Australia 43
Australian Music Centre 39
Austria 162
Averil Smith, Brinton 81

Bach, Johann Sebastian xxxvi, xxxvii, 4, 21, 39, 168
  Goldberg Variations xxxvii
  Inventions and Sinfonias xxxvi
Bach, P. D. Q. 169
Bang on a Can 40–41, 44
Barenboim, Daniel 9
Barthes, Roland 23
Bartók, Béla xxxix, 163, 170
Baumol, William 68
Bayle, Laurent xi, xxix, xlii, xliv
Beach, Amy 189
Beatles, the 16
Beaumont, Sir George 184
Beckerman, Michael xii, xxvii, xxix, xlv
Beckett, Samuel 170
Bedford, Luke 170
Beer, Oliver 187
  Two-Dimensional Sculptures 187
Beethoven, Ludwig van xxxiii, xxxviii, 1, 9–10, 39, 144, 152, 168, 174
  Hammerklavier Sonata 10
  Symphony No. 9 xxxiii, 9
Belgium 160
Benjamin, George 168, 170, 173
Benjamin, Walter 169
Berggruen, Olivier xii, xliv
Berio, Luciano 106, 168
Berliner Philharmoniker 110, 165, 167
Berlioz, Hector 144
Bernstein, Leonard 166
Beyoncé 50
Biber, Heinrich 170
Big Ears Festival 40

BIPOC musicians (pathways for) 20, 25, 90–101
Birtwistle, Harrison 168
Björling, Jussi xxv
Black Lives Matter xlii, 90, 101, 114
Black Pearl Chamber Orchestra 92
Boghossian, Paul xi, xxx, xxxiii
Borda, Deborah xiii, xxx, xli, 42
Boston Symphony Orchestra 20, 92
    Project Step 92
Boulez, Pierre 22, 106, 161, 165–166, 171
Bourdieu, Pierre 115
Bowen, William 68
Bowman, Woods 69
Brain and Creativity Institute at the University of Southern California (USC) xxxix, 29–30, 32
Braxton, Anthony 40
Brendel, Alfred 9
British Broadcasting Company (BBC) xxxi, xliii, 7, 143, 145–148, 150–155
    BBC Orchestras 151–153
    BBC Proms, the 143, 151–152
    BBC Radio 3 143, 145–146, 148–151, 154
    BBC Sounds 147–150, 154
    BBC Symphony Orchestra 153
    curated playlists 147
    Slow Radio xliii, 148–150, 154
    Ten Pieces xliii, 152–154
Britten, Edward Benjamin 23
broadcasts xxvi, 7–8, 11, 83, 145–154
Brönnimann, Baldur 167
Budapest Festival Orchestra 165

Cabezas, Gabriel 97
Cage, John 42, 44, 106, 169, 171–172, 187
    Living Room Music 172
Calabrese, Thad xiii, xli
Cambodia 178
Canada 112
Carnegie Hall xxx, xxxiv, 52, 80, 88, 109, 186
Carter, Elliott 171
Celan, Paul 169

Cendo, Raphaël 44
Central Park 185
Cerrone, Christopher 107
Chamber Music America (CMA) 100
Chanda, Mona 8
Chicago Youth Symphony Orchestra 88
China xliii, 23, 100, 172, 178, 185
Chineke! Foundation 115–116
    Chineke! Orchestra 92
Chin, Unsuk xiv, xxix, xxx, xliii, 42, 157, 167
Christie's 185
Christo 185
Chung, Myung-whun 165–166
Ciconia, Johannes 168
Cincinnati Symphony Orchestra 52, 88, 98
classical music xxvi, xxvii, xxviii, xxxiii, xxxiv, xxxv, xxxvi, xxxvii, xxxviii, xxxix, xl, xli, xlii, xliii, xliv, 1–4, 15, 17–18, 23–25, 31, 40–41, 43–44, 47–49, 52–53, 57, 89–91, 93, 96, 100–101, 105, 107–108, 111–116, 121–128, 130–132, 134, 138–140, 144–146, 148–150, 152–155, 157–163, 165, 174, 177, 179–181, 183, 188–189
    contemporary 5, 42, 157, 161, 162, 189. *See also* new-music
    in video games/gaming 146
    Western xxxvii, 1–4, 17, 23–24, 165
classical music education xxviii, xxxix, 3, 15, 16, 17, 18, 20, 21, 24, 25, 29, 30, 33, 35, 87, 97, 101, 111, 152, 158, 159, 162, 189, 190. *See also* musicology; *See also* research
    conservatory training 15, 20–21, 90, 92, 96, 99, 181
    effects on childhood development xxxix, 16–17, 30–34
    K-12 15, 18–19, 24
    university-level 15, 19, 21, 24
Classic FM 146, 148, 150
Cleveland Institute of Music 100
Colburn School 21
Coleman, Valerie 97
collective bargaining 76, 83, 100

Colour of Music Festival 92
composers xxxv, xxxvi, xxxvii, xliii, 1–3, 7, 20, 22–23, 25, 39–44, 51, 53–54, 89, 91–94, 97, 100, 105–106, 109, 112, 124, 136, 146, 149, 157, 161, 165, 167–168, 170–173, 181, 186–187, 189
concerts xxvi, xxvii, xxviii, xxxvi, xlii, 7, 8, 10, 20, 22, 24, 39, 40, 41, 42, 44, 51, 80, 81, 93, 96, 104, 105, 106, 107, 109, 110, 111, 112, 113, 115, 122, 123, 124, 127, 128, 129, 130, 131, 132, 133, 134, 135, 136, 138, 139, 144, 146, 150, 151, 152, 153, 154, 163, 164, 165, 166, 167, 168, 169, 170, 171, 172, 173, 178, 188, 189, 190. *See also* live performance
concert venues 44, 189
  non-traditional 3, 41, 50, 53, 67, 106–107, 124, 152, 188
conductors xxvi, 108–109, 112, 165–166, 172
Constructivism 184
Couperin, François 170
Couperin, Louis 168
COVID-19 pandemic xxxiii, xxxix, xli, xliii, xlv, 7, 25, 63, 75, 78–80, 82, 85, 90, 92, 94, 100, 143, 160
Cowell, Henry 171
Creative Commons 108
Croatia xxxvii
Croce, Arlene 48
Cuba 135
Cubism 184, 187
Cunningham, Merce 187
Curry, Jessica 146
Curtis Institute of Music 88

Damasio, Antonio xiv, xv
Damasio, Hanna xv, 34
dance music 2, 135
Darboven, Hanne 185
Daugherty, Michael 170
Davey, Alan 148–150, 153
Davidson, Justin 52
Dayton Hudson Corporation 56
Dayton, Kenneth 56
  Governance Is Governance (1987) 56

Dean, Brett 168–170
Debussy, Claude 23, 162, 166
de Grigny, Nicolas 168
Delacroix, Eugène 184
Denk, Jeremy 53
Dercon, Chris 186
Detroit Symphony 98
Deutsch, Bernd Richard 167
Deutsches Symphonie-Orchester Berlin 167
Diaghilev, Sergei 187
  Ballets Russes 187
digital revolution 47, 81, 105, 107, 111, 158
di Lassus, Orlando 168
Dines, Judy 96
Disney Hall 44
di Stefano, Giuseppe xxv
diversity xli, xlii, 22–23, 43, 53, 60–61, 82, 85, 87, 89, 92, 99–100, 150, 160, 163, 165, 169, 181–182, 189
documenta 184
Donaueschingen Festival 40
Doty, Aaron 82
Dudamel, Gustavo 97
Dufay, Guillaume 2
Dun, Tan 5
Dusapin, Pascal 167
Dvořák, Antonín 2, 20
  String Quartet No. 12 (American Quartet) 20

Eastman School of Music 92
Ebert, Roger 48
Eighth Blackbird 22
Elbphilharmonie Hamburg 44
electro 106, 172, 179
Eliason, Olafur 185
elitism 144, 146, 158, 177
Ellington, Duke xxxvii
  Black, Brown and Beige xxxvii
El Sistema project 180
Encounters 135
engagement 9, 21–22, 31, 33, 58–59, 65, 67, 110, 113, 115, 121, 123, 125, 135, 138–139, 144, 147, 150, 152–155

Ensemble Intercontemporain 40
Eötvös, Peter 161, 166–167, 170, 173
equity xli, 60, 82, 85, 87, 92
Europe xxxvi, xliii, 1–3, 5, 7, 15, 20, 25, 40, 43, 47, 160, 168–169, 174, 178, 180, 184

Facebook 49
Fauvism 184
Fedele, Ivan 167
Feder, Susan xv, xlii
Figueroa, Rafael 96
financial health xli, 63–65, 68–70
Fineberg, Joshua 157
Fine, Kit xv, xxx, xxxix
Fires of London 40
Fischer, Iván 165
Fischer, Thierry 166
Flagg, Aaron A. 91
Fleischmann, Ernest 42, 153, 165
Fleming, Renée 53
Floyd, George xxxiv, xlv, 24, 90, 101, 114
folk music xxxvii, 1, 4, 17, 23, 135
Fondation Louis Vuitton 183
France xxix, xliv, 160, 162, 179–181, 184
Freddy and the Dreamers xxxvii
  "I'm Telling You Now" xxxvii
Frick Collection 189
Fujikura, Dai 169
Fure, Ashley 107
Furrer, Beat 173
Furtwängler, Wilhelm 9

Gagosian 185
Galamian, Ivan 20
Gateways Music Festival 92
Gehry, Frank 121, 124
Géricault, Théodore 184
Germantown Performing Arts Center 132
Germany 40, 162, 189
Gesualdo, Carlo 168
Gibson, Randy 50
Gielen, Michael 160
Gilbert, Alan 53, 161

Ginastera, Alberto 166
Glass, Philip 4, 43. *See also* Philip Glass Ensemble
Glen, Hilary 135
Golijov, Osvaldo 5
Google 49
Gordon, Douglas 188
Gotham Chamber Opera 57
Gothoni, Maris xvi, xliii, 157
governance xxviii, xli, 56–59, 61
Grand Rapids Symphony 79, 82
Great American Songbook 3
Grimaud, Hélène 188
Guerrero, Giancarlo 97
Guzelimian, Ara xvi, xxx

Haapanen, Perttu 169
Haas, Georg Friedrich 168, 171
Haas, Michael 9
Habibi, Assal xvii, 29
Hahn, Hilary 42
Hall, Craig xvii, xlii
Hall-Tompkins, Kelly 97
Handel and Haydn Society of Boston 55
Handel, George Frideric 39
Hanslick, Eduard 48
Hardenberger, Håkan 172
Harlem Chamber Players 92
Harman, Chris Paul 167, 170
Harris, Ellen T. xviii, xxx, xxxviii
Harrison, Lou 2
Harth-Bedoya, Miguel 97
Harvard University 23
Hauser & Wirth 185
Haydn, Joseph 1–2, 39
Hearne, Ted 136
Heart of Los Angeles (HOLA) program 31
Herring, Howard xviii, xlii
Hewett, Ivan 173
Hillborg, Anders 167, 170
hip hop 179
Hobsbawm, Eric 162
Höller, York 167
Holst, Gustav 152

Hough, Stephen 7
Houston Symphony 79, 81, 96, 98
Hungary 171
Hussong, Stefan 172
Huyghe, Pierre 185

Ibargüen, Alberto 138
inclusivity xli, 5, 22, 31, 51, 60–61, 82, 85, 87, 89, 92–93, 99–100, 154, 158, 186, 189–190
India xliii, 23, 178
Instagram 110
Institute of Musical Art 20. *See also* Juilliard School
International Conference of Symphony and Opera Musicians (ICSOM) 78–79, 85, 99
Senza Sordino 78
International Contemporary Ensemble (ICE) 22, 41, 44, 85, 107, 109
Italy xxxiii, 160, 184
iTunes 108
Ives, Charles 166, 171

Janáček, Leoš 163
Japan xliii, 4, 23, 172, 178
jazz 16–17, 43, 88, 178
John F. Kennedy Center for the Performing Arts (Washington, D.C.) 132
Johns, Jasper 187
Jolas, Betsy 168
Jones Hall 81
Joplin, Scott 5
Josefowicz, Leila 42
Josquin des Prez 10
Judd, Donald 186
Judge, Jenny xix, xxx
Juilliard School 20, 92
Music Advancement Program 92

Kael, Pauline 48
Kagel, Mauricio 168
Kane, Jon David 136
Kang, Sukhi 166, 168
Karajan, Herbert von 9

Kennedy, John F. 76
Kentridge, William 187
Kentucky Performing Arts Center 132
Kim, Texu 173
King, Martin Luther 11
Kneisel, Franz 20
Kneisel Hall 20
Kneisel Quartet 20
Knight Foundation 122–124, 134, 136–138
Knights Ensemble, The 22, 85
Knussen, Oliver 168
Koons, Jeff 185
Korngold, Erich Wolfgang 189
Kramer, Lawrence 1
Krása, Hans
Brundibár xxxvi
Kronos Quartet 40

labor-management structures 76–79, 82–85
labor unions 76–77
Lachenmann, Helmut 44, 173
Laing, Alexander 96
Lamprea, Christine 97
Latin America xliii, 162
League of American Orchestras 60, 91, 98–99
Catalyst Fund 98
Racial/Ethnic and Gender Diversity in the Orchestra Field 60
Symphony magazine 91
Léonin 22
Levitin, Daniel 8
Ligeti, György 43, 166, 170–172
Lim, Liza 43
Lincoln Center for the Performing Arts 41
Lincoln Theatre 126, 128
LinkedIn 122
literature xli, 56, 63–70, 162
live performance xxvi, xxviii, xxxiv, 2, 3, 5, 7, 8, 9, 10, 11, 12, 13, 25, 85, 105, 109, 123, 133, 146, 169, 172, 188. *See also* concerts

live-streams xxxiv, xxxix, xlii, 25, 104
Lockwood, Annea 106
London Sinfonietta 40
London Symphony Orchestra 180
Los Angeles Chamber Orchestra 98
Los Angeles Philharmonic xxx, xxxi, 29, 31, 42, 97–98, 165
Louisiana Philharmonic Orchestra 77
Louvre 8, 183
Lumet, Sidney
 Serpico xxv
Lutoslawski, Witold 171

Mahler Chamber Orchestra 189
Mahler, Gustav 167, 174
Mälkki, Susanna 42, 161, 166–167, 172
Mangum, John 81
Marsalis, Wynton 5
Massachusetts Institute of Technology (MIT) 19
Massachusetts Museum of Contemporary Art (MASS MoCA) 41
Ma, Yo-Yo xxxvi, 42
 "Songs of Comfort and Hope" xxxvi
McAndrew, Clare 183
McGill, Anthony xix, xxx, xlii, 96
McGill, Demarre 96
McPhee, Colin 2
McQueen, Garrett 89
Meredith Monk and Vocal Ensemble 40. *See also* Monk, Meredith
Merit School of Music 88
Messiaen, Olivier 166, 170–171
Met Breuer 187
Metropolitan Museum of Art 183–184
Metropolitan Opera xxxiv, xxxvi, 50, 53, 78, 88, 96–97, 103
Meyer Sound 132
Middle East xxix, xliii, 43, 178
Milwaukee Symphony 96
Minnesota Orchestra 98–99
Minnesota Orchestral Association 56
Modernism 170, 184

Monk, Meredith 40. *See also* Meredith Monk and Vocal Ensemble
Monteverdi, Claudio xxxvi, 4
 Orfeo xxxvi
Montreal Museum of Fine Arts 185
Morgan, Michael 97
Mortiz, Michael 122
Moser, Johannes 42
Mozart, Wolfgang Amadeus 1, 16–17, 39, 107, 144, 152
Multi-Story Orchestra 152
Mundry, Isabel 168
Murail, Tristan 167
Murakami, Takashi 185
musicology xxvii, xxx, xxxi, 15, 22, 23, 53, 167. *See also* research

Nagano, Kent 161, 173
Nancarrow, Conlon 171
Nashville Symphony 97
National Alliance for Audition Support 98–99
National Broadcasting Corporation (NBC) xxvi
National Conservatory of Music of America 20
National Endowment for the Arts 29, 66
National Gallery 184
National Science and Technology Council 19
Netflix xxvii, 146
Netherlands, the 160
Neuwirth, Olga 44, 171
New England Conservatory 20
New Jersey Symphony 99
new-music xxxvii, xl, 40, 41, 42, 43, 44. *See also* classical music: contemporary
New Music USA 93
New World Symphony xlii, 98–99, 121–141
 Double Take 135–136
 Friends of the New World Symphony 126–127

Magic of Music program 122–124, 133–134, 138–139
  Miami in Movements 137–138
  Mini-Concerts 126–128, 139
  New Audience Initiative 121, 125, 133, 139–140
  partnerships 130, 138–139
  Pulse—Late Night at the New World Symphony 126, 129–131, 134, 136, 138–139
  Symphony with a Splash/Encounters 126–127, 138
  WALLCAST® concerts 131–134, 138–139
New York City Opera 57
New Yorker, The xl, 52
New York Magazine, The 52
New York Philharmonic xxx, xxxi, xxxiv, xlii, 53, 76, 79, 81, 88, 97, 109, 186
New York Times, The xxxi, xl, 48–52, 76, 90–91, 173
Nézet-Séguin, Yannick 80
Nikodijevic, Marko 170
No Child Left Behind Act 18–19
Noguchi Museum 189
nonprofit arts organizations 55–56, 58, 60
nonprofit performing arts 63–65, 68
Norrington, Roger 160
North America xxxvi, xliii, 3, 15, 23, 43, 85, 115, 174, 184
Nott, Jonathan 161
NYU Global Institute for Advanced Study (GIAS) 41

Oberlin College 20
Oberlin Conservatory of Music 19
Oklahoma State University 132
O'Neill, Richard Youngjae 170
Orff Approach 31
Orozco-Strada, Andres 97
Orpheus Chamber Orchestra 98
Ostrower, Francie xx, xli

Pace Gallery 185
Pac-Man xxxvii

Pahg, Sun-Young 169
Palestrina, Giovanni Pierluigi da 4
Paris Conservatory 20
Paris Opera 186
Park Avenue Armory 188
Peabody Institute 19
Peacocke, Christopher xx, xxxi, xxxix
Philadelphia Orchestra 79–80
philanthropy 55, 59, 82
Philharmonia Orchestra 112
Philharmonie de Paris xxix, xliv, 44, 111, 177–179, 181
  Démos Project xliv, 177–179, 182
Philip Glass Ensemble 40. *See also* Glass, Philip
Phoenix Symphony 96
Piatigorsky, Gregor 20
Picasso, Pablo 187
Pintscher, Matthias 161
Poland 40, 160, 189
Poly Group 185
pop music xliii, 47, 108, 146–147, 178–179, 185
Poulenc, Francis 170
President's Committee on the Arts and Humanities 18
Prieto, Carlos Miguel 97
programming xxviii, xl, xlii, xliv, 22, 42, 85, 92–94, 99–100, 106, 113, 145, 147, 149, 151, 163, 168, 173, 189
Prokofiev, Gabriel 152
Prokofiev, Sergei 166
Provenzano, Catherine xxi, xxxi, xlii
Puccini, Giacomo
  Tosca xxv

racial injustice xxxiv, xlii, 24–25, 76, 87, 89–92, 94, 97, 101, 115
Radigue, Eliane 187
rap 179
Rattle, Simon 161
Ravel, Maurice 168
Regional Orchestra Players Association 99
Reich, Steve 40, 43, 152

Reif, L. Rafael 19
research xxvi, xxxix, xli, 15, 22, 29, 30, 35, 40, 49, 63, 64, 67, 68, 96, 109, 111, 112, 121, 124, 125, 126, 130, 133, 134, 139, 181. *See also* musicology
Rice, Tamir 114
Rich, Frank 48
Richter, Max 149
Riley, Terry 43, 171
Robertson, David 161
Rockefeller family, the 184
Rophé, Pascal 166
Rosen, Charles 1
Ross, Alex xxi, xxxi, xl, 173
  The Rest Is Noise 53
Roth, François-Xavier 42, 160, 166–167
Rotterdam Symphony xxxiii
Roumain, Daniel Bernard 97
Royal Academy of Arts 184
Royal Albert Hall 154
Royal Philharmonic Orchestra 145

Saariaho, Kaija 106
Sacks, Oliver 159
Salonen, Esa-Pekka xxxi, 42, 112, 161
Schnabel, Artur 20
Schnittke, Alfred 168
Schöllhorn, Johannes 167–168
Schönberg, Arnold 40, 42, 171
Schubert, Franz 162, 168
Schumann, Clara 189
Scriabin, Alexander 170
Scull, Robert 185
Seattle Symphony 96
Senegal 4
Seoul Philharmonic Orchestra xliii, 42, 157, 163, 165–166, 173
  Ars Nova series xliii, 42, 163–164, 166, 173
Sequoia Capital 122
Serkin, Rudolf 20
Service, Tom xxii, xxxi, xliii
Shakespeare, William xxxvi
  Henry V xxxvi
Shaw, George Bernard 48

Shchukin, Sergei 183
Shed 188
Shelter Music Boston 3
Shepherd School of Music at Rice University 21
Shin, Donghoon 170, 173
Shostakovich, Dmitri 11, 152, 166, 171
  Symphony No. 7 11
Sibelius, Jean 163
Sierra, Roberto 169
Simone, Nina 11
Slocum, Sonora 96
Snow, Jon 7
Snow, Meredith 78–79
social media 48, 53, 90, 110, 129, 145, 150, 158, 188
Sorey, Tyshawn xxxvi, 43
  Perle Noire xxxvi
Sotheby's 185
SoundScape Park 132
South Africa 11
South America 180
South Korea x, xxix, xxx, xliii, 42, 157, 164–173
Sphinx Organization 92–93, 98–99, 115
  LEAD (Leaders in Excellence Arts and Diversity 99
  Symphony Orchestra 92
  Virtuosi 92
Spotify xxxvi, 17, 108, 147–150, 157, 163
Sprott, Weston 96
Steve Reich and Musicians 40
Stockhausen, Karlheinz 44, 106, 166
Strategic National Arts Alumni Project 96
Stravinsky, Igor 4, 23, 144, 163, 166, 168, 170, 187
Südwestrundfunk (SWR) 160
  SWR Baden-Baden Freiburg Symphony Orchestra 160
  SWR Stuttgart Radio Symphony Orchestra 160

Tailleferre, Germaine 189
Takemitsu, Toru 2, 43

Tarnopolsky, Matias 80
Taruskin, Richard 1–2, 53
Tashi Quartet 40
Tate Modern 183, 185–186
Taylor, Breonna 114
Tchaikovsky Competition 21
Tchaikovsky, Pyotr Ilyich 21
technology xxviii, xxx, xl, xlii, 4–5, 16–17, 19, 50, 53, 66–67, 76, 103–107, 110–111, 113–115, 121, 133, 138, 151, 153, 162, 177, 187–190
Thielemann, Christian 9
Thomson, Virgil 7, 48
Thurber, Jeannette 20
Tidal 109
Tiensuu, Jukka 167
Tilson Thomas, Michael xlii, 122–124, 135–136
Tinctoris, Johannes 4
Tommasini, Anthony 51
Traber, Habakuk 167
Trump, Donald 50
Tsay, Chia-Jung 10
Tuuk, Mary 82
Twitter 49, 53, 110

Underwood, Titus 97
United Kingdom 47, 115, 144–145, 151, 160
United States Census 91, 95, 122
United States of America xxxiv, xli, 7, 11, 15, 18–19, 22, 25, 29, 47, 52, 55, 60–61, 75–76, 83, 89–95, 101, 114–115, 122, 132–134
  Congress 20
  Department of Education 18
University of Michigan 132
University of Texas at Austin 64
Urioste, Elena 97

VanBesien, Matthew xxii, xxxi, xli
Van Cliburn, Harvey Lavan 21
Venezuela 31, 180
Venice Biennale 184
venues xl, xlii, 4, 22, 44, 106, 137, 152, 177, 186

Verdi, Giuseppe 152
Vienna School, the 184
Vimeo 110
visual art xxvii, xxviii, 29, 87, 135, 162, 183–186, 190
  sound compositions 188
Vivaldi, Antonio 168
Volkov, Ilan 167

Wallace Foundation 63–64
Wall Street Journal, The 48
Warhol, Andy 185
Warsaw Autumn Festival 40
Washington Post, The 48
Webern, Anton 166, 168
Weber, William 39
Weinberg, Mieczysław 189
Wei, Wu 172
Wen-chung, Chou 43
West, the xxv, 2, 4, 171, 174, 178, 181, 184
Wiggins, Jennifer 68
Wigmore Hall 7
Wilkins, Thomas 97
Wilson, Edmund 48
WolfBrown 126
Wolfe, Julia xxxi, 41
Woolfe, Zachary xxiii, xxxi, xl
World War One 187
World War Two 189

Xenakis, Iannis 44, 106, 166, 171

Yale School of Music 21
Yi, Chen 2
YouGov 145
Youth Orchestra of Los Angeles 31. *See also* Heart of Los Angeles (HOLA) program
YouTube 17, 110, 146, 157, 163
Yuasa, Yoji 43
Yun, Isang 43, 165–166, 171

Zimmermann, Bernd Alois 168
Ziporyn, Evan 2
Zorn, John 169, 171
Zwirner 185

About the Team

Alessandra Tosi was the managing editor for this book.

Adèle Kreager and Melissa Purkiss performed the copy-editing and proofreading.

Jacob More designed the cover using InDesign. The cover was produced in InDesign using Nilland, Montserrat (titles) and Avenir (text body) fonts.

Melissa Purkiss typeset the book in InDesign and produced the paperback and hardback editions. The text font is Tex Gyre Pagella; the heading font is Californian FB.

Luca Baffa produced the EPUB, MOBI, PDF, HTML, and XML editions—the conversion is performed with open source software freely available on our GitHub page (https://github.com/OpenBookPublishers).

This book need not end here...

Share

All our books — including the one you have just read — are free to access online so that students, researchers and members of the public who can't afford a printed edition will have access to the same ideas. This title will be accessed online by hundreds of readers each month across the globe: why not share the link so that someone you know is one of them?

This book and additional content is available at:

https://doi.org/10.11647/OBP.0242

Customise

Personalise your copy of this book or design new books using OBP and third-party material. Take chapters or whole books from our published list and make a special edition, a new anthology or an illuminating coursepack. Each customised edition will be produced as a paperback and a downloadable PDF.

Find out more at:

https://www.openbookpublishers.com/section/59/1

Like Open Book Publishers

Follow @OpenBookPublish

Read more at the Open Book Publishers BLOG

You may also be interested in:

Rethinking Social Action through Music
The Search for Coexistence and Citizenship in Medellín's Music Schools
Geoffrey Baker

https://doi.org/10.11647/OBP.0243

Annunciations
Sacred Music for the Twenty-First Century
George Corbett

https://doi.org/10.11647/OBP.0172

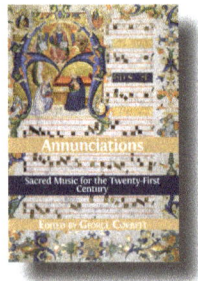

A Musicology of Performance
Theory and Method Based on Bach's Solos for Violin
Dorottya Fabian

https://doi.org/10.11647/OBP.0064

www.ingramcontent.com/pod-product-compliance
Lightning Source LLC
Chambersburg PA
CBHW040903250426
43673CB00064B/1951